CHILD AND ADOLESCENT COUNSELING CASE STUDIES

D1380051

Brenda L. Jones, PhD, LPC, CSC, NCC, is a licensed and certified professional school counselor (CSC), a nationally certified counselor (NCC), and a licensed professional counselor (LPC). She has a doctoral degree in counselor education and supervision. Currently, she is a clinical assistant professor at the University of Texas at San Antonio and is one of the professors on record for master's level school counseling and clinical mental health courses. She is a member of numerous national, state, and local counseling professional organizations. Currently, she is the president-elect of the Texas Association for Counselor Education and Supervision. She has had several professional publications in counseling literature, made numerous peer-reviewed presentations, and has received awards from the American School Counselor Association High School Counselor of the Year Award, the Texas School Counselor Association Rhosine Fleming High School Counselor of the Year Award, and the South Texas Counseling Association High School Counselor of the Year Award. She has been profiled in a feature article on contemporary Black women published by *Ebony* magazine and was recognized in *Jet* magazine's People section. She is an honorary life member of the Texas Parent Teacher Association. She serves on the editorial boards for the *Journal of Creativity in Mental Health* and the *Journal of School Counseling*.

Thelma Duffey, PhD, LPC, LMFT, is professor and chair in the Department of Counseling at the University of Texas at San Antonio and immediate past president of the American Counseling Association. Dr. Duffey was the founding president of The Association for Creativity in Counseling, a division within the ACA, and she served two terms on the ACA Governing Council. Dr. Duffey is a former president of the Texas Association of Counselor Education and Supervision and executive board member for the Southern Association of Counselor Education and Supervision. Dr. Duffey is editor for the *Journal of Creativity in Mental Health* and she served as guest co-editor for a *Journal of Counseling and Development* (*JCD*) *Special Issue on Counseling Men* and the *JCD Special Section on Relational-Cultural Theory*. Dr. Duffey, an ACA Fellow, has received numerous awards from professional organizations such as the Association for Counselor Education and Supervision, the American Counseling Association, the Texas Counseling Association, the Southern Association for Counselor Education and Supervision, the Association for Creativity in Counseling, and the Texas Association for Counselor Education and Supervision. She has over 60 peer reviewed publications; an edited book, *Creative Interventions in Grief and Loss Therapy: When the Music Stops, a Dream Dies*, and a co-edited book, *A Counselor's Guide to Working with Men*.

Shane Haberstroh, EdD, LPC, is currently an associate professor and Doctoral Program Director in the Department of Counseling at the University of Texas at San Antonio. He served on the founding board for the Association for Creativity in Counseling (ACC) and as the ACC President and Treasurer. He is currently the Governing Council Representative for the Association for Creativity in Counseling and the Governing Council liaison for the research and knowledge committee of ACA. Dr. Haberstroh serves as the associate editor for the *Journal of Creativity in Mental Health*. He has published over 30 articles and book chapters primarily focused on Developmental Relational Counseling, online counseling, creativity in counseling, and addiction treatment & recovery. His collaborative research project on relational competencies won the 2010 Texas Counseling Association Research Award, and his collaborative publication on assessment practices in counselor education programs was recognized with the 2014 AARC/CORE Outstanding Outcome Research Award. Dr. Haberstroh began his career in 1992 as a residential technician in a 28-day drug treatment program and worked for many years as a counselor and supervisor in addiction treatments centers, private practice, and criminal justice settings. He has been a counselor educator since 2003 and he joined the faculty of the University of Texas at San Antonio in 2004.

CHILD AND ADOLESCENT COUNSELING CASE STUDIES

Developmental, Relational, Multicultural, and Systemic Perspectives

Brenda L. Jones, PhD, LPC, CSC, NCC
Thelma Duffey, PhD, LPC, LMFT
Shane Haberstroh, EdD, LPC

Editors

SPRINGER PUBLISHING COMPANY
NEW YORK

Springer Publishing Company, LLC
11 West 42nd Street
New York, NY 10036
www.springerpub.com

Acquisitions Editor: Nancy Hale
Compositor: Westchester Publishing Services

ISBN: 978-0-8261-5001-1
e-book ISBN: 978-0-8261-5002-8

16 17 18 19 20 / 5 4 3 2 1

The author and the publisher of this Work have made every effort to use sources believed to be reliable to provide information that is accurate and compatible with the standards generally accepted at the time of publication. The author and publisher shall not be liable for any special, consequential, or exemplary damages resulting, in whole or in part, from the readers' use of, or reliance on, the information contained in this book. The publisher has no responsibility for the persistence or accuracy of URLs for external or third-party Internet websites referred to in this publication and does not guarantee that any content on such websites is, or will remain, accurate or appropriate.

Library of Congress Cataloging-in-Publication Data

Names: Jones, Brenda L., editor. | Duffey, Thelma, editor. | Haberstroh, Shane, editor.
Title: Child and adolescent counseling case studies : developmental, relational, multicultural, and systemic perspectives / Brenda L. Jones, PhD, Thelma Duffey, PhD, Shane Haberstroh, EdD, editors.
Description: New York : Springer, [2017]
Identifiers: LCCN 2016036051 | ISBN 9780826150011 (hard copy : alk. paper)
Subjects: LCSH: Children—Counseling of. | Child psychology. | Teenagers—Counseling of. | Adolescent psychology.
Classification: LCC BF636.6 .C545 2017 | DDC 158.3083—dc23 LC record available at https://lccn.loc.gov/2016036051

Special discounts on bulk quantities of our books are available to corporations, professional associations, pharmaceutical companies, health care organizations, and other qualifying groups. If you are interested in a custom book, including chapters from more than one of our titles, we can provide that service as well.

For details, please contact:
Special Sales Department, Springer Publishing Company, LLC
11 West 42nd Street, 15th Floor, New York, NY 10036-8002
Phone: 877-687-7476 or 212-431-4370; Fax: 212-941-7842
E-mail: sales@springerpub.com

Printed in the United States of America by Gasch Printing.

This book is dedicated to children and adolescents who continuously encounter challenging issues while traversing life experiences. It is also dedicated to the many clinical mental health and professional school counselors, counselor supervisors, and counselors-in-training who serve as ready resources of guidance for children, adolescents, and related systems—family, school, peer, and community. A special dedication goes to all of the dedicated parents including Brenda Jones's daughter, Nicole Jones, and Thelma Duffey's son, Robert Duffey, who continuously foster healthy development for their children.

CONTENTS

CONTRIBUTORS

Norèal F. Armstrong, PhD, LPC-S, NCC, LCDC
Assistant Professor
Montreat College
Asheville, North Carolina

Katherine Bacon, PhD, LPC-S, NCC
Assistant Professor
University of Houston Victoria at Sugar Land
Sugar Land, Texas

Huma Bashir, EdD, PCC-S, LICDC
Assistant Professor
Wright State University
Dayton, Ohio

Lisa L. Beijan, MEd, LPC
Doctoral Candidate
University of North Texas
Denton, Texas

Caroline M. Brackette, PhD, LPC, ACS
Associate Professor
Mercer University
Atlanta, Georgia

Thomas Anthony Chávez, PhD, LMHC (NM)
Assistant Professor
University of New Mexico
Albuquerque, New Mexico

Ernest Cox, Jr., MS, CSC
Director of Guidance and Counseling
Judson Independent School District
Live Oak, Texas

Thelma Duffey, PhD, LPC, LMFT
Professor and Chair
The Department of Counseling
The University of Texas at San Antonio
San Antonio, Texas

Suzanne M. Dugger, EdD, LPC, NCC, ACS, LSC
Professor and Program Coordinator of Counselor Education
University of Mississippi
University, Mississippi

Stephanie Eberts, PhD, CSC
Assistant Professor
Louisiana State University
Baton Rouge, Louisiana

Tamarine Foreman, PhD, LPCC-S, NCC
Assistant Professor
Ohio University
Athens, Ohio

Kristopher M. Goodrich, PhD, LPCC (NM), ACS, NCGC-II
Associate Professor/Coordinator
University of New Mexico
Albuquerque, New Mexico

Shane Haberstroh, EdD, LPC
PhD Program Director and Associate Professor
The University of Texas at San Antonio
San Antonio, Texas

Maria Haiyasoso, PhD, LPC, NCC
Assistant Professor
Texas State University
San Marcos, Texas

Glenda S. Johnson, PhD, LPC, PSC
Assistant Professor
Appalachian State University
Boone, North Carolina

Brenda L. Jones, PhD, LPC, CSC, NCC
Clinical Assistant Professor
The University of Texas at San Antonio
San Antonio, Texas

M. Michelle Thornbury Kelley, MA, CSC
Coordinator, Secondary Counselor Services and Safe School Initiatives
Northside Independent School District
San Antonio, Texas

Alexandria K. Kerwin, PhD, LPC, NCC
Assistant Professor
University of Mississippi
University, Mississippi

Melissa Luke, PhD, LMHC, NCC, ACS
Associate Professor/School Counseling Coordinator
Syracuse University
Syracuse, New York

Jennifer Austin Main, LPC, RPT-S
Doctoral Candidate
University of Mississippi
University, Mississippi

Taryne M. Mingo, PhD, NCC
Assistant Professor
Missouri State University
Springfield, Missouri

Ariel Mitchell, PhD, LPC-S, LMFT, NCC
Assistant Professor
Xavier University of Louisiana
New Orleans, Louisiana

Claudia Morales, MA, CSC
Professional School Counselor
Northside Independent School District
San Antonio, Texas

Jenn Pereira, PhD, LMHC-S, RPT-S, CCPT-S, CT
Clinical Assistant Professor
Arizona State University
Tempe, Arizona

JoLynne Reynolds, PhD, LPC, NCC, RPT-S
Professor
Regis University
Broomfield, Colorado

Michelle Robinson, CSC
Professional School Counselor
Judson Independent School District
Converse, Texas

Mona Robinson, PhD, LPCC-S, LSW, CRC
Professor/Department Chair
Ohio University
Athens, Ohio

Eric Suddeath, MA
Doctoral Candidate
University of Mississippi
University, Mississippi

Donna A. Tonrey, PsyD, LMFT, LPC
Director of Counseling and Family Therapy
La Salle University
Philadelphia, Pennsylvania

Stacy Waterman, M.A., LPC, LCDC
Doctoral Student
The University of Texas at San Antonio
San Antonio, Texas

Tammy L. Wilborn, PhD, LPC-S, NCC
Assistant Professor
University of New Orleans
New Orleans, Louisiana

Angie D. Wilson, PhD, LPC-S, LSOTP, NCC
Assistant Professor
University of North Texas
Denton, Texas

Natasha Young, MEd, LPC
Clinical Supervisor
The Parris Foundation
Houston, Texas

FOREWORD

When I wrote the Foreword for Dr. Larry Golden's third edition of *Case Studies in Child and Adolescent Counseling*, which was published in 2002, I commented about how many more challenges children and adolescents face as they navigate their developmental journey through childhood and adolescence. I noted that Dr. Golden had made a significant contribution to the field with that publication and although his dignified career ended with his death in 2012, Dr. Brenda Jones has recognized the significance of a book of this nature and has resurrected it with new case studies and relevant information that child and adolescent practitioners will profit from on multiple levels.

As I noted in the 2002 Foreword, my first year (1972) as an elementary counselor was a continual learning experience. There were no the Council for Accreditation of Counseling and Related Educational Programs (CACREP)-accredited programs, no internships, very little supervision, and no specific courses in counseling children and adolescents. Suffice it to say that it was a "baptism by fire" year! I will never forget being at a loss for words and thinking that my training had definitely not prepared me for the "real world" when I went into a fourth grade classroom to introduce myself and tell the children about the role of the counselor. I concluded my commentary with "and as your counselor, I am here to help you with your problems." Suddenly a hand shot up and an adorable boy with curly blonde hair blurted out, "My mom's been married three times and my dad has been married twice and now they are getting a divorce. Is this a problem you can help me with?" Now some of you may recall that in the early 1970s, divorce was pretty rare and most of the students I was working with had typical developmental problems that I felt comfortable handling.

But I was less certain about how to help this student. However, when he appeared in my doorway, I knew I had to figure it out by trial and error.

I have thought about that scenario many times, and upon reflection, I realize that "back then" there were so few resources, and what we did with children was basically extrapolated from approaches we would use with adults. It did not take me long to learn that that was extremely inadequate, and I am so thankful that the field has evolved such that today there are specific courses on counseling children and adolescents and a plethora of resources that can be accessed with the click of a mouse. Thankfully, our profession got "up to speed" with specific applications of theories and techniques that work best with the younger population because the problems they present with today necessitate more skill than ever before. In addition to normal developmental problems that all children experience to varying degrees, the number of children and adolescents who deal with emotional or sexual abuse, domestic violence, cyberbullying, homelessness, addiction, and other serious problems is sobering. Unfortunately, so many do not get the help they need and resort to self-destructive behaviors due in part to their sense of hopelessness, their powerlessness, their lack of support, and their developmental level that can impact their ability to fully understand the issues and cope with problems in a self-enhancing, rather than a self-defeating, manner.

Over the years in my private counseling practice, I saw many young clients who came from dysfunctional families and had few, if any, positive role models. Their problems manifested in behavior problems, self-harm, addictions, eating disorders, suicide attempts, and the like. On the other hand, I had clients from healthy families with good role models who were anxious, depressed, dealt with their pain by acting out, refused to eat, or abused alcohol and drugs to numb their pain. Clearly, effective counseling approaches that address not only the individual, but also the system, are needed more now than ever before.

As I read the case studies that Dr. Jones and her colleagues described, I have to admit that I felt some despair and, at the same time, appreciation for the counselors who put so much of their professional expertise to work in order to address the problems on multiple levels. It was disconcerting to read about what 8-year-old Beth had to contend with: her older sister was murdered; her father was incarcerated; her father's friend abused her sexually; her schizophrenic brother physically abused her, and she was bullied at school. How sad to think that a child this age would even consider suicide, let alone attempt it, as an escape from all her problems.

Taryne M. Mingo wrote about her work with Jeffrey, a gifted child who at age 9 stuffed his throat with tissues until he passed out, and Brenda L. Jones described her work with 17-year-old Adam who began drinking at age 9, was using heroin by the time he was 15, and had been in trouble with the law since age 13. Stephanie Eberts presented the case of Darryl, an 8-year-old whose father was incarcerated for assault and was arrested in front of Darryl when he was only 5. His anger and confusion manifested itself in aggressive behavior. Clearly, Taryne, Brenda, and Stephanie recognized the importance of developing rapport with these troubled youth who need someone on their side to help guide them through their troublesome issues. They also consulted with the family and the school, which is critical in delivering effective treatment for young clients.

As I read these case studies, as well as the others in the book, I was impressed that these counselors were nonjudgmental, accepting their clients with their weaknesses and trying to help them find their strengths. They were respectful and mindful about cultural considerations and family characteristics and how these factors affected their clients. Furthermore, they drew from various theories, often integrating them to achieve a better effect. They recognized, as do I, the importance of "counseling outside the lines" and using the expressive arts in their work with these clients.

I appreciated reading the step-by-step description of the problem conceptualization, goals for treatment, and the actual process. I often found myself wondering if I would have arrived at the same conclusions these authors did and whether I would have used similar approaches to treatment. Reading about how the various authors decided on their plan of action was very insightful and thought-provoking, and underscores the notion that there is not "one solution" to a problem. As counselors, we often want what Larry Golden once said was the "magic cure," which is a myth that our field perpetuates but, in reality, rarely happens. Those of us who work with clients on a routine basis know that the road to recovery is often long and winding, and we must draw from a multitude of perspectives and approaches as the authors in these case studies did.

These case studies, albeit difficult to read because of the serious nature of the majority of the presenting problems, illustrated that counseling *can* make a difference in the lives of young clients. I predict that this book will be referred to frequently for ideas about how to address similar problems you have with your young clients, but also for inspiration.

Ann Vernon, Phd, LPC
Professor Emerita
University of Northern Iowa

PREFACE

The purpose of this book is to aid counselor educators, supervisors, and counselors-in-training in assisting children, adolescents, and their families to foster coping methods and strategies while navigating contemporary issues. Past life experiences of children and adolescents continue to shape their present. Counselors who work with children and adolescents serve as ready resources and sources of guidance to help youth traverse life's unpredictable pathways. Developmentally effective counseling is crucial when working with children and adolescents; and when done effectively, provides meaningful, relevant, and transformative outcomes for youth, propelling them forward on paths conducive to mental health improvements. Equally important, effective counseling provides a relational foundation where the connections experienced in counseling teach youth how to relate with themselves and others in more productive ways.

The focal points of this book are not only congruent with national dialogues involving consistency in meeting ethical and accreditation standards, but also with accountability efforts and effectiveness in higher education. This book is designed to be used as a companion piece or supplement not only for child and adolescent counseling textbooks but also for a broad range of other courses in similar disciplines.

Consistent with the literature, this book was written to promote the essence of counselor growth. Case studies were written in contexts that reflect the fact that children and adolescents are part of larger systems—family, school, peer, and community. Systemic context, developmental and relational considerations, multicultural perspectives, and creative interventions were infused in the cases. Time-efficient methods, such as brief counseling, were used in some of the cases. The case studies selected highlight contemporary issues and relevant themes that are prevalent in the lives of youths (i.e., abuse, anxiety, giftedness, disability, social media and pop culture, social deficits and relationships, trauma, bullying, changing families, body image, substance abuse, incarcerated family members, race and ethnicity, and sexual identity and orientation). These themes capture both the child and adolescent perspectives and are designed to provide breadth and depth during classroom discussions and debriefing. They also provide counselors-in-training in clinical mental health and professional school counselors hands-on, useful, concrete, and workable applications that will offer opportunities for skill and theory development.

An impressive roster of contributing authors submitted cases that offer a variety of professional and clinical perspectives. Contributing authors provided:

- An introduction and client background information (i.e., family history, dynamics, and aspects of the client's life that honor diversity and the uniqueness of coping and healing; school and educational concerns; medical information and general health)
- Developmental and relational issues, and personal, social, and emotional status
- Conceptualization of the client's presenting problems along with personal and client goals; theoretical approaches; and creative techniques, strategies, and interventions
- Counseling process describing step-by-step accounting of what happened in counseling sessions including the number of contacts made, with whom, and over what length of time. The counseling relationships were described and, in many cases, included areas such as progress, setbacks, and regressions
- Counseling outcome (i.e., describing results, creative strategies that worked or did not work and why; strategies that the authors would have done differently; and predictions or recommendations for the client)

Several contributing authors have written CACREP signature assignments that appear as appendices to the main text.

Inspiration for this book came from a former professor, colleague, and mentor, Dr. Larry Golden, who recently passed away. In 2002, Dr. Larry Golden wrote the third edition of *Case Studies in Child and Adolescent Counseling,* which served as the model for this book. Dr. Golden was a prolific contributor to the counseling literature. His books are still being used in counseling classrooms today. This book updates and expands Dr. Golden's book and forwards his literary and instructional legacy by remaining responsive to the needs of the counseling field.

ACKNOWLEDGMENTS

Thanks is extended to Dr. Thelma Duffey and Dr. Shane Haberstroh, who have served as mentors for me and co-editors with me in my first book venture. Thanks is also extended to Nancy Hale, Editorial Director, and Mindy Chen, Assistant Editor, Springer Publishing Company. The process of editing this book was made easier by their expert assistance and their exceptional leadership, professionalism, and commitment.

Brenda L. Jones

PART I

CASE STUDIES RELATING TO CHILDREN

CHAPTER 1

SOMEWHERE OVER THE RAINBOW

Maria Haiyasoso

After being released from the state hospital, Beth showed no enthusiasm about being in counseling again. In fact, the first time I met Beth, she referred to me as "another counselor" to see in order for "everyone to leave (her) alone." Beth did not believe that counseling could be beneficial or could help her navigate trauma and difficult familial dynamics. In the following case study, I detail Beth's treatment and the sequence of her engagement in our counseling sessions.

SYSTEMIC INFLUENCES

Beth, an 8-year-old Caucasian female, lived with her stepmother, Alexa. Beth's biological father, Dustin, did not live in the home. He happened to be incarcerated for possessing, manufacturing, and distributing illegal drugs. Alexa's past depicted a history of methamphetamine use; however, she remained sober for several years. Beth's biological mother, Tara, lived in a neighboring town. Beth and her two older siblings shared the same biological mother but different biological fathers. Three years ago, someone murdered Beth's 17-year-old sister during a drug deal. Beth's 22-year-old brother, who doctors diagnosed with schizophrenia, also displayed a history of substance misuse. Beth maintained a strained relationship with her brother due to his erratic behaviors and physical abuse.

Beth disclosed that one of Dustin's acquaintances sexually abused her at age 6. The abuse occurred while Dustin and his acquaintances bought and sold drugs in another room in the house. Beth lived with Tara at the time of the disclosure, and Tara immediately reported the abuse to law enforcement. Since then, Tara discontinued Beth's contact with Dustin. Beth blamed Tara for depriving her of seeing Dustin prior to his incarceration. Beth also resented Tara for being investigated due to Tara's own history of substance use. Throughout Beth's childhood, Tara lost her children multiple times to child protective services. Tara remained sober to create structure in her home and become a present parent to her children. In spite of this, Tara experienced resistance from Beth.

DEVELOPMENTAL CONSIDERATIONS

Cognitive Development

Beth functioned in the concrete operational stage of development. Children with concrete operational skills tend to demonstrate more abstract and inductive thinking (Bee & Boyd, 2007; Piaget & Inhelder, 1969). However, children in this developmental stage often conceptualize from an egocentric perspective and do not fully consider other perspectives or explanations. Beth's caregivers provided no explanations for what happened because they believed "she's too young to understand." Therefore, Beth did not possess the full capacity to assign responsibility to others for their harmful choices. Instead, Beth blamed herself.

Personal, Social, and Emotional Development

Living in a small rural town, Beth's family's criminal activity and arrests became common knowledge. Beth experienced bullying at school and became involved in physical altercations with other students on the school bus and playground. To cope, Beth began pinching her skin on her abdomen until she created a red mark that turned into bruising. In addition, Beth started stealing cigarettes from her brother, mother, and other adults and smoked when unsupervised. Finally, after one argument with Tara, Beth swallowed a handful of over-the-counter pain medication. Doctors treated Beth and later confirmed that Beth attempted to commit suicide. Doctors transferred Beth to a state hospital that diagnosed her with a conduct disorder and an adjustment disorder. The hospital's mental health professionals and Tara agreed Beth should move in with Alexa to reduce environmental stressors. Beth appeared eager to move to a new town and a new school. Beth reportedly did not maintain friends at her old school.

RELATIONAL CONSIDERATIONS

Beth saw drugs consume her sister and her father, and at times, her mother. From a lack of adequate care and supervision, Beth found herself in situations that encouraged sexual and physical abuse and physical neglect. Additionally, students at school bullied Beth. These previous experiences informed her relational images, or images that created templates or expectations for how one functions in relationships with others (Miller & Stiver, 1997). Beth did not feel connected with others. Moreover, Beth's statements in therapy and gestures in her play revealed her self-blame for the havoc in her life. I focused on creating a therapeutic relationship that fostered relational resilience. Relational resilience is demonstrated through attempting to connect with others even after experiencing adversity or traumatic events (Jordan, 2010).

MULTICULTURAL CONSIDERATIONS

Beth and her family lived in a rural area. Beth's entire family resided in a low socioeconomic community except for an extended family member who cut ties with Beth's parents due to their involvement in drugs. Beth's stepmother became the only one in her family who graduated from high school. Being aware of their scarce resources, I made appropriate recommendations and suggestions to Beth's caregivers.

CONCEPTUALIZATION

Beth experienced a childhood riddled with abuse, loss, and addiction. I selected goals that allowed us to work toward incremental change. We targeted three areas rather than divide attention among several.

Goals and Target for Client Change

My work with Beth centered on the following treatment goals: promoting healthy ways of emotional coping, addressing her low self-worth and shame, and attending to her relational functioning. We focused on healthy ways that allowed Beth to cope emotionally with the situations in her life. I based these goals on Beth's participation in self-harm, isolation from others, and smoking stolen cigarettes.

Next, we established a goal to address her self-worth and shame. I based this on my observations and interactions with Beth and her caregivers. My conversation with Beth to get a sense of what she felt was the most important area to focus on in counseling went like this:

> *Me:* "You have a lot of stuff that happened."
> *Beth:* "There is a lot. No one likes me. They kept messing with me. I fought them and went home. I don't like my mom either. She doesn't like me either. (*She slams down a deck of cards on the ground.*) No one likes me."
> *Me:* "No one liked you at school. You and Mom don't like each other. Sounds lonely."
> *Beth:* "Well, it's NOT." (*She runs to the opposite side of the room and picks up a toy dart gun.*)
> *Me:* "You want me to know that you're not lonely."

Beth felt confused and angry with Tara for making choices in the past that repeatedly cost Tara custody of her children. Furthermore, Beth experienced mistreatment, assaults, and a history of abuse at school. Beth questioned whether she caused dysfunction in her family and life in general.

The last treatment goal helped Beth examine her relational images and improve her relational functioning. The adults in Beth's life provided no consistency or stability because they, too, struggled to manage their own difficult circumstances. Also, Beth had been abused sexually by an adult male and physically by her older brother. Even though the bullying stopped when she relocated, she still experienced upsetting memories about how individuals treated her at her previous school. Given how Beth made sense of her exposure to violence and her role in relationships, this last goal seemed fitting.

Strategies for the Client

To work toward the previously mentioned treatment goals, I used various strategies to target each goal. I used an integrative approach and incorporated client-centered play therapy, gestalt play therapy, relational-cultural theory (RCT), and sand tray.

Promoting Healthy Ways of Emotional Coping

The first strategy for promoting healthier emotional coping revealed sensory details that Beth could recognize and identify when she felt happy, mad, sad, scared, or disgusted. If Beth failed to identify these emotions, I made plans to assess them. Children Beth's age may lack a broad (or existent) emotional language, so checking for this in the beginning appeared helpful. Recognizing sensory information (e.g., tingling hands and heaviness in the chest) may assist children in becoming connected and alerted to their bodies' cues to help them gain mastery in controlling their responses. Also, individuals with nonsuicidal self-injury often reported using injury to feel a release because their emotional pain seemed so overwhelming that, at times, they became numb (Choate, 2012). Being attuned to their bodies' sensory cues may help youth reduce that sense of numbness.

Infusion of Creativity
The next strategy for promoting healthier coping involved learning her interests and finding fun, practical ways to utilize those interests when triggered. For Beth, we explored drawing as a creative outlet. Drawing aligned well with her interests. During one parent consultation, I spoke to Tara and Alexa about allowing Beth to take photographs on an old camera and to utilize other media (e.g., newspaper ads) so she could create other kinds of visual art to include in her collection of drawings. Tara and Alexa agreed to help Beth with the visual art projects (i.e., help Beth cut pictures and keep tape and glue stocked and accessible).

Addressing Her Low Self-Worth and Shame

One strategy used to work toward improving Beth's self-worth and reducing shame involved addressing the messages Beth received or did not receive from her caregivers. In a parent consultation, I explained that children Beth's age typically operate from an egocentric perspective. To a degree, Tara and Alexa assumed correctly that Beth would not fully comprehend the minutia of every situation. However, Beth potentially could benefit from developmentally appropriate and honest explanations. Children tend to fill in missing information based on their understanding of the world. Given Beth's developmental stage and the previously mentioned characteristic of egocentrism, she filled in the missing information with shaming messages: "I am bad, and bad things happen to me." Therefore, educating Tara and Alexa on having conversations with Beth about her abuse situations, her sister's death, her father being in prison, and the periods of her mother's absence helped bridge the gaps of Beth's understanding without taking on blame and believing that she seemed inherently "bad."

Infusion of Creativity
I wanted to extend Beth's self-awareness about her self-esteem and overall self-concept as another strategy. I chose to use sand tray to help

Beth express herself beyond her verbal language capabilities. Sand tray appeared to be a helpful medium with Beth because it allowed for emotional expression without verbal expression (Homeyer & Sweeney, 2011). Early on in her treatment, I asked Beth to create a world in the sand. In this session, Beth created a world with a girl sitting in a lawn chair in front of a house. She lined up trees around the back of the house. Across from the girl appeared a rainbow. Beth indicated that the girl sitting outside the house facing the rainbow represented her. As we processed her tray, Beth raked the sand with the rainbow but did not move the rainbow far from its original place. At one point, she moved the girl toward the rainbow and made it possible for the girl to kick it over. In a different sand tray session, Beth created a scene similar to the first sand tray with the girl in the lawn chair facing the rainbow except she omitted the house and trees. As we processed her sand tray, Beth noted that she wanted to be happy and gestured toward the rainbow. A short time later, she took a dinosaur, smashed it into the rainbow, and then placed the dinosaur next to the girl so that they could "sit together." Sand tray sessions like this allowed us to examine her wishes for happiness, barriers to getting there, and self-reflections in that pursuit.

Attending to Her Relational Functioning

I remained careful in pointing out times when Beth demonstrated something in our session that she could employ with others outside of the session. For example:

> Me: "You said everyone is trying to be clean now. What's clean?"
> Beth: "I don't know. No one tried it before."
> Me: "You don't know what clean is. I wonder how you know no one has tried being clean before."
> Beth: "It's just what mom and (Alexa) say."
> Me: "So you are wondering what being clean really is."
> Beth: "No, I don't. I don't care what being clean really is. I just hate that mom is changing the rules at the house now."
> Me: "She is making changes that are hard for you."
> Beth: "Yeah."
> Me: "You know, you corrected me and made me understand a little better what you meant. I sure do appreciate that. When others don't understand you, can you help them like you helped me?"
> Beth: "I guess."

In this example, Beth demonstrated her ability to correct me and share her experience. Using moments like this to encourage her to be authentic with others presented many peripheral benefits such as practicing setting boundaries and communicating her needs.

Infusion of Creativity

Finally, we explored characteristics of healthy relationships using Miller's "Five Good Things": (a) sense of zest; (b) clarity about self, other, and the relationship; (c) sense of self-worth; (d) enhanced creativity and productivity; and (e) desire for further connection with others (Jordan, 2008). I used more developmentally appropriate terms to describe them (e.g., "puts you in a good mood and you have more energy" vs. zest). Even though Beth could not identify relationships in her life that included all of these qualities, she acknowledged that certain relationships possessed some of these characteristics. To practice this, I asked Beth to draw the people in her relationships. Then, she reflected on each relationship. Using slips of paper, each listing a "good thing," Beth placed the qualities that existed in that relationship on the drawings of each person. It became a way to begin actively practicing identifying safe, healthy relationships.

Goals and Strategies for Myself

While consulting with Tara and Alexa, I learned that Beth worked with multiple counselors each time a case emerged that involved a child protection agency. Unfortunately, Beth disclosed information during sessions that warranted the counselor to make additional reports. As a result, Beth regarded previous counselors as people who say, "You can trust me," but "They tell everything you tell them." Therefore, my main goal evolved into earning her trust and contradicting her relational images (i.e., people are not trustworthy). I wanted to be clear with Beth about my role and what to expect with me. I clearly explained the limits of confidentiality throughout our time together, and I revisited the topic of her safety being a priority. Letting Beth know that she held power and influence in our relationship became another goal. To do this, I often informed her of her influence during sessions, and would note her effort throughout her play. I also let her know that I enjoyed our time together.

Systemic Approach

Collaborating with Beth's caregivers and others became integral to her treatment. My work appeared enhanced through partnering with the family and school systems in her life.

The Family System

In our first meeting, Tara and Alexa arrived together and both briefed me on the family history and Beth's current state. Tara and Alexa presented as amicable and respectful toward each other and appeared to be equally invested in Beth's well-being. I immediately noted their unified support as a strength in the family system. Tara and Alexa each verbally committed to prioritizing Beth's counseling and to working as a team to get her to the appointments. Consulting with Beth's caregivers helped in giving me a fuller picture of the family history, their investment in her treatment, and their willingness to be active in her care. As previously mentioned in the section Strategies for the Client, Beth's caregivers and I worked as a team to provide Beth with comprehensive care.

The School System

Furthermore, I obtained written permission to speak to Beth's school counselor when needed. We communicated when Beth experienced difficulties handling outbursts at her new school. He and I worked in tandem to share what appeared to be effective in treatment and educated Beth's teachers on best approaches to address with Beth when she appeared elevated.

COUNSELING PROCESS FLOW

I saw Beth for 30 sessions over a span of 8 months. Given the intricacies of Beth's case, the number of sessions appeared appropriate. I conducted eight parent consultation sessions and three family sessions. Our sessions lasted 35 to 45 minutes, and sometimes, those minutes went quickly. Other times, especially in the beginning, they dragged. I tried to be extra prepared for our sessions and felt great pressure to be present for Beth. At times, I felt like the only person she could rely on. This became the reason why it appeared especially hard when I, like the other counselors, called in a report to child protective services. To call this a setback would be an understatement. For example, in one of our sessions, Beth disclosed learning about a physical altercation between her brother and his girlfriend. The girlfriend carried an infant in her arms while she walked into the home used for "cooking crystal meth." Her brother appeared angry about something, so he "hit her while she carried the baby." I reported possible harm to the proper authorities. I told Beth about my report and explained my ethical obligation to break confidentiality. I could see the color and expression change on Beth's face. It became a process, but we worked our way back to Beth being able to trust me again.

OUTCOME

Beth worked really hard to keep up her defenses. Our work together seemed draining for us both. Beth shared that she smoked cigarettes because her mother indicated that smoking kept her from doing other drugs. So, Beth did the same because she seemed afraid she would want to do other drugs, too. Her attempts to self-protect appeared noteworthy. I examined these strategies she used to protect herself, helped her arrive at new strategies, and watched her reach for her rainbow.

I entered Beth's life shortly after she recovered from a suicide attempt. At the time of termination, she no longer considered taking her life. Instead, she became excited about photography and going to the local civic center for karate lessons. Her mother and stepmother seemed thrilled when Beth got in trouble at school for talking to another girl in the hallway. That meant she began connecting with someone and potentially making a friend! Overall, there seemed to be significant progress, and I believed Beth experienced a successful participation in counseling.

I worked with many survivors of child abuse and neglect, and I often recognized a presence of shame in survivors. Using play and sand tray in counseling children helped me better understand children's experiences. In my experience, I found relying on children to "tell me" proved to be less effective than relying on children to "show me." Also, I incorporated family sessions, parent consultation sessions, and consultation with the school when working with children to provide a continuity of care. I presented these aspects of my previous experience in Beth's case as well. However, in retrospect, I believe I should have attempted a more balanced approach of nondirective and directive play or sand tray interventions. I became fearful of losing ground with Beth if I pushed too hard, so I stayed nondirective for the most part. Additionally, in hindsight, I would encourage more family sessions. It became challenging due to scheduling issues, but the few family sessions seemed impactful.

In terms of prognosis, I expect Beth will experience issues navigating the effects of abuse, loss, and addiction throughout her lifetime. She will need the adults in her life to be supportive and protective. They may need to remind Beth from time to time that she is deserving of happiness and more.

REFERENCES

Bee, H., & Boyd, D. (2007). *The developing child* (11th ed.). Boston, MA: Pearson Education.

Choate, L. H. (2012). Counseling adolescents who engage in nonsuicidal self-injury: A dialectical behavior therapy approach. *Journal of Mental Health Counseling, 34*(1), 56–71.

Homeyer, L., & Sweeney, D. (2011). *Sandtray therapy: A practical manual* (2nd ed.). New York, NY: Routledge.

Jordan, J. V. (2008). Recent developments in relational-cultural theory. *Women & Therapy, 31*, 1–4.

Jordan, J. V. (2010). *Relational-cultural therapy.* Washington, DC: American Psychological Association.

Miller, J. B., & Stiver, I. P. (1997). *The healing connection: How women form relationships in therapy and life.* Boston, MA: Beacon Press.

Piaget, J., & Inhelder, B. (1969). *The psychology of the child.* New York, NY: Basic Books.

CHAPTER 2

GOOD GUYS AND BAD GUYS

Stephanie Eberts

I first met Darryl, an 8-year-old, second grade White male, after his school placed him in an alternative school for children with frequent behavioral issues. Darryl appeared energetic and excited about the prospect of working with me in the playroom. As a doctoral student, I worked under a grant that provided playrooms and play therapy training in several schools in the district. Darryl told me that he always wanted to explore the playroom; and as we walked down the hallway before our first session, it seemed difficult for him to stay next to me. He resisted the urge to run and watched me closely as he politely stayed next to me. Though he stayed in constant motion and seemed open to this new experience, he appeared cautious around new people. I felt him assessing me as we approached the playroom.

SYSTEMIC INFLUENCES

Darryl's mother explained to me that she became concerned about her son's behavior for various reasons. Darryl's father happened to be incarcerated for assaulting (and nearly killing) a man in a bar fight. He also became violent with Darryl's mother. At age 5, Darryl witnessed his father being arrested in front of their apartment, which traumatized Darryl. He maintained a negative view of law enforcement after witnessing his father's arrest. In the 3 years since the arrest, Darryl's mother received counseling and attended a support group. She also met another man whom she planned to marry in the near future. She became extremely concerned about the relationship between Darryl and her fiancé. She said that while they often got along well, Darryl ignored her fiancé at times and begged his mother to end the relationship. She became confused about why Darryl always asked questions about his dad. She explained that she did not like to talk about Darryl's father with him because of Darryl's father's violent history.

Darryl's family, community, and school environments impacted his life. His family system appeared to be in a state of change with his impending new stepfather and the loss of his incarcerated biological father. Darryl's mother felt that her family started to face better financial times with her new job as a secretary for a construction company. Her fiancé's job also appeared stable. For most of Darryl's life, the family moved around a lot. After her partner went to jail, Darryl's mother faced difficulty making financial decisions like deciding between electricity and food.

Darryl's mother also explained that Darryl seemed closest to his sister who attended high school. His sister seemed more introverted than Darryl and appeared very loving and accepting of him. She started to become more involved in extracurricular activities, which allowed her limited time with Darryl. Darryl's mother feared that Darryl would turn out to be like his father, abusive and addicted to alcohol. She indicated that she would do anything to help him.

DEVELOPMENTAL CONSIDERATIONS

Cognitive and Intellectual Development

Darryl seemed very concrete in his view of the world and cognitively functioned like a 5- or 6-year-old. Because of his intelligence, as evidenced by his higher-than-average test scores and high grades, he often used his quick understanding of class material to show his mastery. This behavior often put him at odds with other students. According to his teachers, Darryl seemed very smart and appeared impatient with other students who did not understand the material as quickly as he. This caused problems among his peers who called him a show-off. As a result, Darryl became agitated having to leave the classroom before an altercation occurred. The teacher recognized his leaving the classroom as a temporary solution because Darryl seemed to prefer to be with adults. He understood that if he started to get agitated, he would be sent to one of the specialist teachers, which he enjoyed. Being out of the classroom caused him to miss vital academic material. The teacher tried putting Darryl on a behavior plan. She explained that though this worked at times, she did not observe any lasting changes in his behavior. She estimated that Darryl left the classroom at least once daily. Darryl's teacher noticed that he became more isolated, so forming stronger peer relationships became her hope for Darryl as he worked with me.

The family physician diagnosed Darryl with attention deficit hyperactivity disorder (ADHD). Otherwise, he appeared in good health. Darryl's mother decided not to medicate him for the ADHD because she did not own a health insurance policy and thought that Darryl's medication seemed too expensive. She appeared open to suggestions about how to work with Darryl at home.

Personal, Social, and Emotional Development

On a social/emotional level, Darryl struggled as he functioned within Erikson's stage of emotional development, industry versus inferiority (Erikson, 1950). His struggle to find success in his personal relationships placed him more on the inferiority end of the continuum. The school placed Darryl in an alternative school setting because he threatened his former teacher with a pair of scissors. Though I did not succeed in consulting with the teacher who he threatened, his current teacher and mother gave me the necessary background information regarding this situation. Although Darryl accumulated multiple referrals for disruptive behavior and altercations on the playground, this happened to be his first overtly violent act. He appeared larger than an average 8-year-old, and this act became "the last straw" that prompted this alternative school placement.

As a result of the alternative school placement, Darryl could no longer attend his home school where his friends remained. He stated that he really liked his old school, and he appeared sad about leaving it; however, the alternative school staff appeared more prepared to work with students who experienced challenges that Darryl faced. In spite of this, he faced being placed in a classroom with many other children who also demonstrated behavioral issues. This had a negative influence on Darryl. He often joined in with children who acted out and faced consequences along with the instigators. This new school environment caused additional challenges for Darryl as he struggled to feel successful.

RELATIONAL CONSIDERATIONS

Darryl presented as an extroverted child who sought connection with others. His struggles with peers, teachers, and family members appeared to be a considerable strain on him. His teachers found his outbursts to be frustrating, which impacted their relationship. He attempted to impress me with his knowledge. In his first few meetings with me, he appeared a little despondent while also seeming to be very eager to please. He struggled to find friends at the alternative school because they viewed him as a "show-off."

Darryl took out his anger on his mother at home, and he missed spending time with his sister. His mother described him as a helpful child; but at times, his frustration would get in his way. He would, then, lash out at others. Despite the challenging behaviors that he presented at home, his mother and sister seemed very close with Darryl. They appeared to love each other very much. He maintained a strong relational foundation with both of them; however, Darryl's growth and increasingly violent outbursts put these relationships at risk. Despite this, Darryl's mother and sister remained deeply committed to helping him. The fact that he continued to seek connections with others boded well for our work together. I knew that our relationship would be key to his healing; and his ability to form future relationships and repair some of the fissures in his relationships with family seemed equally important.

MULTICULTURAL CONSIDERATIONS

Darryl's family's socioeconomic situation appeared, at times, dire. Due to his family's financial situation, many of the privileges that are often afforded by White males did not exist in his life. Though the family experienced more stable times during the time that I saw him, their resources still remained limited. Darryl's worldview seemed consistent with other marginalized populations. He seemed weary of authority, and he often felt that he needed to prove himself to others. He seemed to be accepting of other students who appeared different from him. He chose an African American student from his class to be his closest friend. He spoke of wanting money to buy things that he saw in video games and movies, but he did not seem overly preoccupied with the things that he did not own.

I, a White woman who experienced situational poverty for the first time in my life, related to his family's socioeconomic situation. I, fortunately, lived a privileged life not just because I am White, but because of my family's socioeconomic status. Having grown up with parents who did not come from money, they instilled in me the value of working hard, budgeting, and supporting and being supported by community. As a doctoral student living in an expensive city, I struggled a great deal to make ends meet. This understanding and empathy helped me to connect with Darryl's mother. Though she and I underwent different life experiences, our values seemed very similar. I became careful not to project too much of my own beliefs on the family.

CONCEPTUALIZATION

Goals and Targets for Client Change

After consulting with his teacher and mother and after two sessions in the playroom, a clearer picture of Darryl's presenting problem emerged. No one ever presented Darryl the opportunity to explore the loss of his father. With all of the pending changes in his life (i.e., his mother's engagement and his sister's growing interests outside of the home), he faced losses that he could not fully comprehend. No one provided Darryl outlets to express his frustration and sadness; consequently, he externalized these emotions, which emerged as confrontations. Giving Darryl a venue for expressing his feelings that assisted him in regulating his emotions became my goals for therapy.

Strategies for the Client

With this client, play therapy became the most developmentally appropriate intervention to use. Landreth (2012) refers to play as the language of children while the toys serve as their words. I conducted interventions through nondirective play therapy in which my facilitative responses focused on encouragement and reflection of feeling. Though this intervention took place in a school setting, it turned out to be a long-term intervention. I knew that I would be in the school for the whole school year, and my responsibility at this school appeared atypical from the duties of other professional school counselors. The school assigned me, in this alternative school setting, as a counselor for high-need students and their families, which made it possible to work with Darryl once a week for 7 months. This assignment would not be possible if the school assigned me as a regular professional school counselor in this setting. Other responsibilities would pose time constraints.

I also implemented filial therapy as an intervention with the mother and sister. Both women attended a 10-week filial group where they learned how to use play therapy language to better connect with Darryl. I trained in child–parent relationship therapy (Landreth & Bratton, 2005) under Sue Bratton, one of the authors of the protocoled intervention. My school invited her to do a 2-day training with all of the program leaders (professional school counselors and doctoral students). I also received training in play therapy and filial therapy at the university under the supervision of an experienced play therapist. I used play and filial therapy techniques with other students for a year prior to working with Darryl. In a meta-analysis of play therapy interventions, researchers found filial therapy to be the most effective intervention in that it helped parents/caregivers build stronger relationships with their children (Bratton, Ray, Rhine, & Jones, 2005). Knowing this to be an evidence-based best practice for children, I became thrilled to be able to include Darryl's mother and sister in this intervention. As part of the intervention, Darryl's mother spent 30 minutes of special play time with Darryl each week where she practiced her new skills. Since Darryl's mother seemed interested in learning more about how she could help her son, this intervention gave her the support and skills she sought. Conducting these interventions at the school enabled me to stay connected with the mother through face-to-face encounters, which often presented a challenge for counselors who work with students on a regular school campus.

When working with children, it became important to connect with as many parts of the child's support system as possible. After the primary caregivers, the teacher usually becomes the most prominent adult in the child's life. Including teachers in trainings, educational workshops, and consultations develops lasting positive impacts on children like Darryl (White & Stern, 2009). As the third intervention, I empowered Darryl's teacher to learn classroom management skills using play therapy language and techniques. The teacher attended a 2-day workshop and became part of a program called Kinder Training (White & Stern, 2009). This program trained and supervised teachers to use play therapy language to strengthen their connection with students, much like filial therapy strengthens the relationship between parents and children. Afterward, I observed Darryl's teacher in her classroom and gave feedback on using the language. She appeared extremely motivated, and seemed capable of implementing new strategies not only with Darryl but with all of her students.

Goals and Strategies for Myself

When working with students using play therapy techniques, I viewed relationship building as a crucial component in the healing process. I knew that my undivided attention helped Darryl to connect with and trust me. I suspected that there would be times when Darryl would display violent play or images because of his experiences; and though I do not like violence, I became committed to staying with him, offering him "unconditional positive regard." As a doctoral student, I worked under two supervisors, one for the site and one at the university; both held Licensed Professional Counselor Supervisors (LPC-S) as well as Registered Play Therapist Supervisors (RPT-S) credentials. I used both of these experts to help me cope with some of the challenges I faced in the session, as well as help me clinically understand the sessions and the child. Both proved to be invaluable as I worked with Darryl and some of his other classmates.

COUNSELING PROCESS FLOW

Using an Adlerian lens to understand Darryl and nondirective play therapy techniques, I worked with Darryl for approximately 7 months, once a week, except during school holidays and testing weeks. In using nondirective play therapy techniques, the child directs his or her own play, decides what to play with, and determines how he or she will play. The role of the counselor is to use facilitative responses to show the child that the counselor is fully present and understands him or her. The use of tracking, encouragement, reflection of feeling, and limit-setting language became key (Landreth, 2012). Tracking presented a technique where the counselor noticed what the child engaged in and stated it to the child (i.e., "You're looking around the room"). Encouragement appeared different from praise in that it focused on the process rather than the product, and it enabled the child to take ownership of his or her successes rather than the worth being decided by the adult (Kottman, 2015; Landreth, 2012; i.e., "You are working hard to get that the way you want it"). Reflection of feeling helps the child to feel understood while also helping him or her to identify his or her own feelings; and limit setting keeps the child safe while also allowing the child the opportunity to recognize limits and regulate his or her behavior accordingly (Kottman, 2015; Landreth, 2012).

When we entered the playroom, I instructed Darryl that he could play with the toys in many different ways. For the first few sessions, Darryl explored the playroom. In our third session, he began to play out a story that he repeated for nearly 5 months. He created a scene in the sand where many different men fought. One group fought with another group, while another group formed a circle around them, watching and cheering. I tracked the events in the sand, noticing that they became really angry with one another, and they seemed to try to hurt each other. Always there seemed to be one guy who would be on the ground while another miniature man beat him. At this point, he brought the police into the sand. When the police got to the fight, everyone hid from them; and each time, they appeared to be very proud of themselves for successfully hiding from the police. Rather than insert a moral judgment on how fighting appeared wrong and the police needed to be viewed as those who help, I stayed with his story reflecting on their relief that they did not get caught and appeared smarter than the police. One day about 5 months into counseling, I noticed how angry Darryl seemed; and I shifted my reflections from the men in the sand to reflecting his anger. He started to breathe heavily and clench and unclench his fists. I reflected that he worked hard not to use his own fists even though he seemed angry. I stayed with him, trusted that he would not hit me, and assumed him able to go back to his story in the sand. This time the story changed. The scenario now included good guys and bad guys. He made himself one of the miniatures, a good guy. The scenario did not include any cops to hide from, and the fighting became something that the miniature that represented Darryl tried to stop. For the next 2 months, Darryl continued to play in the sand, saving the good guys and punishing the bad guys.

While working with Darryl individually, I taught those same basic play therapy language skills to his mother, sister, and teacher. Darryl's mother and sister began special play time with Darryl, which he loved. Techniques of filial training presented parents a gift of seeing their children differently. Darryl's mother eventually saw her son as a creative and intelligent child who tried to make sense of the violence inflicted by his father while also missing the man he loved. She became grateful for that time with Darryl, and stated that their relationship grew stronger. His teacher also worked hard to incorporate encouragement, reflection of feeling, and limit setting into her classroom setting. The teacher felt that techniques from filial training enabled her to build stronger relationships with her students and created a calmer classroom environment.

OUTCOME

Darryl's behavior started to change about 3 months into our time together. He started to help other students in his class with material they did not understand, and his violent outbursts lessened. About 5 months into our work together, his outbursts stopped completely. His relationships with his mother, her fiancé, his sister, and his teacher strengthened, and he became so successful at the alternative school that the school allowed him to return to his home campus for third grade.

Many factors aligned so that these interventions could be successful. Darryl's mother prepared herself by doing some personal work in order to heal from her own difficult situation. This work really helped with her son. Despite limited financial resources, the family received a level of service from the alternative school counseling department normally reserved for those who worked with a private practitioner. Because the principal of the alternative school heard about the program that we offered through a grant and university support, the family participated in a long-term counseling process that worked with every part of the child's system. They participated at no cost and counseling with Darryl occurred at school.

Trusting that children possess the capability to work through their challenges and can accomplish this on their own time table appears challenging for many adults to understand. Doing this work in the school is not typical. Very often counselors are pressured to work at an accelerated pace. In this case, Darryl took time to process his feelings of grief related to the loss of his father. He also grew more connected to his family and community.

Often in schools we are presented with opportunities to follow up with students after an intervention. In this case, Darryl returned to his home school, and follow-up ended up being an uneasy task to complete. After returning to his home campus, Darryl did not return to the alternative school, which in and of itself appeared to be a success. Shortly after termination, his mother reported that she continued to use her skills and knowledge to strengthen her relationship with Darryl. His teacher continued to use the skills learned in her classroom, and maintained a very strong practice of helping her students return to their home campuses.

REFERENCES

Bratton, S., Ray, D., Rhine, T., & Jones, T. (2005). The efficacy of play therapy with children: A meta-analytic review of treatment outcomes. *Professional Psychology: Research and Practice, 36*(4), 376–390.

Erikson, E. (1950). *Childhood and society.* New York, NY: W. W. Norton.

Kottman, T. (2015). *Partners in play: An Adlerian approach to play therapy* (3rd ed.). Alexandria, VA: American Counseling Association.

Landreth, G. (2012). *Play therapy: The art of the relationship* (3rd ed.). New York, NY: Brunner-Routledge.

Landreth, G., & Bratton, S. (2005). *Child-parent relationship therapy (CPRT): A 10-week filial therapy model.* New York, NY: Routledge.

White, J., & Stern, L. (2009). Kinder training: An Adlerian-based model to enhance teacher-student relationships. In A. Drews (Ed.), *Blending play therapy with cognitive behavioral therapy: Evidence-based and other effective treatments and techniques* (pp. 281–295). Hoboken, NJ: John Wiley & Sons.

CHAPTER 3

A GIFT FOR JEFFREY

Taryne M. Mingo

I met Jeffrey on a uniquely ordinary day. At the beginning of my third week as a first-year counselor, I visited every classroom by grade level and introduced myself as the new counselor at a local elementary school. I scheduled visits to the kindergarten classrooms through the third week of school; and each visit appeared to go smoothly until I visited one particular class. As I closed my lesson, I explained to the students that I needed three volunteers to tell me the essence of my lesson. I noticed a small-framed child, considerably smaller than the others, seated near the back of the rug frantically waving his hand in the air. I called on him. "What is your name, dear?" I asked. "Jeffrey," he said, and began stammering, "I . . . I . . . ," until his teacher jumped from her desk and shouted, "Oh no! Ms. Mingo, I'm so sorry, but I just got a call from the front office, and they need you up front to handle an emergency! Everyone, tell Ms. Mingo goodbye! Jeffrey, have a seat." As I got up from the rocking chair, Jeffrey, who was still standing, watched as I walked to the door. Just before I exited the room, I heard a shrill scream and turned to look back in time to see Jeffrey fall to the floor wailing. His teacher waved at me, and gestured she would tend to him.

Many, including myself, may consider Jeffrey's reaction to be a developmentally appropriate response to disappointment. I did not question this assumption until I returned from the front office nearly 3 hours later and found his teacher in my office comforting a sobbing child—Jeffrey—who sat curled on the floor. "I don't know what to do, Ms. Mingo," the clearly stressed teacher explained. She explained that Jeffrey had continued crying since I had left the room. And this continuous crying appeared typical of his behavior since school had begun

3 weeks earlier. "I just don't know what to do. He cries excessively—every day, all day—and it's distracting for the kids and myself. I can't teach with him in there." I immediately thought it inappropriate to blame Jeffrey, a 5-year-old child, for crying excessively. But as I worked with Jeffrey over the next few months, I began to realize that Jeffrey battled with more than just disappointment.

His teacher scheduled a meeting with Jeffrey's parents a week after my encounter with him in his classroom, and she invited me and the school principal to serve as a support team for Jeffrey. Prior to the meeting, his teacher, the principal, and I felt Jeffrey could benefit from meeting with me when he experienced crying outbursts. After he became capable of composing himself while meeting with me, he could return to class. Jeffrey's parents agreed with our plan. As expected, the teacher brought Jeffrey to my room the very next day of school. He appeared upset when he missed one of the answers on his spelling test and, although he performed better than any other student in his classroom, he focused on that one incorrect answer.

SYSTEMIC INFLUENCES

Jeffrey, an 8-year-old White male student, lived with his mother, father, and two older brothers, ages 14 and 17. His middle-class family resided in the rural Southeast. Jeffrey's parents placed a high value on education and held high expectations for their sons' academic futures. Both parents had received a college education. Jeffrey's dad worked as an engineer at a local factory, and his mother was a stay-at-home mom who frequently attended their sons' school events and conferences.

Jeffrey's parents intentionally exposed their children to events or educational material that they believed furthered their children's academic futures. They expected Jeffrey to be placed in a class for gifted children just as their two older sons had been during their elementary years. Jeffrey's parents played a significant role in his academic development as they consistently encouraged him to read and complete his homework every day after school, and offered him video games that seemed "intellectually stimulating." I asked Jeffrey if he liked television programs on Nickelodeon, and he replied, "No, if I watch television, it's mostly BBC America with my dad. Plus, my mom says those shows [on Nickelodeon] are too childish for me anyway."

Jeffrey excelled academically beyond his two brothers, who often teased Jeffrey about being a "nerd." Although they referred to him as "Jeffrey the Genius," they genuinely seemed to love and be proud of their younger brother. Jeffrey's mother acknowledged that Jeffrey struggled more socially and emotionally than his brothers. Similar to his outbursts at school, Jeffrey's mother stated that when Jeffrey became "frustrated" he hit her or his dad, or hit himself. She, however, minimized this behavior as a negative coping strategy that Jeffrey used to get attention, and saw it as no major concern.

When I suggested psychological testing to see if Jeffrey could benefit from special education services and receive more one-on-one academic and counseling assistance, Jeffrey's mother not only looked surprised, but seemed insulted by this recommendation for her gifted son. Special education, unfortunately, is still viewed by parents, and even teachers, as a negative label and service in educational institutions. Therefore, I quickly attempted to deconstruct the negative association of special education by explaining that special education services meant providing additional opportunities to support Jeffrey's ability to be successful in classroom settings. I also described Jeffrey's decisions to hit himself or other students as a learned behavioral response when he felt anxious and unable to cognitively process his emotions. But the idea that Jeffrey appeared unable to solve any situation in comparison to his peers infuriated his mother even more. She refused testing for special education placement and wrote off his negative behavior as temporary. Lastly, his mother no longer wanted Jeffrey to meet with me for counseling services. The principal and teacher, who also attended this conference, agreed with the mother's decision.

DEVELOPMENTAL CONSIDERATIONS

Jeffrey displays developmental characteristics similar to other children his age, such as becoming upset when dropped off at school by a parent and desiring to play with toys. His intellectual development, however, seemed to mask his maturity level. His ability to effectively communicate gave the impression that Jeffrey could handle more responsibilities than other students his age. However, when Jeffrey encountered an unpredictable situation or when pressed to follow directions he disagreed with, he resorted to excessive crying outbursts and tantrums. Sometimes, he threw chairs across the room, hit teachers or students, or even attempted to hurt himself. On several different occasions, Jeffrey hit himself or verbalized his frustrations by stating, "Jeffrey, stop crying you idiot! You're such a baby!" These types of situations left his teachers confused as to how a gifted child could articulate his thoughts so well but fail to control his emotions on a daily basis.

Cognitive and Intellectual Development

The school recognized Jeffrey as "academically advanced" in comparison to his classmates and identified him as gifted when he reached third grade. He demonstrated a heightened ability in vocabulary, communication, sentence structure, and even proved adept in understanding and evoking sarcasm. He excelled on the examination used to screen for potentially gifted students, earned a near perfect score on each of the state-mandated comprehensive tests, and remained the highest performing student. During his fourth grade year, he won the school- and district-level spelling bee and received the highest score by judges during the *Invent America* science contest.

Personal, Social, and Emotional Development

As I continued working with Jeffrey, I learned that he truly enjoyed reading science-fiction texts and writing fictional stories in his journal. Jeffrey appeared very polite and friendly in environments he perceived as predictable, quiet, and comforting. Even on days when he came to my office after one of his crying outbursts in the classroom, he recognized that I provided a safe space for him. He also knew that we would collaboratively develop solutions for his outbursts.

Jeffrey struggled socially in the classroom with his peers and in other areas of social engagement (i.e., cafeteria, gym, or playground). From kindergarten until second grade, Jeffrey showed no interest in acquiring friends and, according to his teachers, despised any classroom activity that involved group work. Jeffrey often requested to play by himself at recess, kept his eyes on his food during lunch, and only talked to other students when they asked him a direct question. When the school placed Jeffrey in a classroom for gifted students, I noticed Jeffrey's willingness to *tolerate* conversations with other students, particularly with those who shared his interest in science fiction. He also began to participate in group activities within the gifted classroom, as long as his classmates did not challenge or change any of his ideas. Jeffrey and his classmates spent nearly an hour drawing a design for cars of the future. But when his classmates decided to change the design of the rear lights, a change that Jeffrey appeared adamantly against despite being outnumbered by his classmates, he ripped the drawing into multiple pieces and threw them at his classmates.

These incidents indicated that Jeffrey's emotional status hinged on being in control of his environment. He experienced severe anxiety when his environment became unpredictable or uncomfortable. In school settings, children are expected to learn how to navigate social relationships with peers, learn conflict resolution skills, and become empathetic to others. Unfortunately, some students, even those deemed gifted or academically advanced, find these expectations difficult. Ultimately, I decided to monitor him closely to see if he might benefit from the social and emotional support services that the special education program could provide.

RELATIONAL CONSIDERATIONS

Jeffrey demonstrated little to no interest in making friends, and almost always requested to work alone and stay to himself during recess and lunch. Of the few peers he did choose to interact with during class, they shared similar interests related to science and mathematics. However, Jeffrey treated these children as more of a means to an end rather than a desire to acquire social connection or friendly relationships. I believe Jeffrey preferred to isolate himself from peers and even teachers, when not discussing academics, because he wanted to avoid unpredictable and uncomfortable situations. As demonstrated since kindergarten, Jeffrey's emotional response to disappointment, frustration, or any other anxiety-producing situation typically led to harming himself or others. Jeffrey's parents, prior to his admittance to the hospital, viewed these emotional outbursts as attempts for attention, and often encouraged his teachers to find alternative ways to ignore or "work around" these behaviors. During a parent conference, Jeffrey's fourth grade teacher informed his parents how Jeffrey punched a child in the stomach as his class prepared to get in line for lunch. His parents responded, "Yes, Jeffrey told us about this. He said the child took his spot in line. You see, Jeffrey liked to predict what number he will stand in line, and I guess when that child took his spot he became upset. It might be best for you [the teacher] to allow Jeffrey to choose where he wants to be in line first before the class is asked to line-up altogether." This is just an example of the relationship Jeffrey's parents maintained with their son. Unfortunately, most of Jeffrey's peers also began to work around his behavior out of fear that he would hurt them. Nevertheless despite his emotional outbursts and his teacher's attempts to proactively avoid situations that might cause them, he continued to demonstrate violent behavior, and, because he excelled academically, his teacher never referred him to the principal's office.

MULTICULTURAL CONSIDERATIONS

Far too often as a professional school counselor, I met students who identified as gifted through standardized examinations. The school denied some of these students the opportunity to build upon their intellectual gifts because their behaviors in the classroom proceeded the teacher's view of their capabilities. In addition, educational research on teacher perception found that students of color, non-English–speaking students, and students with disabilities seemed to be the least likely student populations to get recommended for gifted classes (Seon-Young, Olszewski-Kubilius, & Peternel, 2010); they are many times viewed as not fitting within the narrow lens of what it meant to be gifted. Therefore, Jeffrey represented many students whom I advocated for in terms of receiving support, not just for academic success, but also for overcoming life's obstacles as they went on to pursue their future endeavors.

In my experiences as a professional school counselor, many presume gifted children to be White, English-speaking children from the United States who live in two-parent, middle-class families. In addition, many assume gifted children to be well behaved and destined for future success with little to no support. Therefore students like Jeffrey, who fit the cognitive and physical expectations of a gifted child, but fall outside the emotional and behavioral expectations may go unsupported due to stereotypes pertaining to gifted children. Many times, the "gifted gate" gets closed on students who demonstrate disruptive behavior, psychological concerns, limited classroom assertiveness, or even limited English proficiency (Peterson, 2015). Kroesbergen, van Hooijdonk, Van Viersen, Middel-Lalleman, and Reijnders (2016) also add that within the education field, teachers' perceptions of what determines a gifted student vary and may pose significant impacts on students' perceived academic capabilities. Therefore, these narrow identity characteristics that seem to define the perceptions about gifted children can unjustly impact gifted children living in poverty, gifted children of color, gifted children with disabilities, and gifted children with emotional–behavioral disorders (Peterson, 2015).

Jeffrey did fit within the stereotyped expectation of gifted students; however, his emotional and behavioral issues did not. These issues stemmed from severe anxiety and fear of failure, and went unsupported by his parents and teachers. Jeffrey demonstrated all of the characteristics of students who identified as having an emotional–behavioral disorder, frequent physical outbursts, self-harm and harm to others, and an inability to control his emotions (Rizza & Morrison, 2002). Nevertheless, his parents, the school principal, and Jeffrey's third grade teacher continued to argue against my recommendation that Jeffrey be tested for special education services for emotional–behavioral support. Because Jeffrey fit perfectly within the stereotypical expectations of a gifted student, he missed out on essential support opportunities because his giftedness masked his emotional and social needs.

CONCEPTUALIZATION

Considering the request made by Jeffrey's mother to discontinue my meetings with her son, I continued helping him through his teachers. I developed goals that enabled the teachers to: (a) recognize triggers that might upset him, (b) perform calming exercises (i.e., deep breathing), and (c) encourage positive self-talk. I chose these goals because I truly felt his emotional outbursts seemed connected to anxiety and an inability to process his emotions in unpredictable and uncomfortable environments. I chose techniques that worked during our previous sessions, and informed Jeffrey's teacher how to meet these goals in the classroom setting. I also consulted with colleagues from my graduate school counseling program, who agreed with this approach. Through a solution-focused therapy approach, I continued to monitor Jeffery's progress within the classroom, and created instructional strategies for his teachers. Based on my counseling notes, his teachers assisted Jeffrey in recognizing barriers to success; given his high-level reasoning skills, this did not appear to be a difficult task for him to achieve.

COUNSELING PROCESS FLOW

Jeffrey's fourth grade year stood out most to me because it became the year that I realized Jeffrey's gifted abilities in academics hindered him from getting the support he needed. Most of his behaviors went undisciplined as his fourth grade teacher never sent him to the principal's office. But one day the principal's office called me for a meeting and, to my complete surprise, I entered the office and observed Jeffrey's mother sobbing. Over the winter break, Jeffrey had become so angry with his parents that he locked himself in a bathroom and stuffed his throat with tissues until he passed out. After the hospital admitted Jeffrey and referred him to a clinical mental health counselor (CMHC) in the area, Jeffrey's mother asked me to talk with this counselor so that we could work together to provide strategies for Jeffrey at his school. They also asked me to consult with Jeffrey's teacher about his progress at school. I agreed.

Systemic Approaches

I provide a description in the following section of how I used an intersectional approach to support Jeffrey as a professional school counselor after his mother recommended I begin working with Jeffrey and his CMHC counselor to support his emotional and academic needs. I presented three systemic approaches: the family system, the peer system, and the school environment system. Each systemic approach detailed which individuals became involved in the counseling process, what happened across counseling sessions, and the anticipated length of involvement for the desired outcome of therapy. In collaboration with the CMHC counselor, I presented the following goals as the desired outcome: (a) help Jeffrey acknowledge and accept responsibility for his negative behaviors, (b) help him understand the source of his frustration, and (c) help him develop new positive behaviors to replace negative behaviors when he felt frustrated.

The Family System

At the family level of my counseling approach, I scheduled a meeting with Jeffrey's mother and father, two brothers, and the CMHC counselor to coordinate a plan that would be consistent in helping Jeffrey achieve one of the outlined goals. I felt it important for Jeffrey to be in attendance at this meeting so that he would recognize all of the individuals supporting him. I also wanted him to feel accountable for improving his behavior. In an effort to empower Jeffrey through the negative images that he possessed of himself, I named the plan we created *The Chronicles of Thompson.* I did this to reflect one of Jeffrey's favorite books that focused on overcoming life obstacles. I wanted to prevent Jeffrey from feeling as though he seemed to be the only family member who needed to make behavioral changes. The CMHC counselor, who received background information on Jeffrey's parents and siblings, used this information during our meeting to address anomalies in the self-care plan for Jeffrey. The counselor and I helped Jeffrey's parents develop new behavioral responses that fostered changes in Jeffrey's behavior and developed a new vocabulary to help Jeffrey deal with his anxiety about failure. This vocabulary consisted of phrases such as, "You are not alone in how you feel," and "When you are ready to talk, I am here for you." Once a month at school for the remainder of Jeffrey's fourth grade year, *The Chronicles of Thompson* met and his family discussed the challenges and triumphs of the time since the previous meeting.

The Peer System

As another means to achieve the outlined goals for Jeffrey, I invited Jeffrey to join a counseling group composed of three other friends whom he trusted. Jeffrey chose three students, two boys and one girl, whom he encountered in the gifted math class he took every evening. These three students—Jeffrey's classmates since kindergarten—developed a close relationship with him. I found his choice of friends to be a great opportunity to teach Jeffrey how to develop new positive behaviors to replace negative behaviors when he felt frustrated. This included not allowing Jeffrey to dictate the rules of a team activity during our group sessions, being open to different ideas to solve problems, and detecting social cues that led to frustrating feelings. Our group met twice a week during lunch for the remainder of his fourth grade year and included teamwork activities geared toward problem solving, learning to communicate through expressive art, and exploring non-academic areas of interest.

The School System

Due to the number of meltdowns and physical reactions to himself or others, testing results categorized Jeffrey with an emotional–behavioral disorder. Once acknowledged that Jeffrey could benefit from additional support to meet his academic needs, his mother gave consent for his teacher to enroll him in special education services so that he could be provided an increased level of direct attention and support. The school placed him in a smaller classroom of five students for 50% of the school day. I worked with Jeffrey on a deeper level after his CMHC counselor sessions. The principal and fourth grade teacher recognized the importance of providing an intersectional approach to meet Jeffrey's emotional needs (rather than focusing only on his academics). Now that we all worked together and operated under the same expectations for Jeffrey, we observed Jeffrey's negative behaviors drastically lessened.

OUTCOME

Recognizing that anxiety appeared to be an underlying factor in Jeffrey's behavioral issues, I wanted to use an approach that incorporated interventions that respected his feelings without empowering his fears of failure. The three intervention systems (family, peer, and school environment) assisted in eliminating Jeffrey's anxiety and helped him manage from a holistic approach. The family system intervention became useful in helping Jeffrey and his family acknowledge how their passive attitudes about Jeffrey's negative behaviors might hinder his attempts to relearn those behaviors. This seemed the most beneficial intervention that we provided to Jeffrey so that he could begin to receive the same level of support at home and school. As a result of this intervention, he demonstrated new positive behaviors when frustrating events happened.

The peer system intervention proved beneficial only in terms of teaching Jeffrey positive social behaviors when he became anxious. Due to his group members' familiarity with his personality, they seemed hesitant to confront Jeffrey about his negative behaviors during group sessions and relied on me to redirect him. Therefore, I made Jeffrey aware of his inappropriate behaviors during group sessions. This became a skill I felt would benefit him in a classroom environment. If given an opportunity to change my intervention, I would still use the group counseling approach. However, rather than let Jeffrey choose his group members, I would select students who could prove beneficial to his social development, but not enable his current pattern of social interaction.

The school environment system intervention also proved beneficial in providing a net of support, and offered Jeffrey long-term support as he moved across grade levels. As a professional school counselor, I found this approach to be beneficial in finding new and creative ways to support Jeffrey without resistance from administration or other teachers who originally found my attempts unnecessary. For example, teachers allowed me extended time with Jeffrey to conduct expressive arts techniques that enabled him to explore self-perception, anxiety triggers, and peer conflict. Once the teachers, administrators, and his parents saw the benefits of counseling interventions conducted by the CMHC counselor and me across the home and school environment, Jeffrey made significant progress in addition to his high academic performance.

Overall, I assessed the interventions as successful approaches that assisted in helping me reach the three goals I outlined for Jeffrey. Additionally, after watching Jeffrey develop socially, emotionally, and academically from kindergarten to fourth grade, I felt that I provided him a gift—needed support—which seemed to elude him because of his giftedness. In addition, I hope to provide awareness about the narrow perception of gifted children and highlight potential missed opportunities when schools overlook the needs of those gifted children. I believe it is important for schools to provide a holistic and supportive framework for all students across all identity groups, including those who are identified as gifted.

REFERENCES

Kroesbergen, E. H., van Hooijdonk, M., Van Viersen, S., Middel-Lalleman, M. N., & Reijnders, J. W. (2016). The psychological well-being of early identified gifted children. *Gifted Child Quarterly, 60*(1), 16–30. http://dx.doi.org/10.1177/0016986215609113

Peterson, J. S. (2015). School counselors and gifted kids: Respecting both cognitive and affective. *Journal of Counseling & Development, 93*(2), 153–162. http://dx.doi.org/10.1002/j.1556-6676.2015.00191.x

Rizza, M. G., & Morrison, W. F. (2002). Uncovering stereotypes and identifying characteristics of gifted students and students with emotional/behavioral disabilities. *Roeper Review, 25*(2), 73.

Seon-Young, L., Olszewski-Kubilius, P., & Peternel, G. (2010). The efficacy of academic acceleration for gifted minority students. *Gifted Child Quarterly, 54*(3), 189–208. http://dx.doi.org/10.1177/0016986210369256

CHAPTER 4

JIMMY IN THE MIDDLE

Claudia Morales

Jimmy, a 10-year-old Caucasian male, enrolled in our school. His family moved to our school community after a deployment in Germany. I first met Jimmy at the beginning of my first year when I conducted a guidance lesson that introduced my role as the professional school counselor. Shortly afterward, Jimmy approached and asked to speak with me about his parents.

A year ago, I interned at a different school and discovered that most of the students I worked with presented issues resulting from being in divorced or separated families. Jimmy became the first student I counseled on this campus regarding his parents' impending divorce. In 1996, divorce affected more than 1 million children (Bryner, 2001). Statistics such as this predict that professional school counselors may face a greater chance of working with children of divorced and separated parents. The major issues surrounding the effects of divorce on children occur in five stages: denial, anger, bargaining, depression, and acceptance (Bryner, 2001). When Jimmy first came to see me, he appeared to be in the denial stage. He appeared to not be able to accept his parents' divorce.

SYSTEMIC INFLUENCES

Because of Jimmy's father's military employment, the family moved frequently. Jimmy disclosed being an only child and that his family did not live near any close relatives. His maternal grandparents lived overseas. Jimmy reported that the frequent moves did not inflict an emotional impact on him; he said that he got used to it. Jimmy described his home life as uneventful, except when he played with video games and friends in the neighborhood. With his parents' impending divorce, the family dynamics changed and affected the way that Jimmy spent time with his parents. Family time no longer consisted of the three of them engaging in activities together. Instead, Jimmy found himself alone or with his mother. He reported spending little time with his father, except for occasionally watching a television program with him.

In my third visit with Jimmy, he reported being angry at his father for his father's infidelity. He lacked comprehension of his father's behavior and felt sympathy for his mother. According to the American Academy of Child and Adolescent Psychiatry (2011), parents can sometimes feel so overwhelmed with their own feelings that they unintentionally put stress on their children by looking to them for comfort or advice. This phenomenon became clear when Jimmy disclosed that the conversations with his mother almost always included a detailed retelling of her discussions with his father. Jimmy felt that he could not turn to others. He felt stuck in the middle of his parents.

DEVELOPMENTAL CONSIDERATIONS

Cognitive Development

Jimmy appeared to be functioning in the concrete operational stage of cognitive development (Huitt & Hummel, 2003; Piaget, 1932). In this stage, egocentric thought processes start to subside, and children begin to develop a sense of empathy (Huitt & Hummel, 2003; Piaget, 1932). At this stage in life, children begin to understand what others might feel or think. This is a pivotal time in developing problem-solving skills.

Academically, Jimmy earned average grades and appeared to be self-motivated to improve in his areas of weakness. Since Jimmy's records came from the Department of Defense education system, his grade equivalents in our district showed that academically, he performed on grade level.

Personal, Social, and Emotional Development

Jimmy met friends in the neighborhood with whom he played after school and on the weekends. Being new to the school, he made a few friends within the first week of school. He seemed tall for his age and appeared skinny, lanky, and wore glasses. He usually displayed a pleasant demeanor, smiling and laughing with his classmates. His teacher described him as a good student who gave his best effort. Jimmy enjoyed playing video games, watching television, and participating in the school's chess club. From a developmental standpoint (Erikson, 1982), Jimmy appeared to function in the industry versus inferiority stage of psychosocial development. This meant that Jimmy seemed susceptible to feeling inadequacy (i.e., his sadness about his parents' impending divorce and his failed attempts to keep them together).

RELATIONAL CONSIDERATIONS

Jimmy presented as an introverted child and maintained few close friends. Yet he did not feel comfortable enough to share his family business with them. Being new to the school, he recently started the process of developing relationships with his peers at school and in his neighborhood. Jimmy reported getting along with both of his parents at home and he enjoyed spending time with them. Jimmy felt comfortable with me and talked with ease about the struggle of coping with his parents' separation. However, Jimmy displayed little emotion when he retold his story. He also used his quirky personality to make light of serious situations. I considered the counseling relationship to be important; therefore, I viewed his quirky personality as a defense mechanism.

MULTICULTURAL CONSIDERATIONS

Jimmy's father came from the East Coast and his mother came from an Eastern European country. Although I did not ask Jimmy specifically, his family appeared to be middle class. His father worked, and his mother stayed at home. The family sent Jimmy overseas to visit family during summer breaks. Living in different parts of the world gave him an opportunity to meet other children of military families. Being an only child, this enabled Jimmy to enjoy playtime and social interactions with children his age.

Jimmy's father traveled a great deal throughout his military career. Jimmy became accustomed to this military lifestyle; in this case, his father traveled and Jimmy and his mother stayed home. Military lifestyle impacts the family unit when it comes to everyday life and relationships. According to the National Center for PTSD (Posttraumatic Stress Disorder; 2016), the parent who stays behind in a military family faces more responsibilities, isolation, and, in general, a sense of feeling overwhelmed. When infidelity becomes an issue, this adds to the family's stress, as in Jimmy's case. As per the *Demographics 2007 Profile of the Military Community* (ICF International, n.d.) report, 3.9% (52,701) of all active duty military showed a divorced marital status.

CONCEPTUALIZATION

One morning as I greeted students in front of the school, Jimmy approached me and asked, "Can I talk to you today?" He did not appear as the jovial student I met in guidance lessons. I became curious about his personality change. While participating in guidance, he behaved well and engaged in the lessons, but appeared hesitant to share too much personal information. I became concerned about the seriousness of Jimmy's request to see me because neither Jimmy nor his teacher previously expressed interest in a counseling referral. After I explained the limits of confidentiality, he started to explain the reason for his visit. This happened to be the first time I spoke with Jimmy in an individual counseling setting. In this session, I used person-centered theory (Reichenberg & Seligman, 2010; Rogers, 1961). This approach appeared effective because Jimmy, being an only child, felt stuck in the middle of a very adult situation. I wanted Jimmy to feel that someone understood him and cared about this life-changing event.

Jimmy informed me that his parents considered getting a divorce and he felt really sad and confused about the whole situation. While we talked, I noticed that Jimmy frequently played with the trinkets on my desk. He even asked me to name some of them and said that they helped him think when he played with certain ones. He revealed that he felt afraid that he could be getting another mom and dad. However, he did not express sadness about this. During our conversation, I used a variety of open-ended questions to understand Jimmy's perspective. For example, I asked, "How would you feel about having another mom and dad?" He responded in a very matter-of-fact way, "That's what people do when they get divorced. They find someone else." After listening to Jimmy express his concerns and revealing that he never thought that he would encounter a situation like this, I noticed him frequently repeating himself. I asked if he would like to come visit me again so that we could work through some of the thoughts and feelings he faced. Jimmy agreed to meet with me, and I let him know I would coordinate with his homeroom teacher to inform her of our next visit.

Goals and Strategies for Myself

While working with Jimmy, I came up with two goals. I created the first goal to establish a positive rapport with him by demonstrating an unconditional positive regard for his thoughts and feelings (Reichenberg & Seligman, 2010; Rogers, 1961). I wanted to make sure that I appeared empathetic to his being an only child in a military family. I wanted him to know that I understood the impact that this might pose regarding his emotional well-being. To engage Jimmy through developmentally appropriate techniques, I established the second goal to incorporate play therapy techniques in our sessions. To do this, I consulted with a fellow professional school counselor who offered her experience with sand tray therapy. Homeyer and Morrison (2008) state that play elicits physical activity that helps the brain transfer memories from nonverbal parts of the brain to the verbal frontal lobes.

Strategies for the Client

I wanted Jimmy to benefit from play therapy type techniques. I also used solution-focused techniques such as the miracle and scaling questions (Brasher, 2009; de Shazer & Berg, 1997). The scaling questions helped me to gauge Jimmy's emotional state when he discussed his parents. Additionally, I incorporated a person-centered approach that allowed me to convey empathy and understanding in the first session.

COUNSELING PROCESS FLOW

In a school setting, professional school counselors are limited in the amount of time allotted with students. Within the school day, students receive their academic lessons from teachers; and the counselors are responsible for delivering guidance, conducting small group counseling sessions, and seeing students individually. While it would be ideal to see each student weekly for an hour, the reality is counselors are allowed limited access to students during regular school hours. Brief therapy techniques seemed to be the most effective approach to use in the school environment because of these time constraints (Brasher, 2009). I saw Jimmy four times over the course of a month. In the first two sessions, Jimmy spent time telling the story of what happened the day he found out his parents contemplated divorce. The following represents a description of the second meeting with Jimmy and what transpired as he told me the story of his troubles and concerns.

Since Jimmy enjoyed using some of the stress-relieving trinkets displayed on my desk, I decided to ask him to try a sand tray activity to assist him in expressing what he appeared to be going through. I wanted to know how his parents' decision to divorce affected him. This provided a little more direction and focus. Jimmy replied, "Sure, why not?" I presented him with a tray of sand and a wide variety of manipulatives to choose from. After sifting through the sand to ensure no items remained, he quickly began to place stones strategically throughout the sand tray. He also chose a toy soldier and two seashells.

The toy soldier represented his father's military status. He used a blue stone to represent himself and a larger blue stone to represent his mother. Jimmy told the story of the night he found out about his parents' impending divorce. He explained this as he moved the stones and other figures around the sand tray. He indicated that his mother and father called him into the living room to tell him that they planned to separate because of his father's infidelity. He moved his stone to the corner of the box with two seashells. Jimmy also placed the stone representing his mother next to his stone. When I asked what the seashells represented, he said, "I was crying so much that night." The seashells came from the ocean, which represented how much he cried. I, then, asked what made him choose a larger stone for his mother and a human-like figure for his father. He said that although his mother presented herself as colder and harder, she still cared.

Jimmy informed me that his mother told him details about what happened. He also stated that he liked knowing, but wished his mother did not tell him everything. Parents do not always appear to be aware of the effects of divorce and children's reaction to it. For example, some parents seem to become dependent on children to compensate for the lack of emotional support from spouses (Bryner, 2001). I kept this in mind as Jimmy told the rest of his story.

As he moved his stone and his mother's stone closer to his father's figure, he placed his stone in the middle. He described the three of them sitting on the couch, his mother on one side and his father on the other. Jimmy said, "It was at that moment I knew I would be in the middle of them." This appeared to be an impactful statement since Jimmy reported being an only child. He could not rely on anyone else at home to talk about this situation. Jimmy began to open up and I became hesitant to contact his parents at this time. I feared he would stop disclosing. I did, however, check with his teacher to see how Jimmy progressed academically. His teacher revealed that Jimmy seemed slightly distracted, but his grades remained in the average range. Although Jimmy maintained his grades, he seemed affected emotionally by the situation he and his parents faced. Eventually, after I noticed Jimmy with his head down one afternoon, I contacted his mother to inquire about how she observed him at home. I let her know that I spoke with Jimmy and became concerned because usually he is quite talkative. She seemed thankful for my call and concern, but did not disclose many details. She also informed me that Jimmy appeared not to be feeling well. She assured me that she would talk with Jimmy.

Even though Jimmy's facial expressions never really displayed sadness, his tone appeared solemn; especially when he expressed that he thought he could do something to convince his parents to stay together.

At that point, I decided to incorporate solution-focused questioning to clarify for Jimmy how much of this situation he could control (or not control; de Shazer & Berg, 1997; Reichenberg & Seligman, 2010). I asked about his plans to keep his parents together. He responded, "I'll just have to convince her to forgive him." It became clear that Jimmy thought that he would be able to talk to his mother into taking his father back and thus prevent the divorce from taking place. Next, using a scaling question, with 1 being not likely at all and 10 being very likely, I asked him about the likelihood of his efforts being successful. He responded by saying, "about a 6," because he planned to really try hard. I asked how he would feel if he tried to talk to his mother and she decided to go through with the divorce anyway. And to my surprise, he told me he would be sad, but at least he tried. I expected him to say he planned on trying again. His short response led me to believe that he, now, appeared to be between the bargaining and depression stages of the divorce (Bryner, 2001).

In the next two sessions, Jimmy revealed a problem with his mother who shared intimate details with Jimmy about the divorce. We reviewed possible "I messages" Jimmy might use to assist him in telling his mother about his level of discomfort with her disclosures. For example, "I feel uncomfortable when you talk about your conversations with my dad." This approach seemed to be effective. Jimmy eventually revealed that his mother began to confide in one of his aunts and less in him.

The last session seemed to come to a standstill as far as emotion and feelings about the matter. Jimmy seemingly became accepting of the situation and said that he "was fine." His verbal expression did not appear to be congruent with his words and actions. He began to spend a lot of time alone at home, and appeared melancholy at times. At the end of my time with Jimmy, I asked if he would be interested in joining a group for students who experienced similar family changes. I explained that sometimes it might be helpful to talk to people around his age who could possibly share great strategies to help him feel better as he worked his way toward a new normal. Jimmy inquired about who would be in the group, what it would consist of, and what he would be able to talk about. After explaining the process of group counseling, Jimmy agreed that he would be interested in joining.

OUTCOME

I sent home a permission slip for Jimmy to be placed in group counseling for students experiencing similar family issues. His parents gave consent to group as well as individual counseling. Another counselor on campus led Jimmy's group. These groups offered students a chance to process emotions and feelings for six to eight sessions. Some of the activities included expressive art therapy and interactive games that included conversation starters.

I saw Jimmy three more times individually as he continued to self-refer to check in from time to time. Sometimes he did not say much and appeared to just want to chat. He enjoyed group counseling and recently said that he felt better with the situation surrounding his parents. He managed his emotions by engaging in activities such as playing video games and hanging out with his friends. Although Jimmy did not completely convince me that he truly accepted his parents' divorce, he learned to cope and focus on other aspects of his life by using some of the techniques he learned in counseling. Sometimes when he popped in to say hello, I wondered if he suppressed his feelings as a defense. Being that he appeared quirky by nature, this could be a reflection of his personality. I continued to ask probing questions in an attempt to bring some emotions to the surface; however, Jimmy maintained "I'm fine." I let him know that I remain available to him if needed.

REFERENCES

American Academy of Child and Adolescent Psychiatry. (2011). *Facts for families: Children and divorce.* Retrieved from http://www.aacap.org/App_Themes/AACAP/docs/facts_for_families/01_children_and_divorce.pdf

Brasher, K. (2009). Solution-focused brief therapy: Overview and implications for school counselors. *Alabama Counseling Association Journal, 34*(2), 20–30.

Bryner, C. L. (2001). Children of divorce. *Journal of the American Board of Family Medicine, 14*(3), 201–210.

de Shazer, S., & Berg, I. K. (1997). "What works?" Remarks on research aspects of solution-focused brief therapy. *Journal of Family Therapy, 19*, 121–124.

Erikson, E. H. (1982). *The life cycle completed.* New York, NY: W. W. Norton.

Homeyer, L. E., & Morrison, M. O. (2008). Play therapy: Practice, issues, and trends. *American Journal of Play, 1*(2), 210–228.

Huitt, W., & Hummel, J. (2003). Piaget's theory of cognitive development. *Educational Psychology Interactive.* Retrieved from http://www.edpsycinteractive.org/topics/cognition/piaget.html

ICF International. (n.d.). *Demographics 2007 profile of the military community.* Washington, DC: Office of the Deputy Under Secretary of Defense, Military Community and Family Policy. Retrieved from http://download.militaryonesource.mil/12038/MOS/Reports/2007%20Demographics.pdf

National Center for PTSD. (2016). How deployment stress affects children and families: Research findings. Retrieved from http://www.ptsd.va.gov/professional/treatment/family/pro_deployment_stress_children.asp

Piaget, J. (1932). *The moral judgment of the child.* London, UK: Routledge & Kegan Paul.

Reichenberg, L. W., & Seligman, L. (2010). *Theories of counseling and psychotherapy: Systems, strategies, and skills.* Upper Saddle River, NJ: Pearson Education.

Rogers, C. (1961). *On becoming a person: A therapist's view of psychotherapy.* New York, NY: Houghton Mifflin.

CHAPTER 5

MICHAEL AND THE CAMOUFLAGE CRUTCHES

Jenn Pereira

Michael, a 4-and-a-half-year-old Caucasian male, lived with his mother and his 3-year-old sister. Michael's mother requested counseling services due to growing concerns surrounding Michael's medical condition, cerebral palsy (CP). She requested me as the therapist to provide emotional support for Michael. She also wanted my assistance in helping Michael understand his disability and the "limitations CP would present on his life."

SYSTEMIC INFLUENCES

It became clear in discussing Michael's issues with his mother that several components played a role in his difficulties. The family was generationally and currently of lower socioeconomic status, making acquisition of health care, therapeutic services, and disability education a struggle. Michael had also not been educated regarding his disability, which began to cause social and emotional difficulties for him. Additionally, it would be imperative that Michael's mother, medical team, therapeutic service providers, and school work together to create an environment of consistent care and education.

DEVELOPMENTAL CONSIDERATIONS

Cognitive and Physical Development

The school diagnosed Michael via early intervention services with only a mild impairment of cognitive functioning. Michael's preschool reported that although his early intervention assessments showed that he tested in the below average range of intelligence, he understood and practiced new concepts well, and he seemed able to assimilate information with visual examples and repetition.

Michael experienced complications early in his young life, including being born prematurely with a low birth weight. Additionally, a pediatrician informed Michael's mother of a diagnosis of CP shortly before Michael's first birthday after she discussed his numerous unmet milestones and muscular control issues. Michael's mother recalled noticing feeding and eating issues around that time as Michael transitioned from baby food to solid food. Michael struggled with issues related to weak muscle tone and poor muscle control and coordination. He lacked the ability to walk with fluidity and struggled to control his arm movements. The school diagnosed him with a mild speech impairment; and Michael received speech and language services at home and, subsequently, at his preschool program.

Personal, Social, and Emotional Development

Michael's teachers noted that when Michael began school, he seemed attentive and cooperative, displayed a good sense of humor, got along well with peers, and appeared to be a pleasure in the classroom. Michael's primary teacher noted that although Michael appeared to be a "happy child," over the past few months, he seemed to experience more frequent "down" or "sad" moods during which he refused to interact with the other kids at gaming and free play times. He cried frequently during the day. He became more and more inattentive during lessons and appeared to get frustrated easily. Michael commented to the school nurse that he found it difficult to play with the other kids "because his legs didn't work like theirs" and he failed to understand why. Michael seemed to view his physical differences as "bad" and "wrong," as though others saw him as defective in some way. He began to make negative comments about himself such as: "I'm dumb"; "I have stupid legs"; "the other kids don't like me"; "I don't have any friends and I can't play right," which the school staff feared to be signs of low self-esteem and possible depression. This negatively affected his ability to accept himself and engage with other children. At this point, the nurse and teacher held a conference with Michael's mother to share their growing concerns and reiterated that it might be helpful for him to better understand what appeared to be happening with his body. Other than the CP, Michael appeared in good health. He reportedly enjoyed a good appetite with the noted minor eating issues being managed by diet, and he slept well. Michael possessed a wonderful sense of humor, creativity, and curiosity.

RELATIONAL CONSIDERATIONS

Michael's mother reported that Michael's CP symptoms began to affect him more negatively on emotional, social, and academic levels, and she felt it necessary to share more details with him regarding his condition. She delayed informing Michael of his CP, telling him instead that his legs and arms seemed a bit weaker than other kids, causing him to sometimes need extra help. She worried that his diagnosis might "make him feel different or scared."

Prior to beginning a preschool program at his local elementary school, Michael experienced limited interactions with other children aside from two mornings a week in a small day-care setting run by a family friend; therefore, his mother disclosed that she "did not see the point" of discussing his condition more fully with him. Michael recently began asking more questions about his condition and seemed to be searching for understanding.

MULTICULTURAL CONSIDERATIONS

Michael's mother and I engaged in several conversations regarding the feelings of grief she experienced upon learning of Michael's disability (i.e., her hopes and dreams for her son, her fears for him throughout his life, and her own concerns about her perceived ineptitude for parenting a disabled child). I learned that his mother failed to seek assistance from the doctor. She contacted the doctor 3 months prior to the doctor fitting Michael for leg braces and crutches that assisted him with coordination and muscle control. She also reported having difficulty keeping up with the physical therapy appointments; consequently, this caused Michael to miss numerous days of services.

Michael's mother reported several concerns in addition to Michael's issues. She selected the family's struggle with poverty as the primary concern. Her financial issues impacted her ability to provide adequate services and care for Michael. She reported living in a "poor, rural farming community" where education appeared not to be a priority. She relied on her Christian faith and felt that it provided support and a caring community during difficult times. The community and Michael's school staff accepted his disability. Michael's mother also reported that although she contacted her family on a limited basis, they provided emotional support for her and Michael. Several members of Michael's family received a disability diagnosis. Because of this, his family seemed supportive of individuals with disabilities. This information provided insight into the personal and educational goals Michael's mother held for her and Michael and her struggle to interact with Michael's doctors and teachers. Eventually, she agreed to work with her own counselor and also began attending parent support groups for caregivers of children with disabilities.

CONCEPTUALIZATION

Michael struggled to understand the changes taking place in his body. His awareness of his mobility and muscle strength issues became more and more apparent, leaving him feeling frustrated and unsure of himself. Additionally, although his mother wanted to protect him from feeling "different," he began to struggle with exactly that.

Goals and Target for Client Change

Assessing the type of information that seemed most helpful to Michael regarding CP and sharing the information in a way that appeared informative and child friendly became my first goals. Although this information did not alleviate Michael's growing emotional difficulties, it provided a basis for his understanding and ultimately an acceptance of his disability. To aid in building relationships, another goal evolved to support Michael in learning to talk about his disability with his peers. In addition to helping Michael better understand his condition, the next goal focused on strengthening his sense of self and helping him understand that having CP did not necessarily mean living a limited life. Working with the school staff to make the environment more accepting and inclusive also served as a goal for me.

Although I designated Michael as my identified client, I felt it necessary to also spend an adequate amount of time with his mother, helping her talk through the worry, fear, and grief with which many parents of disabled children struggle. Embedded in the goal of aiding Michael's understanding, I established an additional goal to help Michael's mother gain further knowledge about CP throughout the life span. Michael's mother reported feeling frequently overwhelmed and not knowing what to do for Michael. I believed that these feelings could be alleviated if she worked more closely with the doctors. This, then, became an additional goal to assist Michael's mother in building a support team of medical professionals (Michael's pediatrician, staff psychologist, the physical and occupation therapists assigned, and the speech therapist) on whom she could rely. It would also be important for his mother to gain a better understanding of how CP could be explained to a child Michael's age.

Goals and Strategies for Myself

As a therapist, this appeared to be a challenging case to accept. At the time, I needed a working knowledge of CP and how it might affect individuals over the course of their lives. As my initial goal, I gathered as much knowledge as possible, which required informational meetings with doctors and extensive reading on CP. It became imperative that a working knowledge of the issues and concerns surrounding CP be in place before I found ways to foster understanding for a 4-and-a-half-year-old. Also important, Michael's mother and the school personnel needed to be on the same page when speaking to Michael regarding his disability; consequently, I created the following guidelines to approach communication with Michael about his disability.

Systemic Approaches

Working With the Parent

It became imperative that Michael's mother respond empathically when Michael expressed feelings regarding his disability (i.e., "It really hurts you that you cannot run like the other kids; I wonder if we can think of some ways you could join"). It also became important for her to be honest, clear, and informative in conversations about disability. Saying "I don't know" and "Let me see what we can do to find out together" is acceptable. I advised her to also consider Michael's developmental and cognitive levels and his emotional abilities when providing information. To help normalize his experience, I encouraged her to provide Michael with examples of other people living with a disability (e.g., disabled actors, athletes, scholars, humanitarians, and artists). I informed her that she could extend his experiences by providing him with opportunities to engage in play, social, and academic activities with other children.

Working With the School

Fostering a relationship of collaboration with Michael's school became a main component in conceptualizing treatment. I found this necessary to boost Michael's self-esteem and create relationships with his peers. I met with Michael's teacher, professional school counselor, and school nurse; together, we created a plan for supporting Michael emotionally during his school day. The plan consisted of the following components: pairing him with a fifth grade peer buddy during free play and lunch several times a week; explaining his disability to the class and deciding the role Michael could play in this conversation; including him in a "Friendship Building Group" run by the professional school counselor; and providing him with "leadership" roles in his classroom where he could serve as an errand runner and morning greeter. We also developed opportunities that allowed Michael to participate successfully with his peers (e.g., scooter tag, partner or small group table games, and games that needed a referee/score keeper/command center). In an attempt to raise the level of awareness and acceptance of differences, the professional school counselor and I also created a series of puppet shows for the Pre-K and kindergarten classes on disabilities and diversity.

THERAPEUTIC INTERVENTION: CHILD-CENTERED PLAY THERAPY AS A CREATIVE PROCESS

I chose the intervention and theoretical orientation, child-centered play therapy (CCPT; Landreth, 2012), because it provided an inherently creative approach to working with children. It allowed me to interact with Michael in a developmentally and culturally sensitive manner that enhanced his self-awareness through the use of experiential and creative means. CCPT, a nondirective therapeutic modality, respects a child's ability to be fully in charge of the therapeutic process (Landreth, 2012; Pereira & Smith-Adcock, 2013). CCPT allowed Michael to lead, creating an open and engaging space in which he worked through issues in ways that provided personal understanding and insight. CCPT is built on the belief that children are innately capable of growth and personal insight when provided an accepting and supportive environment (Axline, 1947; Landreth, 2012; Pereira & Smith-Adcock, 2013). Within this nondirective orientation, therapists are charged with relying on the belief that children are innately capable of knowing what they need from the therapeutic process. The therapist communicates through words and actions that the child is acceptable as he or she is, allowing issues related to or surrounding a disability to take center stage. Children feel free to express their worries, concerns, anger, frustration, confusion, and fear in ways that make the most sense to them, without the therapist imposing his or her views or beliefs on the child. As a play therapist, I felt that CCPT appeared to be an excellent match for Michael, due to his growing struggle with his sense of self, autonomy, and concerns regarding how he understood himself and his interactions with others. Rather than create specific interventions designed to target my perceptions of his difficulties with feelings of being "different" and lowered self-esteem, I wanted to allow Michael to navigate those issues at his own pace and in the ways that appeared most meaningful to him.

COUNSELING PROCESS FLOW

Over the course of our work together, Michael and I conducted 12 individual CCPT sessions and two family sessions where his mother joined us. This appeared to be an appropriate length of time for sessions and family work as the collaboration with the school system supported numerous aspects of the case as well. Michael easily engaged in counseling and the process of our relationship building went very smoothly. During Session 1, Michael asked, "Are you a medical doctor to help me with my legs?" to which I answered, "I am more like a 'Feelings Doctor' who helps people understand and work on their feelings and the things that upset them." He seemed to like that idea and told me that there appeared to be "lots and lots of things that make me sad (and then whispered) and mad too! I get mad at my legs even," to which I replied, "Wow, it sounds like there are things that feel really bad to you right now and make you mad and worried sometimes too, I bet. I would like very much to help you with those things."

I chose one or two individual sessions with Michael to establish rapport before his mother and I sat with Michael to discuss his CP. We began sessions after the intake and I introduced Michael to the playroom with my standard CCPT opening: "Michael, this is a very special room. You can do almost anything in here. If there is something you cannot do, I will tell you, and you can say anything in here." I did not modify the materials or playroom with regard to Michael's motor difficulties (i.e., I did not pre-open the Play-Doh containers, move items to lower shelves, or put floor items up on the table) as I wanted Michael to experience navigating the room for himself, dealing with the successes and struggles that would come. The role of a CCPT therapist is to honor a child's ability to develop the personal strengths and abilities inherent within him or her to find solutions to his or her concerns (Landreth, 2012; Pereira & Smith-Adcock, 2013), which in turn builds a sense of autonomy and personal capacity (Pereira & Smith-Adcock, 2013). Michael, in his first session, spent a great deal of time exploring the materials and telling me how much he "loved his play room." He seemed very interested in the shields and foam swords, excitedly announcing how cool they look, touching them and holding them, but choosing not to play with them. He experienced great difficulty navigating his arm crutches to hold the items, and then simply put them back on the shelf. In keeping with CCPT tenets, I reflected, "Those look pretty cool to you and you would like to try them, but it doesn't seem as though you are sure about them yet. They seem tricky to hold," to which he nodded. He, then, got down on the floor to play with a bin of animals, particularly a small giraffe and its family. After several minutes, he decided to draw a picture of us in the playroom, which is how he ended his time. Michael engaged in the same play during Session 2, spending more time exploring the room. At the start of the third session, Michael informed me of his thoughts about what the animals would be doing. All of the animals appeared on the "playground" running, playing games, and jumping, except for the little giraffe, which Michael placed off to the side. I commented on the little giraffe being left out, to which Michael replied, "Yes, but look at his little tiny legs; so he just stays over there." I made a few more remarks like "So his legs look tiny and not very strong so you feel it might be better, safer maybe, for him to stay over there." "The little giraffe is not even playing by himself. He is just standing watching the other kids play," to which Michael stopped his play, looked at me, and said, "He is lonely. It makes him sad about his tiny legs. But when he grows up, he can have big legs like the kids." After this exchange, I felt the next session would be well spent having a discussion about CP.

Following this conversation, the play themes in Michael's next four sessions consisted of competency play (i.e., displays of knowledge, dexterity, and physical abilities), often leaving him frustrated and acting discouraged, and choosing aggressive play (i.e., battles between "good" and "bad" guys and battles where he needed protection while they attacked us). These battles frequently consisted of his not being able to win the battle, not having the "right" weaponry available, and thinking he killed the "bad guy" only to realize that the "bad guy" came back, leaving Michael needing a great deal of help and support.

During Michael's eighth session, we engaged in another epic battle between good and evil. Michael and I became "holed up" in the fort that we built (to his specifications) for safety, throwing bombs (rolled and taped fabric balls) and shooting foam darts at the "enemy." Michael decided to leave the fort to fight on his own, which resulted in his being "shot" repeatedly by the enemy. I came out from behind the barricade with the first aid kit to "fix him up and rescue him" when he hollered for me. After wrapping his head and leg with ace bandages as directed,

Michael said to me, "Jenn, even when we take this bandage off, my legs still won't really work." I responded, "Even though you are feeling pretty good about yourself lately, that is a tough thing for you to think about; it frustrates you and makes you feel very sad." He nodded and instructed me to pull him to safety behind the fort where he decided to draw for the rest of the session. This theme of needing help continued for two more sessions. During a subsequent session, we constructed the fort again; however, this time Michael requested that I help him don the plastic breastplate and arm shields, as he held both his crutch and a sword. He decided to fight the battle outside the safety of the fort, telling me to "stay there where it's safe; I can fight." During the "battle," Michael struggled to hold the sword and manipulate his leg braces to navigate around items on the floor. He fell several times, dropped his weapons, struggled with his braces and crutches, but would not allow me to assist. He fought alone—telling me he would protect the fort. He exerted so much energy in this session that he appeared red faced and sweaty toward the end. The battle came to a head with him "fighting the leader of evil—the last bad guy" whom he finally defeated. He emerged triumphant, prompting me to cheer for him and clap. He, then, suddenly turned to me and exclaimed, "Jenn! I'm strong! I'm a strong boy! My outsides might not work right—but my insides feel all fixed up!" We then formed a parade where all the "thankful villagers" cheered the hero for saving them. The remaining sessions consisted of competency play, where he strove to display skills such as drawing, counting, and reading. The aggressive play themes ended.

OUTCOME

Providing Michael with information on CP allowed him to better understand what came to light about his body and why he experienced difficulty. He enjoyed hearing stories about disabled athletes and their ability to engage in many physical activities. He also seemed very excited that his mother agreed to his birthday request, "camouflage-colored" leg braces and crutches; and helped us wrap them with camouflage grip-tape in session. He gained a lot of positive attention from his peers at school, and he appeared very proud of his braces. During the course of the 5 months of treatment, Michael experienced changes in the school environment as well. Michael began to engage his peers in the classroom and his teachers noted that he became invested in the school day and learning activities. He cried less and less frequently, with no tears at all during the last month; invited classmates to play with him; and seemed included by his peers, thanks to the efforts of the teachers in building a wonderfully inclusive atmosphere. The puppet shows performed by the professional school counselor and me helped the children talk about disabilities in more positive ways and displayed helpful behaviors (i.e., helping Michael carry things and choosing him to participate in games). The professional school counselor continued to run the Friendship Building Group, which he reported helped Michael further his skill development.

Michael's mother, after the initial conversation with Michael regarding CP, became much more comfortable attempting to respond to his questions and providing information, contacted the doctors when she faced questions or concerns of her own, made a concerted effort to be sure Michael received his physical and occupational therapy services, and felt better able to advocate for him. Michael, over the course of therapy, began to understand and integrate his diagnosis with his sense of self. He continued to become frustrated at times when he seemed unable to do all the things his peers did, but he found success and pride in his current abilities and activities. As Michael's frustration and anger lessened, his sense of humor became more present, as did his very engaging personality. Michael displayed an ability to note his own successes; and when unsuccessful, he remarked positively on how hard he tried. He became interested in testing limits to discover his physical capabilities, and came up with alternate behaviors that seemed easier. He felt positive about that. Michael's statement about his insides being "all fixed up" appeared to be a poignant cue that he understood the permanence of his disorder but possibly also felt that this did not define him as a person.

I recommended Michael engage in the counseling process as he grows older so that additional support during future developmental and life-oriented milestones can be provided. It is crucial that the services be continued to further develop fine and gross motor skills as well as manage the effects of his speech impediment. Additionally, Michael and his mother would benefit from this continued support so that they can best advocate for Michael's needs as he grows and matures.

REFERENCES

Axline, V. M. (1947). *Play therapy*. New York, NY: Ballantine Books.

Landreth, G. L. (2012). *Play therapy: The art of the relationship*. New York, NY: Routledge.

Pereira, J. K., & Smith-Adcock, S. (2013). An evaluation of a child-centered play therapy workshop for school counselors. *International Journal of Play Therapy*, 22(3), 129–142.

CHAPTER 6

CREATING SPACE FOR DOMINIC'S PEACE

Ariel Mitchell

Dominic was a 9-year-old Caucasian child who lived with his paternal grandparents, Mr. and Mrs. Lowe, in a small rural community for the past 8 months. Mr. and Mrs. Lowe reported that Dominic regularly assaulted them verbally and physically. According to Mr. Lowe, "He hits us, throws things at us, and curses at us when he does not get his way." Dominic's latest aggressive episode occurred 2 days prior to his office visit, after being suspended from school. This recent outburst happened because his grandparents asked him to work on his suspension packet. Mrs. Lowe stated that Dominic sat at the table to work on his packet while she cooked dinner and Mr. Lowe worked in the yard. Dominic began to play by jumping up from the table and running around the house saying, "I'm not doing it." Mrs. Lowe demanded that Dominic complete his work or he would not be allowed to go fly-fishing with his grandfather. Dominic became irate at the thought of being punished and began screaming, "No, don't punish me . . . I don't want to be punished . . . I'll do my work." When Mr. Lowe walked in to the house to wash up for dinner, Mrs. Lowe approached Dominic in an attempt to calm him down and reiterated to Dominic, "You are not punished, but if you do not complete your homework before dinner, you will be." Dominic began to yell out to his grandmother, "You're being a bitch," and then he stabbed her with his pencil. Mr. Lowe ran from the bathroom and immediately restrained Dominic. Once Dominic calmed down, he began to sob and yell out, "I'm sorry grannie" over and over again. He sunk down into a corner of the living room and continued to sob for over an hour. Mrs. Lowe explained that this experience was common and happened regularly at times when Dominic was asked to perform any task.

SYSTEMIC INFLUENCES

Mr. and Mrs. Lowe reported that they knew little about Dominic's history prior to him coming to live with them. Although Mr. and Mrs. Lowe were Dominic's paternal grandparents, they reported a strained relationship with their son, Pete. Pete's relationship with Dominic's mother ended shortly after Dominic was born due to her drug abuse. I did not know if Dominic's mother abused drugs while pregnant with him. Dominic lived with his mother for 3 years while his father began a new relationship. Pete obtained custody of Dominic when he was 4 years old due to complaints of parental abuse and neglect while in his mother's care. At age 4, Dominic transitioned into the home with his father and stepmother, Thalia. Dominic remained with Pete and Thalia until he was 8 years old. According to Mrs. Lowe, she only saw Dominic about twice per year, but she always felt that his family treated him unfairly in their home.

DEVELOPMENTAL CONSIDERATIONS

Dominic attended a local private school where he received individualized education accommodations based on school-level evaluations, asserting that his learning is being impacted by behavioral deficits. Teachers at Dominic's school reported that he was like a "ticking time bomb" around his teachers or other adult administrators. Ms. Tina, his English and Math teacher, reported that she immediately knew "something was wrong." She wrote that Dominic was known for antagonizing other kids, moving about the classroom, and not focusing on the tasks at hand. She noted that he did not handle corrective feedback well. Ms. Tina stated that Dominic threw desks, tried to break the classroom window, shoved her, spit at the principal, and threw shelves of books to the floor. This behavior typically ensued directly following a directive that Dominic refused to follow.

Dominic received a 7-day suspension from school for charging at Ms. Tina and shoving her into her desk. This incident happened when Ms. Tina asked Dominic to return to his desk following a group exercise. Dominic began to yell at her and stated, "I'm not ready to go back." Ms. Tina then explained to Dominic that he had 10 seconds to begin moving to his seat or she would refer him to the office. Dominic remained on the floor for the entire 10 seconds and when Ms. Tina called the front office, Dominic jumped up and shoved her into the desk. After this incident, Dominic was removed from Ms. Tina's classroom and his grandparents picked him up from school. A hearing was scheduled for the following day and it was determined that Dominic would be suspended for 7 days. The school also informed Mr. and Mrs. Lowe that if Dominic engaged in any more aggressive behaviors, he would be expelled from school.

RELATIONAL CONSIDERATIONS

Shortly after Dominic moved in with his father and stepmother, his baby sister was born. Mrs. Lowe recalled an incident about 3 to 4 years before Dominic came to live with her when he tried to kick his then-pregnant stepmother in the stomach. According to Mrs. Lowe, once his sister was born, the family constantly monitored him and allowed limited interaction with his sibling. Dominic recalled that his family locked him in his room at bedtime and he was not allowed out until it was time for breakfast. Mrs. Lowe stated that Dominic acted verbally and physically aggressive with his dad and stepmom until Thalia threatened to take Emme and leave unless Pete "did something with Dominic." It was at that point that Pete asked his mother and father to take Dominic or he would be placed in a residential facility because, according to Pete, "My wife is scared for her life and we can't keep living like this." One week following that conversation between Pete and Mrs. Lowe, Dominic moved in with his grandparents. When I asked how Dominic interpreted the situation, Mrs. Lowe stated, "Dominic feels like he has been abandoned by his mother and his father." Regarding his father and stepmother, he would constantly make comments such as, "She (Thalia) is a bitch and she is why my dad doesn't want me." Dominic verbalized that he was happy with his grandparents and did not want them to "leave him like everybody else."

MULTICULTURAL CONSIDERATIONS

Dominic resided in a small rural community with his middle-class elderly grandparents that believed in a traditional way of life. The community and household both seemed patriarchal in gender beliefs. Mr. Lowe admitted that when Dominic first came to live with them, he dismissed Mrs. Lowe's complaints about Dominic's aggressive behavior by saying, "Boys will be boys." Dominic did not begin to be punished for his behaviors until after a few weeks when his aggressive behaviors were directed toward Mr. Lowe. Once consequences were implemented for Dominic's behavior, he became more aggressive, according to Mr. and Mrs. Lowe. It would seem that the initial underlying belief was that aggressiveness was "normal" for young boys. However, Dominic's aggressiveness became an issue once it threatened the elder male, Mr. Lowe.

Media outlets also played a large role in Dominic's life as he reportedly spent a large amount of his formative years locked inside of his bedroom with a television and video games. Mrs. Lowe reported that Dominic owned several violent video games that came with him from his father's home. In addition to the violent video games, Mrs. Lowe believed that Dominic was able to watch the television at his own discretion and without adult supervision. What Dominic remembered and/or understood from his exposure to violence in the media was unknown at the onset of treatment.

CONCEPTUALIZATION

According to Erikson's theory of psychosocial development, at 9 years of age Dominic was in the industry versus inferiority stage of development. However, Dominic's behavior was consistent with the initiative versus guilt developmental stage. He exhibited aggressive behaviors toward family and friends in an effort to exert control over self and others. Almost immediately following his aggression, Dominic showed extreme remorse and guilt about his decisions. Dominic also experienced previous abuse in his foundational relationships. This abuse may have impacted his ability to form healthy attachments with authority figures. Based on Dominic's developmental level and age, I used a child-centered play therapy modality to facilitate the therapeutic process.

Goals and Target for Client Change

Consistent with the child-centered play therapy model, the goals of our sessions were for Dominic to gain respect for himself, accept his feelings, express his feelings responsibly, assume responsibility for himself, develop creative problem-solving skills, and gain self-control (Davis & Pereira, 2014; Kottman, 2001; Landreth, 2012). Throughout the process of Dominic achieving his session goals, individual growth toward developing congruence with his perceived and ideal self should become evident.

COUNSELING PROCESS FLOW

We spent time during the initial sessions focusing on rapport building and developing an atmosphere where Dominic felt accepted. I wanted Dominic to experience the freedom to express himself and be heard as I tracked and reflected his feelings. I hoped that active and empathic listening would help him gain insight into his own emotional processes. I allowed Dominic to lead the conversations, and I set limits as necessary.

Infusion of Creativity

When Dominic first entered the play therapy room, he immediately began to pick up objects and explore the toys and room. He never became engaged with one object for any period of time; instead, he touched many objects in the playroom. He commented about the physical attributes of the objects as he randomly selected them. Approximately midway through the first session, I noticed that Dominic started to remove items from where he found them and move them to a different place. He looked at me as though he assumed I would address his actions in some way. Instead, I continued to track and reflect his feelings, and he never replied back. He then continued with his earlier pattern of behavior for the remainder of the session.

During the second session, Dominic began to spend more time with objects before moving on to the next. I noticed that Dominic's attention shifted constantly from one thought to another, and there seemed to be no logical sequence to his statements. I also noticed that although he did not invite me into his play, he frequently looked at me as though he was seeking validation of some sort. My role at this point in the therapeutic relationship was to continue tracking Dominic's actions, reflecting content and feelings, and showing Dominic unconditional positive regard. Given Dominic's prior experiences of neglect and abandonment, as well as his perceived need for constant validation, expressing unconditional positive regard toward Dominic was the most immediate need at the onset of his therapeutic process. Dominic needed to experience and understand the message that I will accept him as he is, so that the therapeutic process could commence and hopefully lead to his own self-acceptance.

At the onset of the third session with Dominic, I believe we developed good rapport. Instead of being led to the playroom, Dominic took the lead and began to give me instructions based on our physical placement in previous sessions. During this session, Dominic began to push limits in the playroom by engaging in more aggressive play and throwing figurines about the room. I set a soft limit for Dominic by simply stating that the toys were not for throwing. After the limit was set, he began to softly push a figurine in the air and catch it. While he was engaging in this behavior, I continued to track his actions. When Dominic threw the figurine up and across the room once again, a hard limit was set. I stated directly to Dominic, "The toys are not for throwing and if you choose to continue throwing the toys, you are choosing to end our time in the playroom for today." Dominic verbalized that he did not want our time to end, but he continued to push the limits that were set for him. When he decided to throw the figurine for the third time, I promptly ended our session by reminding him about the limit. I stated to Dominic, "Since you choose to throw the figurine, you choose to end our session for today." I opened the door of the playroom and stood in the hall until Dominic exited the room.

When Dominic returned to my office for our fourth session, he stated, "I decided that I won't throw any toys today." This statement illustrated that Dominic was beginning to take responsibility for his actions. He realized that his choices would lead to consequences based on his choices. As a result, Dominic engaged in therapeutic play through-out the entire session, acting out clear themes of abandonment and abuse. He played out one particular scene where he placed a figurine behind a Lego wall. He told the figurine, "You are punished" and then yelled, "You are stupid, you are ugly, you don't do nothing right!" As I reflected Dominic's feelings, he began to cry and said, "I'm not stupid." Dominic had experienced an abreaction, and this was the end of Session 4.

We began our fifth session as usual, with him directing where I should sit and where he would start in the playroom. During that session, I noticed that Dominic was unusually somber. His speech was slurred and he stayed occupied with items in the playroom for extended periods of time. At points during the session, Dominic stared blankly into space for minutes on end. His behavior seemed much different from his usual functioning. When our time ended, I sought out Mrs. Lowe with hopes of gaining some clarity about Dominic's behavior. Mrs. Lowe explained to me that Dominic had been on the wait list to see the local psychiatrist for weeks and he finally got an appointment about 5 days ago. She explained that the psychiatrist prescribed Dominic medication, but she could not remember the name or dosage. She said, "Dominic has been doing better since he began his work with you but he is still all over the place and his school requested for me to seek medication to help calm him down." I empathized with Mrs. Lowe and explained that I appreciated her being forthcoming with me about why she sought medication. I also asked her to complete a release of information so that I could coordinate services with Dominic's psychiatrist. Mrs. Lowe signed the release and left the office with a gloomy child I did not recognize.

Prior to the sixth session, I received a phone call from a hysterical Mrs. Lowe stating that Dominic had been admitted into an inpatient facility out of town. She explained that they had an altercation as she was trying to make Dominic take his medication. Mrs. Lowe commented that he refused to take his medication and she threatened him with punishment. "I can't recall what happened next, but all I know is he ran into me and pushed me so hard that I fell and broke the table in the living room," she explained. Mr. Lowe heard the commotion, came into the living room, and immediately restrained Dominic. Mrs. Lowe then called the police and asked for an ambulance to take Dominic to the nearest hospital. The ambulance transported Dominic to the same hospital where his new psychiatrist worked. Dominic remained in the hospital for 24 hours and was to be discharged, but Dominic's psychiatrist recommended that Mrs. Lowe seek inpatient treatment for Dominic. She began to cry again and said, "I didn't know what else to do." Mrs. Lowe and Dominic's psychiatrist signed paperwork to have him admitted to an inpatient psychiatric hospital. I did not know if I would ever see Dominic again.

OUTCOME

Based on Mrs. Lowe's report of Dominic's behavior, Dominic developed some of the skills needed for treatment to be considered successful. He reduced the frequency of his aggressive behaviors from a daily occurrence to approximately twice per week. Mrs. Lowe reported that Dominic better expressed himself verbally, and began to track his own actions at home. The improvement in Dominic's behavior mirrored what I noticed in session, but I was unsure if Dominic's behavior transferred into his school environment.

Given the limited amount of time that I worked with Dominic, there were two things that I would have done differently. First, I would have started working with Dominic's teachers at the onset of counseling instead of waiting. Second, I would have incorporated family sessions into Dominic's treatment plan to focus on developing effective communication between Dominic and his grandparents. Infusing parent management training into the family therapy model could have also helped to improve communicative interactions.

Looking back at Dominic's treatment, I cannot help but wonder if I collaborated with teachers, family therapy, and parent training earlier in the therapeutic process than I usually did, things might have ended differently. In retrospect, I understand why Dominic's grandparents needed to see immediate change, even if the change was short lived. I believe that Mr. and Mrs. Lowe needed to see Dominic's capability to change to deepen their investment of the therapeutic process. Although Mrs. Lowe verbalized understanding at the onset of counseling that the process would take time, I now understand that she was in crisis mode and needed immediate de-escalation of Dominic's maladaptive behaviors. I believe that Dominic's case is an example of why I believe constant collaboration with caregivers and other vested individuals represents the best approach when working with children.

REFERENCES

Davis, E. S., & Pereira, J. K. (2014). Child-centered play therapy: A creative approach to culturally competent counseling. *Journal of Creativity in Mental Health, 9*(2), 262–274. http://dx.doi.org/10.1080/15401383.2014.892863

Kottman, T. (2011). *Play therapy: Basics and beyond*. Alexandria, VA: American Counseling Association.

Landreth, G. L. (2012). *Play therapy: The art of the relationship*. New York, NY: Routledge.

CHAPTER 7

CONQUERING THE WORRY BULLY

Huma Bashir

Drew was an 11-year-old male whose supportive parents brought him to counseling with concerns about how Drew's anxiety significantly affected his daily life. Drew was the third of four children in his family. He attended the sixth grade with his twin sister, but they spent time in different classes. His father directed theater in a local community college and his mother worked at a local university. His parents reported that anxiety and depression ran in their family.

Drew expressed feelings of fear about his life, and isolated and withdrew from others as a consequence. When I first met Drew, he had trouble staying in his chair as we talked. He seemed mildly distractible, stopping in the middle of our conversation to play with a toy he noticed behind him. He spoke quickly, and showed mild difficulties with articulation. Drew spoke about having a "foggy head," which characterized his attention issues at school. However, he felt these concerns improved because of his new medications for attention deficit hyperactivity disorder (ADHD) and epilepsy. He said he fell behind when he started fifth grade because of this fogginess, and experienced a very difficult year. Drew's parents reported they did not believe Drew had cognitive issues, but did agree that he appeared easily distracted at times.

The initial concerns about Drew's learning surfaced in second grade. In the third grade, he received an Individual Education Program (IEP). His current plan outlined goals for writing and math, which were below level, and recommended occupational therapy services. His parents agreed that his math and reading skills were about one grade level behind. Drew's school records indicated problems with focus, but with intervention, he made substantial progress in reading. Unfortunately, according to his parents, he felt "almost phobic" about math. Drew avoided getting extra help, and sometimes declined accommodations because he feared the social stigma of needing academic help.

SYSTEMIC INFLUENCES

Drew's family system is considered nuclear, as he lives with both of his parents, who have been married for 25 years. Both parents have college degrees, and he has three siblings. His family is very supportive of Drew and helps him with his day. They have developed a routine for him that starts early in the morning going to school, and upon return he does his homework first, and then he is allowed to watch TV or play. Drew and his older brother, who is attending college, are movie buffs and especially *Star Wars* fans, and Drew watches the movies and anything related to the series. Drew loves watching his siblings in plays because theater is a big part of their upbringing. His parents and siblings are very hands-on and understand how they could be of help to him. They plan their activities and communicate them to Drew so that he has time to process and prepare. For example, his older sister, who recently finished middle school, is able to prepare Drew about what to expect in middle school because he has a lot of anxiety about the transition. His twin brother is very athletic and keeps Drew engaged with physical activities.

DEVELOPMENTAL CONSIDERATIONS

Drew exhibited no physical issues at birth and as an infant. However, during his early years, his parents reported he showed inconsistent behavior—there were days where Drew appeared cognitively "foggy, unmotivated, and exhausted," and on other days, his behavior seemed the opposite. When Drew was 10, he received a diagnosis of complex partial epilepsy, without impairment of consciousness; however, his parents never witnessed him have a seizure. About a year later, Drew received diagnoses of ADHD and an anxiety disorder. The report stated that epilepsy put him at high risk for both of these problems, and it was likely that both ADHD and anxiety contributed to his difficulty paying attention and controlling his own behavior.

RELATIONAL CONSIDERATIONS

Relationally, Drew tended to be overly sensitive and eager to please. He focused heavily on his peers' fondness for him. He struggled making transitions and regulating his emotions. He apologized excessively to his parents, sometimes without even knowing if he had done anything wrong. Drew shared that he worried a lot and was stressed at school, and he teared up when we talked about it. Drew was aware of his inability to control his emotional reactions, and understood the impact this had on himself and others, but did not know how to implement change.

Drew enjoyed playing trumpet in the school band, participated in student council, and worked with his sister at a church youth group. He shared a group of friends with his brother, but over the course of a year those friends seemed to distance themselves from him. He told me he just wanted to be "normal" and worried that he would not do well in middle school. The neuropsychological evaluation helped support my initial concerns and gave more direction to my plan for Drew. His parents voiced concerns about Drew's tendency to become fixated; to avoid or completely withdraw from stressful situations (especially math at school); and to be ostracized from school peers because of his behavior.

MULTICULTURAL CONSIDERATIONS

Drew came from a Caucasian family. They were middle class in their socioeconomic status (SES). Both parents worked and instilled in the children the value of education. I used more general interventions based in Western values. I did not notice any conflict with Drew's values and worldviews. He seemed to be a well-adjusted young man who tried to fit in with his peers, who were predominantly Caucasian. From his discussions with me, he appeared very open to other cultures and values and had classmates from different cultures. Because of their background in literature and theater, his family seemed very open to those from different cultures.

CONCEPTUALIZATION

After our initial few sessions, it became apparent that Drew's anxiety should be the focus of our work. I found the neuropsychological evaluation helpful in that it supported my initial concerns and gave more direction to my plan for Drew. His parents voiced concerns about Drew's tendency to become fixated; to avoid or completely withdraw from stressful situations (especially math at school); and to be ostracized from school peers because of his behavior. After evaluating Drew, speaking with his parents, and meeting with the school counselor, I determined that a holistic approach that included therapy, medication, school accommodations, and family support would offer the best possibility for success.

Drew's Goal

Drew's tendency to fixate on things surfaced early in counseling. He fixated on things and experienced difficulty breaking from that. For him, it became all or nothing, often working himself into exhaustion. Ruminating until he fell asleep became his coping mechanism, often regardless of location. He understood that he functioned better with overt plans or instructions, sharing that he "can't go with it" and "can't come up with something on the fly."

The adults in Drew's world reported significant problems with inattention and hyperactivity, depressed mood, and somatic problems, along with a broad executive dysfunction affecting his ability to regulate his own behaviors. Drew's self-rating also identified significant problems with shifting attention/making transitions and controlling emotional reactions. Drew seemed to be in a fortunate position in that adults in his circle appeared attentive and caring, offering support and willing to seek appropriate medical care.

Clinician's Goal

I determined decreasing Drew's anxiety by containment, and helping him learn new coping skills to work with his anxiety and ADHD to be my goals. Drew learned how to make meaning with his thoughts. To achieve these goals, I implemented sand tray therapy, art therapy, and playing games. My session framework evolved into checking in with him and his parent, and setting the agenda for the session and working with Drew individually. I gauged his anxiety using a Likert scale of 1 to 10; and based strategies and techniques on CBT principals. Based on research on anxiety and ADHD, CBT confirmed a larger effect-size.

Working with Drew gave me the chance to utilize my cognitive behavioral training, which reframes his intrusive thoughts about anxiety. The inward expression of distress, symptoms of anxiety are called internalizing or intrusive. ADHD and anxiety disorders overlap in symptomatology. For example, restlessness, irritability, and difficulty in concentrating are observed in both patient populations. Current research suggests that anxiety may either precede or follow ADHD, depending on the developmental pathway (Appleton, 2008).

I needed to use interventions that were downward extensions of successful adult treatments. These strategies worked because Drew seemed articulate, insightful, and wanted to diffuse his symptoms. In children, cognitive interventions are not sole interventions; rather, cognitive strategies are used in combination with behavioral interventions (Beidel & Alfano, 2011). I used developmentally appropriate homework, worry time, and analogies, for example, a growing plant needs water, what if you do not water it, what happens, being the same as the case with worrying thoughts; if you do not attend to them, they will go away.

COUNSELING PROCESS FLOW

I started seeing Drew in May of 2015 and met with him 20 times over the course of the year. We established a trusting, open relationship where Drew felt comfortable sharing his successes, worries, and failures. I determined my goals for Drew were to decrease his anxiety by containment, and help him learn new coping skills to work with his anxiety and ADHD. To achieve these goals, I implemented sand tray therapy, art therapy, and playing games.

Working with Drew gave me the chance to utilize my cognitive behavioral training, which reframed his intrusive thoughts about anxiety. Drew appeared articulate, insightful, and wanted to diffuse his symptoms. In children, cognitive interventions are not sole interventions; rather, cognitive strategies are used in combination with behavioral interventions (Beidel & Alfano, 2011). I employed homework, worry time, and analogies that were developmentally appropriate for him. For example, a growing plant needs water. What if you do not water it? What happens? This is a metaphor with worrying thoughts. If you do not attend to them, they will go away.

I utilized cognitive behavioral therapy (CBT) adopted for children combined with a humanistic approach (HA). I focused on helping Drew feel like he had control over his fears, and that he controlled his anxiety/intrusive thoughts rather than the anxiety controlling him. I emphasized that the way he thought influenced the way we felt (Clark & Beck, 2012). We developed an action plan at the end of each session. This helped him structure his week and reduced his anxiety about the upcoming events. This strategy helped him with his ADHD symptoms as well.

Infusion of Creativity

One of the most successful techniques in our sessions focused on using physical activities to regulate the limbic region of Drew's brain.

We employed "tossing the ball" in session to facilitate our talks while he played. We used a ball to mimic intrusive thoughts and thought-stopping strategies. He learned that as soon as an unwanted thought entered his brain, he could throw it out. By throwing a ball back and forth and increasing its speed, we could model how automatic thoughts happened, and demonstrate that he had some power over letting his thoughts go. I also used relaxation-breathing exercises that Drew utilized when he realized the emergence of anxious feelings. Another strategy we developed for work at home included a "STOP" sign Drew made that he held up to counter intrusive thoughts. The stop sign signaled his parents to intervene and help him in the moment, so he could work to manage his thoughts and shift back to homework.

OUTCOME

Drew progressed well in counseling. He seemed engaged. He reported he enjoyed our meetings, and found himself responding to the strategies. His anxiety level steadily decreased and he showed success with completion of tasks. Our conversations and activities gave Drew more confidence to self-regulate and implement coping strategies. He adopted a more realistic look at situations, retaining and using what we worked on in counseling outside of our sessions. While he still relied on an old coping skill of putting his head down and taking breaks for a short time, he used a squishy ball when he felt overwhelmed or worried his anxiety might take over. Squeezing it while counting numbers backward seemed useful for Drew.

In his school, Drew's overall performance improved. He accepted additional assistance, experienced reduced math anxiety, and failed no classes. Finally, he reported no episodes of fixated behaviors or shutdown. He participated in more school activities, and was elected as a student counsel officer for his grade. He attributed part of his success to the team of adults who supported Drew at school. The team consisted of the school psychologist, behavior interventionist, professional school counselor, Drew's parents, and me. We met to discuss interventions for schoolwork, homework, and social activities, which were integrated into Drew's IEP. Some of the agreed-upon accommodations were to include an aid in all classes, offer preferential seating away from distractions, allow frequent breaks, provide small group instruction to minimize distractions, and allow time extensions. Our goal with these accommodations focused on increasing Drew's independence over time.

He responded well to all of the interventions because I allowed him to fully express his feelings and troubling thoughts. He learned to trust me and, more importantly, trust himself to defuse his worries. He learned to call his worries a "worry bully," and he used a fly swatter to "mush" them. We used drawings so he can create a visual image of what those worries look like and talk about how he can ignore them. I also have a scheduled "worry time" of his desire to talk to his parents only once a day.

Drew learned to recognize and reevaluate his uncertainty and to differentiate which thoughts were not true. This skill allowed him to dismiss troubling beliefs and thoughts. Drew expressed relief when he understood he had control over his thoughts. He said he felt like he could now be seen as more normal instead of someone with an uncontrollable disease. Drew saw himself as an intuitive and sensitive person.

REFERENCES

Appleton, P. (Ed.). (2008). *Children's anxiety: A contextual approach.* New York, NY: Routledge.

Beidel, D., & Alfano, C. (2011). *Child anxiety disorders: A guide to research and treatment* (2nd ed.). New York, NY: Routledge.

Clark, D. A., & Beck, A. T. (2012). *The anxiety and worry workbook: The cognitive behavioral solution.* New York, NY: Guilford Press.

CHAPTER 8

PAULA'S PICTURESQUE PERSONA

Katherine Bacon
Natasha Young

Paula Jimenez came to counseling following a referral from her mother and professional school counselor. They reported concerns about her social deficits and relationship issues when she was 9-and-a-half years old. Paula was a Hispanic female of Mexican descent. She was the middle child of three girls, and lived at home with her two sisters, mother, and father. Her family primarily spoke Spanish at home. Her mother was from Monterrey, Mexico, and was a U.S. citizen. Her father was from Mexico City, Mexico, and at the time of treatment, sought U.S. citizenship. Paula previously received treatment for separation anxiety after she witnessed her father's arrest followed by a 3-month deportation. She improved while receiving counseling for separation anxiety but regressed during the summer months following treatment. Finally, Paula was hospitalized and diagnosed with juvenile type 1 diabetes. Her mother described Paula as "not being happy" and "not wanting to do things with the family." Paula's teacher and professional school counselor noted Paula engaged in minimal social interactions with her peers. Furthermore, Paula's pediatrician diagnosed her with attention deficit hyperactivity disorder (ADHD), inattentive type, and prescribed Focalin XR. Paula's school retained her in third grade the following academic year.

SYSTEMIC INFLUENCES

To enhance the likelihood of increasing Paula's self-efficacy and long-term success, we used a systemic approach. To assist Paula in addressing social deficits and relationship issues, we engaged Paula's systems of family, peers, and school.

The Family System

In addition to her nuclear family, Paula also had extended family in Mexico City and Monterrey, Mexico, which she visited once every few years. Paula's family system played a significant role in her case. Outside of school, Paula rarely interacted with persons other than her nuclear family of origin. Paula's family would take road trips periodically, which Paula enjoyed. When Paula and her mother described Paula's interactions with her family, we discovered evidence of Paula's self-efficacy and ability to have positive, meaningful social interaction and relationships. We used these successes as an opportunity for strength building and as examples Paula could use to assist her in addressing the social deficits and relationship issues she experienced at school.

The Peer System

Paula's peer system consisted of students in her grade level at the charter school she attended. Teachers reported Paula being withdrawn in the classroom, and observational assessments of Paula during recess and lunch revealed the same level of withdrawn behavior. We engaged Paula's peer system during counseling through Paula's participation in small group counseling with other students from her school. Specifically, Paula participated in a psychoeducational group for girls that focused on self-esteem, confidence-building, and social skills. Group counseling provided the opportunity to practice new skills in a safe environment.

The School System

Paula attended a charter school that included grades kindergarten through 8, with kindergarten through third grades having both English as a second language (ESL) and non-ESL classrooms. The charter school enrolled approximately 350 students, many of whom were siblings from the same family. The school served predominately low-income, first-generation families. One third of the families attended the after-school program sponsored by the community center, which shared building space with the charter school.

DEVELOPMENTAL CONSIDERATIONS

Paula followed a strict diet and took insulin for type 1 diabetes. I considered Paula's development when conceptualizing her case and developing counseling goals and interventions. For example, counseling sessions were 30 minutes in length and included expressive arts so that Paula did not feel pressured to sit still and talk for 45 minutes. When I considered interventions for utilization, the developmental appropriateness of the intervention/activity served as a determining factor for whether I utilized a particular intervention. For example, when considering the "Me Tree" activity (Propes, 2011) to facilitate the therapeutic process, I reviewed the developmental level of the normed population for the intervention.

RELATIONAL CONSIDERATIONS

At the time Paula began treatment, her family served as the primary significant relationship in her life. Paula struggled with developing trusting relationships with her teachers and with peers at school. To assist Paula in strengthening her self-efficacy to develop healthy relationships with teachers and peers, I used specific interventions during the counseling process that focused on healthy relationship building.

MULTICULTURAL CONSIDERATIONS

From a multicultural perspective, when developing the treatment plan, we considered culturally appropriate goals. We avoided goals that would possibly conflict with her cultural norms. We also addressed multicultural aspects in counseling by using toys reflective of persons' clothing and skin tone from her family of origin. We also played musical instruments that represented different cultures to enhance her cultural experience. We ensured these items were in the playroom so that she could choose any of them as part of her play and therapeutic experience. Additionally, when tracking Paula's play and identifying themes, we were careful to not interpret her play from an ethnocentric perspective, but considered her cultural experience when identifying themes within her play.

CONCEPTUALIZATION

Paula's Concerns

Paula's social deficits seemed rooted in the initial unexpected loss of her father (Miller, 2003). Although her mother reported Paula "always struggled with making friends at school," Paula's disconnection at school became distinctly more noticeable by her teachers and the professional school counselor following her father's arrest and deportation. Because Paula was showing improvement after receiving counseling for the trauma and separation anxiety after witnessing her father's arrest and deportation, her new diagnosis of type 1 diabetes, the unsuccessful test performance, and grade retention, Paula met the diagnostic criteria for 309.28 (F43.23) adjustment disorder, with mixed anxiety and depressed mood, persistent (chronic).

Paula's Goals

Working from an integrated approach (Mauer, 2006), the care team identified Paula's treatment goals. In addition to continued compliance with prescribed medication for ADHD, the team identified three main treatment goals: (a) build a consistently positive self-image; (b) demonstrate improved self-esteem by accepting compliments, by identifying positive characteristics about herself, by being able to say no to others, and by eliminating self-disparaging remarks; and (c) increase her social skill level. The team estimated it would take 6 months to accomplish the treatment goals.

To achieve the treatment goals, three objectives were identified: (a) identify positive traits and talents about self; (b) identify negative automatic thoughts and replace them with a positive self-talk message to build self-esteem; and (c) positively acknowledge and verbally accept praise or compliments from others.

Counselor Goals

As a counselor, the goals I set for myself with this case centered on ethically participating in an integrated health care (IHC) approach to Paula's case. Since the integrated team was co-located (Mauer, 2006) and not fully integrated using the same electronic health records (Mauer, 2006), I remained mindful of the ethics and logistics of maintaining confidentiality. For example, the team developed a process to secure consent to release information for each entity/organization on the integrated team. However, just because I had full consent to discuss

Paula's case with anyone from the pediatric clinic and anyone from the charter school, that did not mean full disclosure to all persons would assist in Paula's progress.

COUNSELING PROCESS FLOW

We met for individual 30-minute counseling sessions biweekly during the fall semester. After returning from the winter break, we transitioned individual counseling to a weekly psychoeducational group. The closed group consisted of four girls from the elementary charter school Paula attended. The group lasted for 7 weeks and utilized Trice-Black and Taylor's (2007) social skills curriculum for grades kindergarten through 5.

Theoretical Approach

The theoretical approach we used for Paula's treatment included solution-focused counseling integrated with cognitive behavioral and play therapy. We initially used child-centered play therapy for the first counseling session with Paula. In the first session, we introduced Paula to the playroom and observed and noted the themes from her play. We employed nondirective play therapy for the first session as a way to assess Paula's psychosocial–emotional status. The themes that surfaced during the intake session centered on family (people and pets), nurturing/caretaker, and outside activities.

Infusion of Creativity

We provided counseling services in an integrated setting that included an elementary charter school, a counseling center agency, and a pediatric primary care clinic, as well as an after-school community center. Using an integrated approach, individual counseling sessions occurred during the school day. The counselor coordinated the time and date of the counseling sessions with Paula's teacher to help minimize the academic impact of being removed from class to receive counseling. In an effort to not make Paula feel like she was being punished for receiving counseling, we did not hold sessions during lunch or recess.

Following the initial nondirective assessment session with Paula, during the second individual session, we used a sand tray to facilitate the therapeutic process so Paula could describe her life. We prompted Paula to make a tray about "your life now." Paula used miniatures of people to represent herself and her nuclear family in the tray. The children, which included Paula, were evenly distributed as a partial circle around the miniatures representing Paula's mother and father. Paula's mother and father stood closer together "in the kitchen." She placed the family members on the left side of the tray. On the right side of the tray, Paula placed miniatures representing activities; the family dog; the family car, which competed in car shows; and the beach. During this session, Paula demonstrated progress toward her objective to identify positive traits and talents about herself.

For the third individual session, we used paint to facilitate the therapeutic process so Paula could describe her goals from her perspective. We prompted Paula to paint her "miracle day." Paula used several different shades of blue, purple, yellow, orange, and red to paint "snow" on the majority of the canvas. Paula painted a house and persons in the center bottom half of the canvas. When asked what Paula would change about the day, she reported wanting to tell her parents the truth about breaking an item in the house. During the session, we processed Paula's perception of her parents' reactions to the truth and Paula's feelings related to the incident.

During Session 6, the last session before the winter school closure, we used the "Me Tree" activity (Propes, 2011) to facilitate the therapeutic process. During this session, Paula demonstrated progress toward her goals of identifying positive traits and talents about herself; identifying negative automatic thoughts and replacing them with positive self-talk messages to build self-esteem; and positively acknowledging and verbally accepting praise or compliments from others.

During the first individual session, following the winter school closure, Paula painted a picture to describe her progress and life as she experienced it now. Paula painted two pictures: one with warm colors, the second with darker colors. The first painting included a ballerina and tree and sunshine. During the session, we processed the ballerina and tree metaphors related to relationships, self-esteem, and positive attributes. The second painting included a car, bridge, and water. Paula described the second painting as a family trip to New Orleans and Florida. We further processed family interactions during the trip.

Group Counseling

To assist Paula in transitioning from individual to group counseling, the new counselor held an orientation session. During this session, Paula shared that she "does not get to do fun things" because her mother does not have a lot of money. She discussed not being "able to leave the house to go to the mall because [they] would have to take the bus." Other than having limited resources, Paula expressed that her "home life was good." Paula also verbalized that she was establishing new friend-ships with other people in her class at school.

Throughout the group counseling process, Paula presented with euthymic mood but reluctance to engage with the group members. However, she identified positive traits about herself during several of the group sessions. Paula attended all but the third group session. During Session 5, the group members worked to build the tallest free-standing tower they could with provided supplies. Paula had difficulty working with her group mate. Paula's partner attempted to help her with the activity; however, Paula's reaction suggested little interest. Paula continued to work alone.

During the sixth group session, Paula created two masks. The first mask was "an outer mask," which reflected what Paula thought people saw when they looked at her or what Paula thought she reflected toward others. The "inner mask" reflected how Paula felt about herself. Paula identified and shared that on the outside she is "happy," but on the inside she felt "sad." Paula's ability to share personal vulnerability publicly with the group demonstrated that Paula's self-confidence had grown and she felt safer with a group of her peers. By group termination, Paula listened to group members' positive attributes about her and accepted those compliments.

OUTCOME

Individual counseling sessions utilizing directive play therapy fol-lowed by psychoeducational group counseling appeared to provide Paula with the most success in developing a stronger sense of self, enhanced social skills, and reduced anxiety in social situations. The integrated approach used with Paula's case was helpful. She showed improved academic performance, increased positive self-esteem, and improved ability to describe and identify healthy social skills and rela-tionships. She also reframed her perception of juvenile diabetes from a wellness perspective. However, Paula would have likely shown more improvement if her mother and father engaged in the therapeutic pro-cess. We encouraged Paula's parents to participate in a parent education and support group. We also provided referrals for couples counseling. We suggested that Paula's parents participate in parent consultation to discuss Paula's progress, systemic dynamics impacting Paula's prog-ress, and strategies they could implement at home. Paula's mother seemed motivated to attend couples counseling. Neither parent wanted to join the parent education and support group. Overall, Paula's health and wellness improved. Observations of Paula's social interactions during the school day such as during recess and lunch also suggested an improvement in social skills, decreased anxiety, and the development of healthy peer relationships.

REFERENCES

Mauer, B. J. (2006). *Behavioral health/primary care integration: The four quadrant model and evidence-based practices.* Rockville, MD: National Council for Community Behavioral Healthcare.

Miller, J. B. (2003). *Introducing relational-cultural theory: A new model of psychological development.* Wellesley, MA: Stone Center. Retrieved from http:// www.tribal-institute.org/2004/download/pppresentations/C10%20 -%20Pamela%20Burgess-Responding%20to%20Violence%20Against%20 Native%20LGBT-Handouts.pdf

Propes, A. (2011). Me tree. In L. Lowenstein (Ed.), *Assessment and treatment activities for children, adolescents, and families: Practitioners share their most effective techniques* (Vol. 3, pp. 18–19). Ontario, Canada: Champion Press.

Trice-Black, S., & Taylor, J. V. (2007). *Girls in real life situations: Group counseling for enhancing social and emotional development: Grades K-5.* Champaign, IL: Research Press.

CHAPTER 9

FINDING SHAY

Melissa Luke

The following presents a case study of Shay, a 9-year-old girl with whom I met for weekly counseling sessions over a 4-month period in my private practice. Synthesizing developmental, relational, and systemic perspectives, I describe Shay's initial presenting concerns related to gender nonconformity, as well as how I conceptualized Shay and her needs within her familial, school, community, and cultural contexts. Additionally, I describe the creative arts and expressive treatment approach I utilized within a relational-cultural framework, and the outcomes related to Shay's developing gender identity.

Shay and her family sought counseling when Shay was in third grade. Shay's struggles began with the school's expectations that students begin changing into gender-specific uniforms for physical education (PE) classes. Although Shay had no prior history of behavioral acting out, she began to receive a series of referrals for frequently not having her PE uniform, reports of disobedience and escalating insubordination, refusal to enter the locker room, and, ultimately, hiding in the girls' bathroom during PE class. After numerous phone conversations with Shay's classroom and PE teachers, Shay's parents met with her principal, social worker, and school psychologist. They explained that Shay identified as female since the age of 4. From her parents' perspective, Shay's recent behavior was in direct response to the school's insistence she wear a male uniform, change in the male locker room, and, at least in PE class, use her birth name of Shane. Increasingly, Shay's parents did not feel that the school supported her emotional and social needs, or that the staff understood or appropriately responded to Shay's needs as a child who was gender nonconforming.

These issues reached a crescendo when the school personnel informed Shay and her parents that hiding in the girls' bathroom room was a safety violation and they suspended Shay from school for several days. Further, they said that given the ongoing challenges, a "psychological assessment" might be warranted because such behavior could be a sign of potential "sexual deviance." Shay's parents understood the importance of affirming relationships and supportive contexts in a child's development (Alessi, Dillon, & Kim, 2015). They felt more worried about the possible negative impact of the school's misrepresentation of Shay's behavior on her self-concept than they were of either Shay's gender nonconformance or school referrals. Shay's parents shared that the challenges in school escalated and included several incidents of harassment by her peers. Shay felt intense feelings of sadness, isolation, and hopelessness by the time we engaged in counseling. In the first session, Shay shared, "I just want to be treated like everyone else and not have to stick out. It shouldn't be that difficult for my PE teacher to just drop the 'N' sound in my name."

SYSTEMIC INFLUENCES

My understanding of how family, school, and cultural systems influenced Shay informed how I conceptualized her presenting concerns and my counseling approach. As research supports that 10% of children are gender nonconforming at some point, many families and most schools and communities include gender-nonconforming children (Roberts, Rosario, Slopen, Calzo, & Austin, 2013). However, to date, gender identity models promote gender as binary and do not represent the experiences of persons who are gender nonconforming. Therefore, most adults are not informed about and ill prepared to respond to the needs of gender-nonconforming children (Goodrich, Harper, Luke, & Singh, 2013; Luke & Goodrich, 2012). Even though research strongly suggests that having family members, mentors, and a supportive community can be a positive factor in development (Lewis, Derlega, Griffin, & Krowinski, 2003), gender-nonconforming children continue to be marginalized and family or school personnel often mandate them to counseling (Goodrich & Luke, 2015).

By the age of 8 or 9, children begin to develop a more sophisticated self-concept through social comparisons with peers. Peer groups increasingly influence their development, and concurrently, the range of children's emotional experiences expands to include a more diverse range of complex emotions. That said, the gender sorting that is endemic in P–12 schools can unintentionally create significant challenges for gender-nonconforming children and plays a significant role in their long-term development (D'Augelli, Grossman, & Starks, 2006). Competent and affirming counselors work to help children feel safe in counseling and to fully engage in the counseling process (Goodrich & Luke, 2015).

DEVELOPMENTAL CONSIDERATIONS

Even before meeting Shay, I conceptualized her situation and concerns with an understanding that expression of and exploration of gender identities and roles are a normative part of child development (Institute of Medicine, 2011). This is particularly relevant because such changes in personal and social identity can influence the dynamics and progression of counseling (Goodrich & Luke, 2015). Unless my assessment of Shay revealed that she felt uncomfortable with her gender identity, I sought to understand her identity as part of a natural continuum, and then work with her and her family to examine how systemic and contextual factors shaped her development.

RELATIONAL CONSIDERATIONS

Relational-cultural theory (RCT) informed my work with Shay and her parents. I recognized and strove to establish meaningful, mutual, and empathic relationships to facilitate therapeutic growth (Jordan, 2010; Miller & Stiver, 1997). Using an RCT framework, I postulated that Shay lacked meaningful and mutually empathic relationships in some aspects of her life. According to RCT, mutually empathic relationships foster feelings of connection, growth, and a renewed sense of energy. Further, I believed that through the counseling relationship, Shay would develop a deeper understanding of herself and others, experience increased self-esteem, and desire additional meaningful relationships. In addition, Shay's parents also expressed anger at the school, guilt about not protecting Shay better, and fear about how withdrawn they perceived she had become in the last few months. Given Shay's parents' description of depressive symptoms, my initial intake would need to assess suicide risk, and begin to determine what aspects of her life might be endogenous, an adjustment reaction, internalization of negative attitudes, or a functional response to her relationships and relational oppression at school.

MULTICULTURAL CONSIDERATIONS

Culturally aware and responsive counselors possess a sensitivity to and understanding of the lived experiences of gender-nonconforming children (Goodrich & Luke, 2015). In this case, I intentionally communicated in developmentally appropriate ways to Shay and her parents. I shared my awareness of the conflicting messages about gender identity within the media and culture more broadly. In addition, I knew that it would also be necessary to assist Shay and her parents to deconstruct the ways in which heterosexism, homophobia, and transphobia may be impacting Shay's identity development and peer interactions (Luke & Goodrich, 2012), as well as the familial functioning. Further, "access (or lack thereof) to strength-based wellness resources and community connections" (Goodrich & Luke, 2015, p. 41) would be helpful. Given the salience of the intersection of identity (Luke & Goodrich, 2014), I endeavored to continually consider the ways in which Shay's age, race, religion, and social location contributed to her intra- and interpersonal experiences. Lastly, I sought to encourage Shay and her family to incorporate this multicultural complexity into their understandings as well.

CONCEPTUALIZATION

Although gender has been falsely dichotomized as a male–female binary system (Association of Lesbian, Gay, Bisexual, and Transgender Issues in Counseling [ALGBTIC], 2009), the World Professional Association for Transgender Health (WPATH, 2011) recognized gender nonconformity as a common human experience. Still, people who are gender nonconforming face social and cultural stigmas (Gray, Carter, & Levitt, 2012; Reiger & Savin-Williams, 2012). Recognizing these social biases, I intentionally work to provide an open and affirming environment. As a lesbian, gay, bisexual, and transgender (LGBT) affirming counselor with a specialty in working with children and adolescents, my informed consent communicates my validation and affirmation of the full range of gender identities (ALGBTIC Competencies Task Force, 2013). Shay's parents reported that reading the informed consent was a relief, and a reason why their pediatrician had urged them to consider traveling 45 miles for treatment. Although I spoke with both of Shay's parents by telephone twice, I met with them for a 90-minute consultation prior to meeting Shay. During the initial consultation, Shay's parents completed intake forms and shared medical records, and I explained my approach to child counseling including confidentiality and parent consultation. Together, we also discussed Shay's developmental history and their approach to parenting, which included their affirmation of Shay's gender identity.

COUNSELING PROCESS FLOW

Given that the therapeutic relationship predicts treatment retention and accounts for a substantial amount of client success (Eyrich-Garg, 2008), I intentionally attended to building, maintaining, and repairing the therapeutic relationship with Shay. These strategies began by connecting with her to find out what was important to her from her perspective, to inquire about her ambitions and hopes, and to support her in determining who was significant to her (De Jong & Berg, 2007). I was transparent with Shay about her power (Goodrich & Luke, 2015) to determine the focus of our counseling, and I attended to the complex and sometimes conflicting thoughts, feelings, and messages that accompanied this material. Because I knew children often uniquely communicated about the therapeutic alliance and related processes (Everall & Paulson, 2002), I infused creative and expressive interventions into our work.

Infusion of Creativity

Creative arts and expressive modalities effectively engage child clients (Schimmel & Jacobs, 2011) and counselors employ them across diverse theoretical frameworks (Sommers-Flanagan, Richardson, & Sommers-Flanagan, 2011) including RCT. Therefore, I included a variety of creative and expressive mediums available for Shay, starting in our first session. These elements included puppets and other props, sand tray, and art supplies. While Shay gravitated toward many of the creative approaches on her own, I invited her to experience more intentional expressive activities. For example, when she struggled to explain the multitude of events during a previous day, I invited her to use some of the materials in my office to construct a symbolic obstacle course to represent the various events. In addition to reflecting and tracking her experiences, I shared my process observations to which she offered additive responses. Instead of just verbally describing or recounting what each object represented, Shay actually demonstrated in vivo what it was like to navigate obstacle after obstacle in sequence. The visual and nonverbal symbolism was powerful. Our connection grew when she invited me to accompany her through the obstacle course. Through repeating her motions, gestures, and kinesthetic movements, I provided a more nuanced verbal mirror for her, wherein she remained the expert in her own experience.

TREATMENT

In addition to a strong therapeutic alliance, treatment for gender-nonconforming children includes actively combating negative messages by educating others, seeking resources, and fighting stereotypes about the LGBT community (Goodrich & Luke, 2015). Even with such resources, many gender-nonconforming children experience some ambivalence about their identity and/or others' judgments of their identity. However, many gender-nonconforming adolescents reported that they gained self-awareness (Riggle, Whitman, Olson, Rostosky, & Strong, 2008), recognized their fortitude through experiences of adversity, and gained a sense of community through relationships with other LGBT persons.

Accordingly, treatment recommendations often include a combination of psychoeducational and process interventions, wherein the in vivo biopsychosocial factors that may have more enduring impacts on child development and the maintenance of a positive identity can be addressed. Therefore, my work with Shay incorporated interventions such as "Learned Agency" and "Advocacy in a Bottle" (Goodrich & Luke, 2015, pp. 71–75) modified for individual child treatment. Both interventions rely upon creative and expressive techniques to support clients in gaining insight and developing communication and advocacy skills. As I continued to consult with Shay's parents, I infused Van Vliet's (2008) five steps to overcome some of the shame associated with internalized oppression. Through this work, I discussed the ways in which Shay's parents could intervene with her as well as within the various systems to which she belonged. Relatedly, they became active in an LGBT parent support group and worked to educate school officials. Their advocacy efforts positively influenced some new PE regulations. Despite this achievement, they explored the possibility of enrolling Shay in a private or charter school.

OUTCOME

After 4 months of counseling, Shay's depressive symptoms abated considerably, and she received frequent and less flagrant behavioral referrals at school. Shay continued to display gender-nonconforming behavior and identity. She remained actively engaged in the individual counseling process, and discussed potential interest in joining a short-term group. Gender-nonconforming children report lower self-esteem and increased risk for social and emotional challenges (Dziengel, 2010). The marginalization and misunderstanding that gender-nonconforming children experience, combined with their intrapersonal challenges (Toomey, Ryan, Diaz, Card, & Russell, 2010), makes counseling a much needed resource (Fitpatrick, Euton, Jones, & Schmidt, 2005). As such, it is imperative for all counselors to be clinically, ethically, and multiculturally competent to ally with (Goodrich & Luke, 2015), and effectively respond to, the needs of gender-nonconforming children.

REFERENCES

Alessi, E. J., Dillon, F. R., & Kim, H. M. (2015). Determinants of lesbian and gay: Affirmative practice among heterosexual therapists. *Psychotherapy, 52*(3), 298–307.

ALGBTIC Competencies Task Force. (2013). Association of lesbian, gay, bisexual, and transgender issues in counseling competencies for counseling lesbian, gay, bisexual, queer, questioning, intersex, and ally individuals. *Journal of LGBT Issues in Counseling, 7*(1), 2–43.

Association of Lesbian, Gay, Bisexual, and Transgender Issues in Counseling (ALGBTIC). (2009). *Competencies for counseling with transgender clients.* Alexandria, VA: Author.

D'Augelli, A. R., Grossman, A. H., & Starks, M. T. (2006). Childhood atypicality, victimization, and PTSD among lesbian, gay, and bisexual youth. *Journal of Interpersonal Violence, 21,* 1462–1482.

De Jong, P., & Berg, I. K. (2007). *Interviewing for solutions* (3rd ed.). Pacific Grove, CA: Brooks/Cole.

Dziengel, L. (2010). Advocacy coalitions and punctuated equilibrium in same sex marriage debate: Learning from pro-LGBT policy changes in Minneapolis and Minnesota. *Journal of Gay and Lesbian Social Services, 22,* 165–182.

Everall, R. D., & Paulson, B. L. (2002). The therapeutic alliance: Adolescent perspectives. *Counseling & Psychotherapy Research, 2*(2), 78–87.

Eyrich-Garg, K. M. (2008). Strategies for engaging adolescent girls at an emergency girls shelter in a therapeutic relationship: Recommendations from the girls themselves. *Journal of Social Work Practice, 22*(3), 375–388.

Fitpatrick, K. K., Euton, S. J., Jones, J. N., & Schmidt, N. B. (2005). Gender role, sexual orientation, and suicide risk. *Journal of Affective Disorders, 87,* 35–42.

Goodrich, K. M., Harper, A. J., Luke, M., & Singh, A. A. (2013). Best practices for professional school counselors working with LGBTQ youth. *Journal of LGBT Issues in Counseling, 7*(4), 307–322.

Goodrich, K. M., & Luke, M. (2015). *Group counseling with LGBTQI persons.* Alexandria, VA: American Counseling Association.

Gray, S., Carter, A., & Levitt, H. M. (2012). A critical review of assumptions about gender variant children. *Journal of Gay and Lesbian Mental Health, 16,* 4–30.

Institute of Medicine. (2011). The health of lesbian, gay, bisexual, and transgender people: Building a foundation for better understanding. Retrieved from http://www.nationalacademies.org/hmd/~/media/Files/Report%20Files/2011/The-Health-of-Lesbian-Gay-Bisexual-and-Transgender-People/LGBT%20Health%202011%20Report%20Brief.pdf

Jordan, J. (2010). *The power of connection: Recent developments in relational-cultural theory.* New York, NY: Routledge.

Lewis, R. J., Derlega, V. J., Griffin, J. L., & Krowinski, A. C. (2003). Stressors for gay men and lesbians: Life stress, gay-related stress, stigma, consciousness, and depressive symptoms. *Journal of Social and Clinical Psychology, 22*, 716–729.

Luke, M., & Goodrich, K. M. (2012). LGBTQ responsive school counseling supervision. *Clinical Supervisor, 31*(1), 81–102.

Luke, M., & Goodrich, K. M. (2014). Recognizing the needs of sexual minority boys and adolescents in school. In M. Kocet (Ed.), *Counseling gay men, adolescents, and boys: A strengths-based resource guide for helping professionals and educators.* New York, NY: Routledge.

Miller, J. B., & Stiver, I. P. (1997). *The healing connection: How women form relationships in therapy and life.* Boston, MA: Beacon Press.

Reiger, G., & Savin-Williams, R. C. (2012). Gender nonconformity, sexual orientation, and psychological well-being. *Archives of Sexual Behavior, 41*, 611–621.

Riggle, E. D. B., Whitman, J. S., Olson, A., Rostosky, S. S., & Strong, S. (2008). The positive aspects of being a lesbian or gay man. *Professional Psychology Research and Practice, 39*, 210–217.

Schimmel, C. J., & Jacobs, E. (2011). Ten creative counseling techniques for helping clients deal with anger. Retrieved from http://counselingoutfitters .com/vistas/vistas11/Article_53.pdf

Sommers-Flanagan, J., Richardson, B., & Sommers-Flanagan, R. (2011). A multi-theoretical, evidence-based approach for understanding and managing adolescent resistance to psychotherapy. *Journal of Contemporary Psychotherapy, 41*(2), 69–80.

Toomey, R. B., Ryan, C., Diaz, R. M., Card, N. A., & Russell, S. T. (2010). Gender nonconforming lesbian, gay, bisexual, and transgender youth: School victimization and young adult psychosocial adjustment. *Developmental Psychology, 46*, 1580–1589.

Van Vliet, K. J. (2008). Shame and resilience in adulthood: A grounded theory study. *Journal of Counseling Psychology, 55*, 233–245.

World Professional Association for Transgender Health (WPATH). (2011). Standards of care for health of transsexual, transgender, and gender nonconforming people (7th version). *International Journal of Transgenderism, 13*, 165–232.

CHAPTER 10

WHITNEY AND ROOK: FINDING CONNECTION IN PLAY THERAPY

Suzanne M. Dugger
Jennifer Austin Main

Whitney was 3 years old when I met her, and I must say I felt surprised by my first impressions. Having already met with her foster mother for an intake interview, my image of Whitney stood in stark contrast to her actual appearance when I greeted her and her foster mother "Carol." Despite enduring enough abuse and neglect as an infant to have been removed from her birth mother's care at 18 months of age, and despite living in six different foster homes since that time, Whitney appeared no worse for the wear. In fact, Whitney appeared more like a treasured, privileged child who lived a charmed life than like an abused and neglected child who had spent half of her life in the foster care system.

Sadly, Whitney's case was one in which her looks belied the true abuse she experienced in her life. By the time Whitney arrived in our clinic for play therapy services, the years of abuse, neglect, and inconsistency indelibly marred her life. In this chapter, we offer a conceptualization of Whitney's case, describe the process of play therapy with her, identify treatment outcomes, and offer our reflections.

SYSTEMIC INFLUENCES

From a systemic perspective, Whitney's early experiences in her family seemed clearly fraught with difficulties. Her experiences of abuse and the time she spent in the foster care system exacerbated her growing attachment problems. Whitney seemed unable to attach to her various foster parents, in large part due to the extent of abuse and neglect she had experienced, but also perhaps due to the impact of subtle cultural differences between Whitney and the families that fostered her.

DEVELOPMENTAL CONSIDERATIONS

Whitney was born in rural Mississippi. Her single, 19-year-old Caucasian mother raised Whitney alone after her boyfriend Justin "hit the road" when he learned of the pregnancy. We knew little about Whitney's first year of life, but court records indicated that the Department of Human Services (DHS) initiated an investigation just after Whitney's first birthday. Although initial complaints of suspected abuse and neglect went unsubstantiated, a trip to the emergency department (ED) ultimately resulted in a DHS decision to remove Whitney from her birth mother's care. Apparently, Whitney's birth mother had been routinely using sedatives in place of babysitters. Whenever Whitney's birth mother wanted to go out with friends, she administered sedatives to Whitney, who would fall into a deep sleep while her mother "was out partying." One morning, however, Whitney did not wake. Terrified, her mother rushed Whitney to the ED and revealed her strategy for "child care."

In accordance with state child protection laws, the physicians immediately notified DHS. Armed with the mother's confession and a file full of unsubstantiated but very concerning complaints, DHS immediately removed Whitney from the home and placed her into foster care. Rather than fighting this action, Whitney's birth mother seemed relieved and did not contest the decision. Within 6 months, she voluntarily surrendered her parental rights.

Although a novice counselor may view this as a success and conclude that Whitney would be much better off, experienced counselors know all-too-well about the challenges often involved with foster care. In Whitney's case, for example, she arrived in her first foster home at 18 months of age and stayed less than a month. The first set of foster parents described Whitney as inconsolable, highly emotional, and so "out of control" that they felt unequipped to provide adequate care for her. Over the course of the next 15 months, Whitney would be placed in—and soon removed from—five additional foster homes. It was not until she lived with Carol and Ben that Whitney experienced any consistency of care. When Carol and Ben first sought play therapy services from our clinic, Whitney had been with them for 3 months.

RELATIONAL CONSIDERATIONS

From a relational perspective, Whitney's early relationship with her primary caretaker had been insufficient at best. Rather than offering the consistent and loving care and attention needed to build strong attachments, Whitney's mother remained inconsistent, often inattentive, neglectful, and sometimes abusive. When removed from her birth mother's care, Whitney was already at risk for attachment-related difficulties.

MULTICULTURAL CONSIDERATIONS

Although they all identified as Caucasian, differences related to socioeconomic status (SES) may have contributed to the difficulties early foster parents had in relating to Whitney. The foster families benefitted from the privilege afforded by a middle-class lifestyle and had no real understanding of the impact of poverty on Whitney's birth mother. They had no real understanding of how poverty, both in terms of financial and social capital, might contribute to a mother's decision to choose inexpensive sedatives purchased on the street over a human babysitter. This may have resulted in them villainizing Whitney's birth mother and having great difficulty in responding to Whitney's emotional distress over the separation from her mother.

Thus, although the foster care system had the potential to help Whitney heal from her early family experiences and begin forming healthy attachments, this did not occur with Whitney. Instead, Whitney experienced foster care as "repeated changes of primary caregivers that limit[ed] opportunities to form stable relationships" (American Psychiatric Association [APA], 2013, p. 266).

From a developmental perspective, Whitney manifested some delays, which were unsurprising given her life history. For example, in the context of psychosocial development, Whitney struggled with the development of trust in herself and others, and she also exhibited low tolerance for frustration. Additionally, Whitney displayed some cognitive delays, most clearly evident with regard to language acquisition.

Diagnostically, I conceptualized Whitney as displaying symptoms consistent with reactive attachment disorder (RAD; APA, 2013), which were etiologically related to the lack of consistency and care in her early relationships (RAD criterion D). Additionally, as sessions progressed, Whitney demonstrated symptoms consistent with a diagnosis of posttraumatic stress disorder (PTSD; APA, 2013).

As such, despite her perfect, almost doll-like, physical appearance, Whitney arrived for play therapy with an array of developmental, systemic, and relational deficits related to many unmet needs. Especially given the delays related to language acquisition, I chose to approach the counseling process using an adaptation of child-centered play therapy (CCPT; Axline, 1969; Landreth, 2012).

CONCEPTUALIZATION

Conceptualizing Whitney's case, I was profoundly struck by her unmet needs. Indeed, Whitney's life history seemed to represent a 3-year saga of unmet needs from relational, systemic, and developmental perspectives.

CREATIVE TREATMENT APPROACH: CANINE-ASSISTED PLAY THERAPY

As a Licensed Professional Counselor (LPC) and a Registered Play Therapist Supervisor (RPT-S), I base my work with children in the theory and practice of CCPT (Axline, 1969; Landreth, 2012). CCPT may be described as a nondirective, Rogerian approach to play therapy in which the child leads the session and the play therapist trusts the child to take the process where he or she needs to go. However, whereas Rogerian approaches to counseling adults rely upon word-based conversation, CCPT views play as a child's language and the toys as the medium of expression (Axline, 1969; Landreth, 2012).

In addition to using CCPT as the foundation for my work with children, I received training in canine-assisted play therapy (CAPT), an adaptation of CCPT that has received increasing attention over the past few years (Chandler, 2005; Lange, Cox, Bernert, & Jenkins, 2007; Thompson, 2009) but has its origins in much earlier work (Levinson, 1962, 1969). For the past several years, I have integrated a trained therapy dog, named Rook, into my play therapy sessions with children. Rook acts as an extension of me and offers children his attention and genuine, positive regard.

COUNSELING PROCESS FLOW

Fortunately, Whitney responded quite well to play therapy with me and Rook. She fully engaged in the process and her time in the playroom allowed her the freedom to explore and express herself. Over the course of 34 sessions spanning 11 months, Whitney's play shifted with regard to themes and seemed to reflect her reactions to both past and present life circumstances. Themes included early exploration and non-committal play (Sessions 1–3); ambivalent play that alternated between protective, nurturing play and control-oriented play (Sessions 4–12);

dissociative and regressive play (Sessions 13–29) after visitations with her biological father began; and, after another significant systemic disruption, trauma play (Sessions 30–34).

Exploration and Noncommittal Play (Sessions 1–3)

I met Whitney for the first time in the waiting room of our university-based clinic. When I introduced myself and Rook to Whitney and invited her to join us in the playroom, she eagerly hopped down from Carol's lap, wrapped her tiny fingers around my hand, and accompanied me to the playroom. Although this warm response was not typical of children exhibiting symptoms of RAD, it has been my experience that even children with attachment difficulties seem to respond well to Rook's presence.

Whitney appeared to embrace the play room quickly and showed no signs of distress being away from Carol. Instead, Whitney displayed curiosity and thoroughly explored the playroom, carefully examining each of the toys and often asking me about them. Although her play during these sessions was mostly noncommittal and nonexpressive, the ability to explore the playroom and decide things for herself seemed freeing to Whitney. Given her background and lack of control over her life, Whitney seemed to appreciate the play room as a space in which she felt empowered to make decisions.

Ambivalent Play (Sessions 4–12)

By our fourth session together, Whitney's play became more expressive and seemed to reflect her ambivalence about relationships. Specifically, Whitney alternated between protective, nurturing play and rejecting, control-oriented play.

Examples of nurturing play could be seen in numerous interactions with me and Rook. Early on, she often sat in my lap while she played in the sandbox or with various toys. Whitney would brush Rook and pretend to give him a bath. She also pretended to wash my hair and apply makeup to make me "look pretty." Other instances of nurturing play were evident in Whitney's concern about protecting us. For example, when Whitney pretended to feed Rook, she checked to make sure that there was nothing on his plate that could hurt him. Also, Whitney would use the doctor kit to check both of us. If we were "sick," she would prepare us food and give us a "shot" to make us feel better.

As our sessions progressed, however, her nurturing and protective play shifted to themes of anxiety about cleanliness. Whitney became increasingly preoccupied with anything "messy," described many items in the playroom as "nasty," and quickly engaged in cleaning behavior. Also, she would lie on the floor and look up to check Rook's underside to see if he urinated on himself and would reassure me that he had not. Whitney's nurturing play with Rook then became more controlling and rejecting. Although she never became physically abusive of Rook, Whitney began to verbalize threats of punishment or rejection. For example, her admonishments included, "If you don't eat your food, you can't play with any more of your toys" or "Go away, you can't play with us."

As a play therapist struggling to understand the communications embedded in Whitney's play, I found myself with several unanswered questions. Was her behavior toward Rook mimicking treatment she had endured? Did her need for cleanliness and repeated washing reflect that she had experienced sexual abuse? If so, was this abuse current or from the past?

A Systemic Disruption

Five months into Whitney's counseling, Carol and Ben informed me that Whitney's biological father, Justin, had contacted the court to seek custody of Whitney. They were crushed by this news as they had hoped to adopt Whitney, and they felt confused about why Justin would now seek custody of Whitney because he had expressed no interest until now in having a relationship with her. To their dismay, the judge ordered Carol and Ben to allow Whitney to begin visitation with Justin and his wife Rachel every other weekend.

Although they complied with this court order, Carol and Ben claimed that Whitney would cry, scream, and resist going with Justin for their scheduled visits. When Whitney returned from Justin's care, she appeared dirty, disheveled, tired, and emotionally reactive. Carol and Ben reported that it would take a few days to help Whitney adjust to being with them again. They stated that Whitney started biting her nails again, experiencing night terrors, and regressing in her toilet training. Whitney also began to make comments such as, "You are not my mom" or "I don't have to listen to you." It seemed that this oppositional behavior became even more problematic during visitations with Justin and Rachel. Rachel revealed to Carol that Whitney slapped her and acted disobediently and defiantly in their home.

Carol denied ever seeing Whitney act aggressively toward someone else and speculated that "something must be going on" at Justin and Rachel's home to cause this new behavior. As a play therapist, I also saw a significant change in Whitney. I, too, had concerns about the negative impact of this systemic disruption in Whitney's life.

Dissociative and Regressive Play (Sessions 13–29)

Over the course of the next 5 months, the themes in Whitney's play became noticeably more aggressive, demanding, controlling, and messy. At times, her play appeared chaotic and disorganized. Whitney's speech became more difficult to understand, and she began to exhibit regressive behavior as well as signs of possible disassociation. Specifically, Whitney would "zone out" and, during these times, she seemed not to hear me talking to her. Rook was so attuned to Whitney that I began to watch him for early indicators of Whitney's dissociation. Rook seemed to sense when Whitney began to disassociate and, when she "zoned out," he would leave her side, go to the other side of the room, and lie down.

During these times, Whitney began having whispering conversations with herself while playing in the sandbox. Whitney would suddenly look at me and sincerely ask, "Who are you?" or "What is your name?" On one particular occasion, she had spent the majority of her time in the sandbox just rubbing her hands through the sand, barely talking. She looked at me with concerned eyes and asked, "Where is Ms. Jennifer? I have to find her." Clearly distressed and not feigning concern, Whitney left the playroom on a quest and ran halfway down the hall before turning around and saying, "There you are! I found you. Where did you go?"

During these sessions, Whitney also began displaying regressive behaviors. For example, she began using the pacifier for herself and would suck on it periodically throughout her play. In one session, after stubbing her toe as she entered the playroom, Whitney wanted to sit in my lap until she felt better. She filled a baby bottle, crawled into my lap to drink her bottle, and stayed there until she felt better.

As our sessions continued, the unanswered questions continued to mount. Was Whitney actually dissociating during our sessions as I suspected? If so, was this indicative of the psychological avoidance recognized as a hallmark symptom of PTSD? Why was she regressing? To what extent were the visits with her father and Rachel contributing to these symptoms?

Another Systemic Disruption

As if Whitney had not experienced enough instability in her life, she then experienced yet another systemic disruption. When contacting Carol and Ben after a rare no-show, I learned that Whitney had been removed from Carol and Ben's custody and placed in a new foster home. Apparently, the judge ordered this placement in response to the custody battle between them and Justin in order to determine whether Whitney had developed an attachment to her biological father.

I immediately contacted Whitney's guardian ad litem and discussed the importance that Whitney continue to receive services. She agreed and provided me with contact information for the new foster mother, "Sasha." When I called Sasha to introduce myself, Sasha told me in no uncertain terms that she would not have time to bring Whitney to the clinic as her own "real" children were her priority. It was quite some time until the guardian ad litem was able to arrange transportation for Whitney to resume sessions with me.

Trauma Play (Sessions 30–34)

When Whitney finally returned to play therapy, a full month later, I could immediately tell she was in a different foster home. Her hair was not brushed, her clothes were torn, and her behaviors in our play sessions revealed themes of abuse and trauma. Whitney was also angry with me. She complained, "You left me." I had been a consistent and stable figure in Whitney's ever-changing life, and she struggled to understand why she did not see me for a month. Over the next five sessions, Whitney's play themes revolved around abuse and trauma.

In one session, Whitney sat in the sandbox and asked me to bathe her. Concerned that this could be an inappropriate interaction between the two of us, I returned the responsibility back to her by saying, "In here, you can bathe yourself." She proceeded to pour sand all over her body and head and began washing herself with the sand. When she finished, Whitney asked me to turn around so I would not see her get dressed. When Whitney climbed out of the bathtub, she said, "Baby hurt your pee-pee. You need to check your pee-pee. Moms know about a lot of stuff. I know about pee-pees and I want you to know about pee-pees, too." She demonstrated for me how to check her pee-pee by bending over and looking at her groin area. Whitney then squatted down and pretended to urinate. Then, as if nothing profound had just happened in the session, Whitney redirected our play and we pretended to get in the car and go to Walmart so she could buy groceries.

During her next session, Whitney used Play-Doh and water to create what she eventually called her "baby." As Whitney rubbed her hands on the Play-Doh and added water to the mixture, she stared at the wall and appeared to zone out, not responding to my verbal reflections. After several minutes, Whitney turned to me and said, "This is not done yet. It's going to be a baby, but isn't one yet. Baby is going to be bad, but it's not bad yet. I'm going to have to push this baby out." Whitney proceeded to clean the baby by adding more water to it, but then exclaimed, "Ewww, it's gross, it has doo-doo on it." She continued to clean the baby by adding more water to it and then wrapped the baby in numerous paper towels. She explained to me that "I am the mom and I am not hurting the baby, but I might hurt the baby later. I'm going to cook that baby." She took a wet paper towel, soaked the baby, and placed it in the microwave. Whitney cooked the baby, placed it on a plate, and with flat affect said, "I've made baby soup. Come and eat."

In another session, Whitney selected a baby to care for and her selection seemed to suggest that this baby was her identified self-object (Gil, 1991). After gently holding the baby and caressing the doll, Whitney said, "Oh no, it's going to get all dirty again." She then took the baby and poured red paint all over it. Next, she filled a container with water and washed the baby off. For most of the session, Whitney cycled through the process of pouring sand and paint all over the baby and then cleaning it. Finally, she took the baby and threw it into the trash can and said, "You pee-pee'd in the water. That's right, you are not good." She filled a container with water and exclaimed, "Where is baby? Baby has to come back now. Baby, I missed you." She retrieved the baby from the trash can and poured sand all over the baby and washed it again. She then took the baby back to the trash can, threw it in, and stated, "There, that's where you belong." At this point, she turned her focus to me. Whitney gave me a shot and said, "This won't hurt you" and tried to put a pump up my nose. She instructed me to pretend to cry. While I cried, she took the syringe again and said, "Oh no, please don't cry. Let me give you this stuff. It will make you go to sleep."

Once again, I found myself with several unanswered questions. To what extent did Whitney's play reflect her actual experiences? Was Whitney now experiencing sexual abuse, either in her new foster home or while visiting her father and Rachel? Did Whitney remember, on some level, her biological mother's administration of sedatives?

OUTCOME

I wish I could conclude this case study with a happy ending. Unfortunately, my work with Whitney ended prematurely. As with too many other cases in which children must depend upon adults for their access to mental health services, Whitney stopped coming to our clinic. Despite my calls to her guardian ad litem and my expressions of concern for her safety, I have been unsuccessful in scheduling any future appointments for Whitney. My profound concern for her well-being leaves me with a deeply unsatisfying sense of unfinished business and a deeper understanding of compassion fatigue.

CONCLUSION

This chapter shared details about an all-too-common case of unmet needs, unanswered questions, and unfinished business. It is our hope that readers will benefit from our analysis of Whitney's unmet needs and gain deeper insight into the impact of systemic disruptions in a child's life. We also hope the discussion of the themes, which emerged during Whitney's sessions, will support play therapists in recognizing possible signs of dissociation and abuse. Finally, we hope this chapter has normalized feelings other play therapists may experience when frustrated by the premature ending of a counseling relationship and the unfinished business that remains for our child clients. Although many unanswered questions invariably arise during the practice of CCPT and CAPT, we implicitly trust that Whitney took the play therapy process where she needed it to go and that it would have continued to a therapeutic end had it been allowed to progress to its natural conclusion.

REFERENCES

American Psychiatric Association (APA). (2013). *Diagnostic and statistical manual of mental disorders* (5th ed.). Washington, DC: Author.

Axline, V. M. (1969). *Play therapy*. New York, NY: Ballantine Books.

Chandler, C. K. (2005). *Animal assisted therapy in counseling*. New York, NY: Routledge.

Gil, E. (1991). *The healing power of play: Working with abused children*. New York, NY: Guilford Press.

Landreth, G. L. (2012). *Play therapy: The art of the relationship* (3rd ed.). New York, NY: Brunner-Routledge.

Lange, A. M., Cox, J. A., Bernert, D. J., & Jenkins, C. D. (2007). Is counseling going to the dogs? An exploratory study related to the inclusion of an animal in group counseling with adolescents. *Journal of Creativity in Mental Health, 2*(2), 17–31.

Levinson, B. M. (1962). The dog as a co-therapist. *Mental Hygiene, 46*, 59–65.

Levinson, B. M. (1969). *Pet-oriented child psychotherapy*. Springfield, IL: Charles C. Thomas.

Thompson, M. J. (2009). Animal-assisted play therapy: Canines as co-therapists. In G. R. Walz, J. C. Bleuer, & R. K. Yep (Eds.), *Compelling counseling interventions: VISTAS 2009* (pp. 199–209). Alexandria, VA: American Counseling Association.

CHAPTER 11

ZARACK AND THE LAND OF DREAMS

JoLynne Reynolds

I received a phone call one Friday afternoon from Sophia Martinez (a pseudonym), a woman desperate to find a counselor for her 11-year-old son, Mateo. She told me that Mateo experienced suicidal thoughts but said he did not want to die. After getting a brief history of Mateo's past health and a summary of recent events in his life, we developed a safety plan for her and her husband to implement over the weekend. I instructed her to keep Mateo with family members at all times, and to engage him in structured pleasant activities until I could meet with them on Monday. I also gave her information on where she could take him for an immediate psychological evaluation if needed, and told her to call me over the weekend with questions or if Mateo needed to talk to me.

SYSTEMIC INFLUENCES

Both Sophia and Matt served as professionals in the community with advanced academic degrees. They showed pride that all three children excelled in school and athletic activities. Alicia, the oldest child, enjoyed a busy social life and spent less time with the family. Mateo and Michael shared a bedroom and Mateo often expressed annoyance toward his younger brother about the invasion of his space and time. They saw Mateo as musical, gifted academically, and as someone who enjoyed baseball and running cross-country. Mateo's maternal grandparents resided in the family's basement apartment and enjoyed a close and loving relationship with the family.

DEVELOPMENTAL CONSIDERATIONS

An Adlerian view of Mateo helped me consider the impact of the family constellation and birth order on Mateo's developing cognitive map (Adler, 1928; Carlson & Yang, 2008; Kottman & Meany-Walen, 2016). As a middle child with a successful older sister and an attention-getting younger brother, Mateo's experience made sense to me. Research on birth order from an Adlerian perspective supports Adler's view that developing middle children struggle with finding their place in the world, feeling sandwiched in between their older and younger siblings, and are at risk for developing feelings of not belonging (Eckstein et al., 2010). Considering Mateo's age and stage of cognitive development proved important. Piaget's theory of cognitive development (Piaget, 2003) placed Mateo in the concrete operational stage of development, characterized by logical concrete thinking and an egocentric perspective of events. All of these factors considered together—his birth order, family constellation, and his cognitive developmental stage—contributed to the likelihood that Mateo developed a negative view of himself with mistaken conclusions about the cause of stressful events in his life (Kottman & Meany-Walen, 2016).

RELATIONAL CONSIDERATIONS

Mateo's family possessed many qualities characteristic of "growth-fostering relationships" defined in RCT (Jordan, 2014). However, beginning in third grade he developed a negative relational image of himself, becoming withdrawn and disconnected from others, hiding aspects of his pain, and losing his sense of voice and connection. Telling his parents about his suicidal thoughts indicated his resilient nature and was a strong step toward experiencing the benefits of the many growth-fostering relationships available to him (Jordan, 2014).

MULTICULTURAL CONSIDERATIONS

Sophia portrayed Mateo as a healthy young boy with few developmental problems or health concerns. She described her family as Hispanic, with a Catholic heritage and strong ties to their extended family. Sophia and Matt had been married for 20 years with three biological children: Alicia, age 15; Mateo, age 11; and Michael, age 7.

CONCEPTUALIZATION

I began to formulate a partial picture of Mateo by considering his symptoms and strengths in the context of his age, and his family constellation with respect for his family's Latino cultural background (Withrow, 2008). I found an integration of various theories helpful in this process including relational–cultural theory (RCT; Chu, 2014; Jordan, 2014); Piaget's cognitive theory of development (Piaget, 2003); and Adlerian theory (Adler, 1928; Carlson & Yang, 2008).

Infusion of Creativity

Mateo came to his first session with his mother and father. Mateo seemed small for a fifth grader, with dark, curly hair and large brown eyes that quietly assessed me. I invited him and his parents into my office where I engaged them in a conversation about the events on Friday and over the weekend. I discussed counseling, confidentiality, and its limitations to Mateo and his parents. Mateo politely listened and remained quiet during the conversation with his parents and cooperated in answering the questions his parents and I asked of him. We talked together about a safety plan, and Mateo agreed to let his parents or his school counselor know if any thoughts of self-harm came to him during any day or night.

After his parents left the counseling room, Mateo quietly looked around the shelves full of toys and miniature figures. I wanted to diffuse the stress he might be experiencing from the conversation with his parents, so I began by directing the conversation to things he enjoyed doing. He told me about running cross-country, learning to draw anime, and reading books, especially books about magic and dragons. As we continued, a small smile let me know he felt more relaxed. I gently directed the conversation back to his troubling thoughts. He said that he thought about killing himself since third grade, but refrained from telling his parents until now. I asked him about his eating and sleeping, and he replied that he did not sleep well. Chronic nightmares almost every night for the whole 2 years caused him worry, which made it hard to fall asleep. He looked down at the floor and said, "I feel tired almost every day."

I felt immense compassion for Mateo and said, "I think it's awful for you to have all these nightmares. Maybe you and I can work together and find a way to make the nightmares go away." He looked up at me and I sensed his hopefulness at this suggestion. He told me how his dreams would start out okay, and then they would start changing into nightmares. The nightmares sometimes began when he would dream that his parents expressed anger toward him. They would yell and scream at him, saying they did not love him. Other nightmares consisted of Mateo being grabbed and pulled into a van, after which a man would kill him, at which point he would wake up. My heart went out to him, hearing how much he suffered. I wanted to validate his pain and said, "I agree with you, these are some pretty scary dreams. I can see why you don't want to have them anymore."

We both paused and I sensed that he felt connected and that I cared about him. He told me the nightmares and bad thoughts started in third grade when he did not have very many friends. I decided to begin to assess if any of the contents of his nightmares might be flashbacks related to real-life traumas or if they originated from high levels of anxiety (Gil, 1991; Luis, Luis, Varela, & Moore, 2008; Muris & Merckelbach, 2000). I looked at him closely and asked, "Has anything bad ever happened to you or has anyone ever hurt you in any way?" He told me that some of the boys at school behaved aggressively and would make fun of him, but no one ever grabbed him or hurt him like in his dreams. He also said his parents never told him they did not love him. I felt tentatively reassured, but still puzzled about the frightening content of his dreams. I asked him about school and he told me that he had several good friends and liked his teachers. He smiled and shared he recently won an art contest for his drawing of a close up of a dragon's face. He proudly said, "I got first place!" He also told me about a book series he really liked that featured a boy and his pet dragon.

I read one of the books and we shared what we liked about the stories. We talked about how cool it would be to have a pet dragon. I asked, "What kind of dragon would you choose if you could have one?" He smiled and decisively said, "A red dragon that I could ride anywhere. It would breathe blue fire!" I smiled back, enjoying the image with him. Internally, the powerful theme of his fantasy and the excitement he expressed about flying with his pet dragon impressed me. Because it seemed such a contrast to the helpless and trapped experience of the past 2 years for him, I asked him, "Would you like to write a story with me about a boy and his pet dragon? What if in the story the dragon could help the boy whenever he needed it? Maybe the dragon could even come into his dreams and help him get rid of nightmares." He seemed excited and smiled.

I then acted on another impulse to plant a therapeutic suggestion and said, "You know, I bet you could even try that out before I see you next week with your own dreams. You could call your dragon into your dream if you need help." He smiled a really big smile and said, "Okay." I gave him a piece of paper and asked him to write down his answers to the following: If I could have three wishes, I would wish . . . . He wrote down the following three wishes that poignantly described his humor as well as his problems: *"(1) destroy wasps and replace them with something kind; (2) feel better about myself; (3) have a good night's sleep all of the time."* As we ended the session, we reviewed our safety plan and I told him, and then his parents, they could call me if he needed to come in before the next week's appointment. After Mateo and his parents left that day, my thoughts wavered between concern and hope. His long-term silence worried me, yet I also felt encouraged that he finally reached out for help to his parents and opened up to me.

COUNSELING PROCESS FLOW

The priorities for Mateo's counseling goals included: (a) to assess the risk that Mateo might harm himself and put in place interventions for safety; (b) to determine what significant life events contributed to his anxiety and depression; (c) to increase his feelings of connection to others; (d) to reduce the occurrence of his nightmares; (e) to support him in developing a stronger voice in order to ask for help when he needed it and to express his needs. The plan included 10 weeks of counseling; 8 weeks of individual counseling for Mateo and two scheduled parent consultation meetings. I also included specific things for his parents to do as part of the treatment plan, including scheduling positive one-on-one time with Mateo, and taking him to his doctor for a physical exam to rule out any medical concerns for his anxiety.

I planned to use Adlerian play therapy that would include four phases of counseling: (a) building a positive egalitarian relationship; (b) exploring his lifestyle; (c) helping him gain insight; and (d) providing reorientation and reeducation for him and his parents (Kottman & Meany-Walen, 2016). Because his nightmares caused such negative consequences for his health and well-being, I used a variation of the mutual storytelling technique (Gardner, 2002; Kottman, 2011) to help him experience power and competency over them. I received no phone calls from his parents following our first session, and wondered about Mateo's progress. When Sophia arrived with Mateo, I spent the first 10 minutes of the session with both of them together. Mateo seemed relaxed and calm, and reported no suicidal thoughts during the week. He also gave a big smile and said he slept well during the week with no nightmares. He and his mother shared the week's events that included several positive conversations and activities between Mateo and his parents. After Mateo's mother left the session to wait outside, I asked Mateo if he thought any more about his dragon story. He said yes, and even drew a picture of his dragon. We created the following story together. The phrases in italics are the story parts he contributed as a cowriter.

Zarack and the Land of Dreams

Once upon a time, there was a boy named Mateo. He lived in the land of *Agilealth*. One remarkable thing about Mateo is that he had his very own pet dragon named *Zarack*. *Zarack is a red dragon with yellow and orange eyes. His scales are stronger than armor and his fire is dark blue. Zarack* could do many things that only dragons can do including: *he could not be hurt by swords, he could fly, and he could breathe fire.* One special power *Zarack* had was that he could immediately tell if someone was lying or telling the truth, which was a great power to have. Mateo and his dragon did many things together. They liked to *swim in the lake and fly everywhere together.* They also used their power to help people who needed it. They helped *many villages detect threats of danger and helped them get the food and water they needed.*

Dragons do not sleep, but because boys always have to sleep each day, Mateo would have to go to the land of dreams without his dragon. For most of Mateo's life, the land of dreams was fun. In the land of dreams, he could do anything he wanted. He loved to dream about *adventures to far places.* One day, an evil *Or'k* put a spell on dreamland. He divided dreamland into two sides with a river running through it. On one side was the happy place Mateo loved to visit. But the other side of the river was the side of lies. On this side, the evil *Or'k* ruled. He plotted and planned terrible ways to trap Mateo and then created terrible events that would make Mateo feel sad and scared. Mateo found out about this bad part of dreamland one night as he slept. Somehow the evil *Or'k* pulled him over to the scary side of dreamland. As Mateo entered this part of dreamland he immediately knew something was not right. His parents, who he knew loved him very much, yelled at him, they even said: *leave we don't want you.* Mateo felt confused. He felt *lonely.* As he wandered through this lonely place a terrible man in a van stopped and pulled him inside. Just when the man started to hurt Mateo, Mateo woke up and left dreamland. He was so upset and scared. He was afraid to go back to sleep now that dreamland wasn't safe for him anymore.

Mateo didn't know that these parts of dreamland are all lies. None of them were genuinely true, but the evil *Or'k* loved to play his tricks and cast his evil spells. Mateo told his dragon *Zarack* about dreamland and the terrible things that happened there now. His dragon decided Mateo needed his help. He told Mateo that, even though dragons didn't dream, he could come to dreamland and help Mateo whenever he needed him. Mateo simply had to call out his name and he would fly to Mateo and they would end the bad things together. Knowing now that he had help, Mateo decided to go back to dreamland. That night, as he fell asleep, he started to enjoy the beautiful part of the dream. He saw *rainbows* and got to *go to the beach*. All of a sudden, he fell into the dreamland river and found himself on the other shore of dreamland . . . the dream of lies. Scary things started to happen right away. He saw a jail and then he saw and heard *screaming and yelling*. He started to be scared, very scared, but then he remembered his dragon's promise. In his loudest voice he yelled out *ZARACK!* Immediately *Zarack* appeared. *The sun shown behind Zarack, making him look like an angel. He looked awesome! Zarack* said, "These are all lies made up by the evil *Or'k*. We will battle him and return dreamland back to its peaceful state." *Zarack* used his power of telling lies from truth. He breathed his magical fire on the lies that *Or'k* had created. Immediately *everything turned beautiful and the sun shone like it was August.* With one final blow, Mateo and his dragon flew together to where the evil *Or'k* lived. When they found him hiding in his cave *they banished him from dreamland forever.* From that time on, dreamland became a peaceful, happy place for Mateo to visit. Never again did the evil *Or'k* come to spread his lies. And Mateo knew that if anything ever scared him again, he could call out his dragon's name, and together they would conquer any enemy that tried to hurt him.

After his first session, Mateo continued to be nightmare free, with no further thoughts of self-harm, and he ate and slept well. In his third and fourth sessions, I continued to explore his life events and his view of himself and asked him to do a timeline of his life. From his life timeline, he did not relate any significant traumas or abuse of any kind. I also asked Mateo to construct a kinetic family sand tray scene, a variation of the kinetic family drawing (KFD) assessment (Cook, 1991). I asked Mateo to select miniatures to represent each member of his family, including himself, and to situate them each doing something in the scene. The sand tray scene revealed Mateo's feelings of distance from his family and his internal view of self as someone insignificant and alone. I helped him explore these feelings and suggested alternative views about his family to promote insight. Mateo began to build a more positive view of himself.

The fifth session involved a parent consultation session attended by his mother, Sophia, and his father, Matt. Both parents expressed relief that Mateo's symptoms and his sleep improved. Much of the session focused on ways we could work together to help Mateo feel more valued in his family, and how we could help him develop a positive self-image. I suggested they continue the increased one-on-one time with him and to use encouragement in place of praise to help him appreciate his strengths (Kottman & Meany-Walen, 2016).

In the sixth through the ninth sessions, Mateo continued to improve. He slept free of nightmares and seemed relaxed and happy with no suicidal thoughts. Two areas of discouragement emerged from these sessions. One concern surrounded his desire for his own room away from his younger brother. He felt if he asked his parents, nothing would change. The second concern we discussed involved the bullying incidents at school. He again felt he could do nothing to change things. We began to explore his options and ways he could begin to speak up for himself. I used encouragement (Kottman & Meany-Walen, 2016) to help him develop a view of himself as a resourceful and courageous person, just like the character in his dragon story. By the end of our ninth session, Mateo shared both these concerns with his parents. They helped create a space for his own bedroom, and set up a meeting with his school counselor to address the bullying incidents.

OUTCOME

At our last session, Mateo proudly took the book he wrote home and planned to continue writing new chapters about his adventures with Zarack. The final session involved a parent consultation meeting where we reviewed Mateo's successes and his parent's new insights to his needs. Both expressed appreciation for the counseling and told me that if Mateo needed help in the future, they would bring him back for more sessions. I asked them to let me know if they needed anything and to follow up with me as needed.

Adlerian play therapy and mutual storytelling proved to be a good fit for Mateo, and helped me understand his view of self and his world. I did not find any evidence of abuse, but I did feel that his family overlooked his emotional needs for some time. Mateo's sibling position made it difficult for him to compete with his siblings for his parents' attention. Because Mateo did well in school and was a quiet child, I believed that his emotional needs became almost "invisible" in his family constellation, resulting in his mistaken conclusion that he did not matter as much as others. He completed counseling without any reoccurrence of nightmares or suicidal thoughts, and held a new view of himself as a courageous and resourceful person with parents who loved and cared about him.

REFERENCES

Adler, A. (1928). Characteristics of first, second, and third child. *Children: The Magazine for Parents, 3*(5), 14–52.

Carlson, J., & Yang, J. (2008). Adlerian family therapy. In K. Jordan & K. Jordan (Eds.), *The quick theory reference guide: A resource for expert and novice mental health professionals* (pp. 197–208). Hauppauge, NY: Nova Science Publishers.

Chu, J. Y. (2014). *When boys become boys: Development, relationships, and masculinity.* New York, NY: New York University Press.

Cook, K. M. (1991). Integrating kinetic family drawings into Adlerian life-style interviews. *Individual Psychology: The Journal of Adlerian Theory, Research and Practice, 47*(4), 521.

Eckstein, D., Aycock, K. J., Serber, M. A., McDonald, J., Van Wiesner, V., III, Watts, R. E., & Ginsburg, P. (2010). The role of birth order in personality: An enduring intellectual legacy of Alfred Adler. *Journal of Individual Psychology, 68*(1), 60–74.

Gardner, R. A. (2002). Mutual storytelling. In C. E. Schaefer & M. Cangelosi (Eds.), *Play therapy techniques* (pp. 257–268). Northvale, NJ: Jason Aronson.

Gil, E. (1991). *The healing power of play: Working with abused children.* New York, NY: Guilford Press.

Jordan, J. J. (2014). Relational-cultural therapy. In R. VandenBos, E. Meidenbauer, & J. Frank-McNeil (Eds.), *Psychotherapy theories and techniques* (pp. 325–333). Washington, DC: American Psychological Association.

Kottman, T. (2011). *Play therapy: Basics and beyond.* Alexandria, VA: American Counseling Association.

Kottman, T., & Meany-Walen, K. (2016). *Partners in play: An Adlerian approach to play therapy* (3rd ed.). Alexandria, VA: American Counseling Association.

Luis, T. M., Luis, R., Varela, E., & Moore, K. (2008). Parenting practices and childhood anxiety reporting in Mexican, Mexican-American, and European-American families. *Journal of Anxiety Disorders, 22*(6), 1011–1020.

Muris, P., & Merckelbach, H. (2000). Fears, worries, and scary dreams in 4–12-year-old children: Their content developmentally. *Journal of Child Psychology, 29*(1), 43.

Piaget, J. (2003). Cognitive development in children: Piaget development and learning. *Journal of Research in Science Teaching, 40*(S1), S8–S18.

Withrow, R. L. (2008). Early intervention with Latino families: Implications for practice. *Journal of Multicultural Counseling and Development, 36*(4), 245–256.

PART II

CASE STUDIES RELATING TO ADOLESCENTS

CHAPTER 12

RENEWED THROUGH CHARTED MEMORIES

Alexandria K. Kerwin
Eric Suddeath

As a newly graduated counselor working at a community mental health agency in the rural South, I became acquainted with Kristen, a 15-year-old White female, and her family. At first glance, Kristen seemed to be a confident and secure young lady. She earned straight As, played trumpet in the high school marching band, and appeared popular among her peers. During our time together (2008–2010), we covered much ground from drug use to a suicide attempt and, eventually, a teen pregnancy. We ultimately identified residual effects of childhood trauma as the root cause of her presenting issues. Using trauma-focused cognitive behavioral therapy (TF-CBT), we began to see a reduction in her symptoms.

SYSTEMIC INFLUENCES

Kristen hailed from a small southern town where she lived with her mother, stepfather, and two younger siblings, ages 12 and 10. The family dynamics appeared patriarchal as her stepfather called the shots. Kristen and her 12-year-old sister resented him, but her 10-year-old brother did not. Although her mother seemed happy with the dynamics, she showed empathy toward the girls' feelings. When I first met Kristen, the U.S. Army had deployed her biological father to Iraq. I met him several months later upon his return, and he provided a consistent and calming presence during Kristen's treatment. Her biological parents divorced early in her life, but Kristen still remembered the intense conflict between them. The divorce greatly impacted Kristen and damaged the trust she once experienced with her mother and her father. In addition to her nuclear family, her paternal grandmother appeared as a supportive presence in the family. Kristen frequently talked about the love and support she felt from her grandmother. Despite her many strengths and supports, Kristen encountered struggles. Police placed her maternal grandfather in prison for molesting Kristen and her younger sister.

From a strengths-based perspective, Kristen appeared socially adept despite the fact that some regarded her friend base as the "wrong crowd." She enjoyed her friendships in the marching band and at school, but preferred to party with her 18- and 19-year-old friends. Her teachers cared about her and expressed concerns about her recent increased absences from class. Kristen seemed well aware of her intelligence and wanted to become a doctor. She responded to her teachers' concerns by saying, "If I can make the grades, then everyone should get off my back about it."

DEVELOPMENTAL CONSIDERATIONS

Counselors distinguish themselves from other helping professionals by embracing a developmental perspective rather than a medical model. For example, in my approach, I assessed for strengths and helped the client recognize and build upon them. Fortunately, Kristen reported having overall good physical health without any concerning medical history; however, she reported having intense mood swings. Prior to my meeting Kristen, a psychiatrist diagnosed her with bipolar disorder and prescribed medication for her. Applying a developmental perspective with Kristen became one of my tasks. Table 12.1, which takes eclectic concepts from Rathus (2016), compares and contrasts Kristen's development with what is considered normal development.

RELATIONAL CONSIDERATIONS

Kristen's ability to connect well with others impressed me. Most, including me, enjoyed her company. She appeared easy to connect with because of her ability to articulate, her intellect, and her good sense of humor. Even though she ran with the wrong crowd, she demonstrated her ability to form peer relationships, which I distinguished as one of her strengths. Additionally, Kristen described her mom as her best friend despite the fact that they argued constantly; however, she *despised* her stepfather, describing him as overbearing and harsh. She engaged in explosive arguments with her sister, but her younger brother appeared

TABLE 12.1 Developmental Considerations for Kristen

Type of Development	Typical Adolescent Development	Kristen's Developmental Experience
Physical (Female)	Puberty: Increased hormonal activity resulting in growth spurts, breast development, menstruation, body hair, and so on.	Female puberty occurred at a younger age. However, Kristen appeared to be on the tail end of a healthy puberty at age 15.
Cognitive	Abstract thinking, advanced information processing, self-reflection, reasoning and decision skills, and more advanced problem-solving skills. Increased potential for engaging in risky behavior despite these progressive cognitive shifts.	Kristen appeared cognitively more advanced than her peers, and exhibited a high level of intelligence. She made a 27 on the practice ACT in the eighth grade and consistently made the school's honor roll. She eventually graduated from high school as the salutatorian. Even though her high-risk behavior (unprotected sex and drug use) caused problems, it served as an indicator of normal development.
Social	Attachment shifts from parents to peers and there is an emerging desire to fit. Rebellion, detachment, and parent–child conflict expected. The importance of sexual attraction and romantic relationships is displayed.	Her high-risk behavior caused conflict with her parents. Compared to the average adolescent, Kristen appeared highly sexually active with 10+ sexual partners by age 16. She frequently discussed loving sex and wanted to experiment with as many partners as possible. Her interest in sex began earlier than most when her grandfather began sexually abusing her at age 9. She described it as a game she looked forward to because it felt good.
Emotional	Fluctuating emotions due to hormonal shifts, and coping skills needed for exposure to new situations.	Psychiatrists diagnosed Kristen's emotional dysregulation as bipolar disorder. She lacked the ability to cope with anger and sadness and her psychiatrist labeled her high-risk behavior as mania. She displayed frequent anger outbursts and depressive episodes.
Moral	Values and morals of their parents chosen to integrate into their self-concept. Behavior aligned with ideas of what is right and wrong. Shift from avoidance of consequences to reward seeking. Moral behavior promoted by	Kristen struggled with her moral development. The trauma inflicted by her grandfather, a trusted adult, skewed her interpretation of right and wrong. However, at age 12, she knew that informing her mother about the abuse appeared to be the right thing to do,

(continued)

TABLE 12.1 Developmental Considerations for Kristen (*continued*)

Type of Development	Typical Adolescent Development	Kristen's Developmental Experience
	positive feelings, such as empathy and kindness.	especially after she discovered that her sister became her grandfather's next target.
Identity	Exploration of various identities. Goals for committing to a congruent identity. Unchanging identity indicating stability or distress.	Kristen did not explore her identity. I saw a shift in her identity when she became a mom at age 17. She no longer appeared to be the "wild child." She described it as having to "grow up fast." "Growing up fast" is also the phrase she used to describe her reaction to the sexual trauma she experienced. She appeared to be living in her grown-up identity when we terminated counseling.

Adapted from Rathus (2016).

uninvolved in the family drama. She also expressed feeling incredibly close to her paternal grandmother who, according to Kristen, always "spoiled" her. Kristen experienced positive relationships with her teachers due to her academic achievement and likable personality. When they expressed concerns, it appeared genuine.

MULTICULTURAL CONSIDERATIONS

Counseling practitioners adhere to professional ethics and competencies to better understand clients within contexts. For generations, Kristen's family resided in a small southern town with a population of approximately 2,100 people. Southern Baptist prevailed as the dominant religion in the area. Although her family identified with this religion, they did not attend services regularly. Kristen described the religion as judgmental and harsh; from Kristen's point of view, the services also appeared as a breeding ground for gossip. Additionally, racial tensions tended to be salient in this part of the country. Though half of the school consisted of African American students, Kristen chose to associate with White friends. She noted, "It's not meant to be racist, that's how it is."

Kristen's family struggled financially. Even though both of her parents graduated from high school and worked hard, they found it difficult to make ends meet. They also fought to maintain employment because of the economic crisis of 2008. Fortunately, her biological father served in the army and paid for her counseling through TRICARE.

When I considered cultural differences, I noted many similarities between Kristen and me. I am a White female from a small, southern, predominantly Southern Baptist community characterized by a low socioeconomic status (SES). However, at the time of our counseling relationship, I lived in the second largest city in our state, and since meeting Kristen I gained more social currency by way of education. Categorized as a college town where the average SES seemed much higher, the attitudes in this community appeared more liberal than Kristen's. I commuted 30 miles to work in her community, and the differences seemed palpable. Compared to Kristen's small town, I felt as though I lived in a bubble of privilege. My agency offered a considerable amount of free supervision, and I took advantage of it when dealing with cultural issues.

CONCEPTUALIZATION

Client's Problem

A tearful Kristen and her mother stepped into my office for the initial intake, and their story began to unfold. She skipped school, got high, and engaged in risky sexual behavior. In regard to unprotected sex, she bluntly stated, "I like the way sex feels, and it feels better without a condom." After numerous attempts to improve Kristen's situation, I researched childhood trauma and discovered literature on TF-CBT that identified previous trauma as a frequent underlying cause of behavioral and emotional problems experienced by children and adolescents (Cohen, Mannarino, & Deblinger, 2006). I found this to be important information in conceptualizing Kristen's presenting problem—the past sexual abuse by her maternal grandfather. My training as a certified TF-CBT therapist and my meeting the criteria set by the TF-CBT Therapist Certification Program proved invaluable. During my training, I completed live training collaboratives, engaged in consultation with the trainers for 6 months, completed three TF-CBT cases, used standardized measures to assess progress, and passed the TF-CBT Therapist Certification Program Knowledge-Based Test.

During my training, I learned three principal goals that guided my trauma work with Kristen: (a) assess TF-CBT for its appropriateness for Kristen; (b) create a plan of action; and (c) empower Kristen to reduce levels of related distress by confronting traumatic memories. I also emphasize that the following is an abbreviated explanation of TF-CBT, and I encourage counselors to become trained if TF-CBT is determined as the most appropriate approach.

Strategies for the Client

TF-CBT is an evidence-based treatment used to treat posttraumatic stress disorder (PTSD) experienced by children ages 3 to 18 (Cary & McMillen, 2012; Cohen, Mannarino, Kliethermes, & Murray, 2012; Lawson & Quinn, 2013). As the name indicates, the theoretical base lies in the cognitive behavioral school of thought. The overall focus of TF-CBT is to build physical, emotional, and cognitive coping skills; bolster the parent–child relationship; gradually expose and desensitize; and create new meaning surrounding the trauma. Most importantly, it is used to help the child to not be defined by the trauma (Cohen et al., 2006).

The culminating event in TF-CBT, the creation and sharing of a trauma narrative (TN), is actually a two-pronged intervention: (a) exposure and (b) meaning making. Before beginning the TN, it is essential that the client practices and feels comfortable using physical, emotional, and/or cognitive coping skills. Tailoring coping skills to the client's needs is important to help him or her feel increased control during the exposure (Cohen et al., 2012). These skills help the client combat the intense experiences that arise during the TN. The goal of the TN is to help "youth to understand themselves, their relationships and their past experiences in new and more positive ways" (Cohen et al., 2012, p. 536). Rather than proceeding chronologically or focusing on a specific traumatic event, exposure during the TN is focused on themes and difficult thoughts and feelings that arise out of the client's trauma experience(s) (Cohen et al., 2012). The therapist supports and guides the client as the client is exposed to the previous trauma through the TN and makes new meaning of the trauma. The process of creating the TN also helps the client to develop greater understanding about the experience and to challenge previously held negative core beliefs (Cohen et al., 2012).

The client progressively authors his or her experience of the event to become gradually exposed and desensitized to the distressing memories associated with the trauma. The client, then, engages in meaning making by re-authoring an empowering survival story and sharing it with a trusted adult (Cohen et al., 2006). To develop the TN, the client and counselor discuss the trauma little by little each session. The gradual exposure happens by reviewing shared experiences about the trauma in each session. This process continues until the child no longer displays signs of distress when discussing the traumatic memories.

Goals and Target for Client Change

Clients in TF-CBT write their experiences in first person, present tense, and repeat the narrative with the counselor in an effort to face their fears and become desensitized. Kristen recalled seeing her sister's abuse as the worse image. The abuse happened sporadically to Kristen from age 6 to 8. She stated that it did not feel traumatizing at the time because "He made it like a game and it felt good." However, seeing her grandfather molest her sister surfaced as the worst memory of the abuse. Kristen saw her sister in distress and reported that she no longer enjoyed "the game." This became the deciding point to tell her mother.

Assessment

The assessment process began with utilizing Foa, Johnson, Feeny, and Treadwell's (2001) Trauma Screen and Child PTSD Symptom Scale to measure Kristen's trauma history and level of distress. Kristen indicated items such as, "Someone older touching your private parts when they shouldn't." The scale then asks, "Which one is bothering you the most now?" After she identified her most distressing trauma, we explored her situation further. To do this, we moved on to the UCLA PTSD Index for the *DSM-IV*, Adolescent Version (Pynoos, Rodriguez, Steinberg, Stuber, & Frederick, 1998). At this point of the assessment, I used the instrument that aligned with the *DSM-IV-TR*. The American Psychological Association updated the index in 2010 to accommodate the *DSM-5*.

I used the UCLA PTSD index to measure PTSD in Kristen by creating a trauma history profile and identifying levels of continued distress. She indicated continued distress items such as, "I have trouble feeling happiness or love," and "I think that some part of what happened is my fault" (Pynoos et al., 1998, p. 4). After discussing the results and implications of the formal assessments, Kristen and her mother decided to move forward.

COUNSELING PROCESS FLOW

I wish I could tell you we did this in a clean and linear fashion and provided a session-by-session account. This did not happen. As with most counseling, my experience with Kristen seemed circular rather than linear. Most notably, her pregnancy threw us off the TF-CBT linear protocol track, but we backtracked as needed. However, I managed to provide a general outline of the counseling process flow.

Sessions

The format used for treatment entailed individual and joint sessions with both mother and child. Each meeting with Kristen began with an

assessment of her emotional status. I became intentional in not imposing the TF-CBT agenda when it did not seem appropriate for Kristen.
The approach detailed a checklist to help guide the therapist (Cohen
et al., 2006, 2012; Lawson & Quinn, 2013). The acronym for the eight-
item checklist is PRACTICE: (a) psychoeducation and parenting;
(b) relaxation; (c) affective modulation; (d) cognitive coping; (e) TN
and cognitive procession of the narrative; (f) in vivo exposure; (g) con-
joint sessions; and (h) enhancing safety. Because Kristen and I established a positive therapeutic relationship, my immediate focus became
the preparation for the TN work.

Infusion of Creativity

I preferred to use simple metaphors in counseling because they make
complex ideas approachable, especially for children and adolescents. To
explain the purpose of gradual exposure, I used toe testing in a swim-
ming pool as a metaphor, which resonated well with Kristen. I explained
that instead of doing a cannonball into the deep end of the pool, I preferred to start with one toe in the shallow end and gradually work our
way into the water. After sessions of solidifying her affective modulation and cognitive coping, I focused on the heart of TF-CBT, the TN
(Cohen et al., 2006).

The manual provided no specific ways to construct the narrative;
rather, we approached the trauma work with an understanding that clients
can express themselves through a variety of mediums (e.g., write, illustrate, collage, sing, sand tray, video recording, audio recording). This
is where the client's creativity comes into play. It is also important to
note that the TN is developed in session and *not* assigned as homework. The academically minded Kristen chose to write her narrative in
essay form, and she became highly motivated and engaged during
most of our TN sessions. After all, her work ethic earned her a salutato-
rian ranking.

The Trauma Narrative

In Chapter 1 of the narrative, she began the task of crafting her TN with
the neutral prompt, "About Me." This section allowed her to warm up to
the process without having to delve into painful memories of the trauma.

Chapter 2 initiated the exposure of her experience. This section
included elements of the first time, worst time, and last time, as well as
when she disclosed her abuse and explained how others reacted (Cohen
et al., 2006). At times, she wrote several paragraphs at once; at other
times, she did not want to write at all. In each instance, we continued

to revisit her coping and relaxation skills. My role evolved into observing and helping her deal with any overwhelming emotions during exposure using an array of relaxation skills. While she wrote, I essentially "disappeared" by providing her physical space. I spent time reading or drawing, which assured her that she did not need monitoring. However, I observed the emotions she displayed and how she managed them as she wrote. It became necessary to help her stay grounded in the present.

Chapter 3 transitioned into meaning making and empowerment (Cohen et al., 2006). Kristen wrote advice to other kids who experienced similar trauma in the past and at present. The most salient piece of advice she gave involved shame. She stated, "Don't feel ashamed if you enjoy it. Sex feels good. It's not your fault, and it doesn't make the things they do right." Letting go of anger toward her mother for not knowing about the abuse, not knowing the warning signs to protect her own child, and not demonstrating self-compassion became the themes of her meaning making.

After the TN, Kristen shared her narrative with her mother. The sharing built trust and intimacy in the parent–child relationship (Cohen et al., 2006). Not only did I work with Kristen to build relaxation techniques, I also assisted her mother in using similar ones. I grew confident in her mother's ability to be a steady presence in the room, and she proved me right. It is important to note that the client is not required to share the narrative with a guardian. This event can take place with any adult the child deems trustworthy (e.g., an aunt, coach, or a night orderly at an inpatient facility).

OUTCOME

When I terminated with Kristen, her levels of distress significantly decreased and relationships with her family improved. She also graduated from high school with high honors and enrolled as a pre-med major at a nearby university despite being a teen parent. The odds seemed stacked against her, as she became a teen parent during our TF-CBT work. Unfortunately, I could not follow up with Kristen; however, I can only hope our work together bolstered her ability to live her best life.

This case study outlined the process of finding healing through charting memories utilizing an evidence-based treatment. I hope the examination of Kristen's case from systemic, relational, and developmental lenses shed light on the complexity of childhood trauma. Finally, I hope that I offered an alternative way to conceptualize and treat adolescent behavioral and emotional problems when other interventions do not seem to alleviate presenting problems.

REFERENCES

American Psychiatric Association. (2013). *Diagnostic and statistical manual of mental disorders* (5th ed.). Washington, DC: Author.

Cary, C. E., & McMillen, J. C. (2012). The data behind the dissemination: A systematic review of trauma-focused cognitive behavioral therapy for use with children and youth. *Children and Youth Services Review, 34*(4), 748–757. http://dx.doi.org/10.1016/j.childyouth.2012.01.003

Cohen, J. A., Mannarino, A. P., & Deblinger, E. (2006). *Treating trauma and traumatic grief in children and adolescents*. New York, NY: Guilford Press.

Cohen, J. A., Mannarino, A. P., Kliethermes, M., & Murray, L. A. (2012). Trauma-focused CBT for youth with complex trauma. *Child Abuse & Neglect: The International Journal, 36*(6), 528–541. http://dx.doi.org/10.1016/j.chiabu.2012.03.007

Foa, E. B., Johnson, K. M., Feeny, N. C., & Treadwell, K. H. (2001). The Child PTSD Symptom Scale: A preliminary examination of its psychometric properties. *Journal of Clinical Child Psychology, 30*(3), 376–384. http://dx.doi.org/10.1207/S15374424JCCP3003_9

Lawson, D. M., & Quinn, J. (2013). Complex trauma in children and adolescents: Evidence-based practice in clinical settings. *Journal of Clinical Psychology, 69*(5), 497–509. http://dx.doi.org/10.1002/jclp.21990

Pynoos, R., Rodriguez, N., Steinberg, A., Stuber, M., & Frederick, C. (1998). UCLA PTSD index for *DSM-IV* (Adolescent Version)[©]. Retrieved from http://www.irct.org/Admin/Public/Download.aspx?file=Files%2FFiler%2Fglobal%2FTraining%2FIstanbul+2009%2FUCLA_PTSD_Adolescent.pdf

Rathus, S. A. (2016). *Human development*. Boston, MA: Cengage Learning.

CHAPTER 13

HOPE DEFERRED

Caroline M. Brackette

Hope, a 14-year-old Caucasian female, came to see me for counseling during my time as a clinical therapist in an outpatient counseling agency located inside a medical hospital. The hospital also offered counseling and short-term inpatient psychiatric treatment. Hope came to counseling because her mother expressed concerns that Hope seemed withdrawn. Her mother further reported a reoccurrence of Hope's depressive symptoms displayed in counseling approximately 2 years ago. As a result, Hope agreed to return to counseling.

SYSTEMIC INFLUENCES

Hope lived with her mother and 10-year-old brother, who also received counseling for behavior-related concerns. Hope's parents never married, and no consistent contact or established relationships existed with her biological father. The family lived on the border of a neighboring state. Hope's family previously lived in my state; during that time, another counselor worked with her prior to her coming to counseling with me. Her current school and her mother's current job appeared closer to the agency she previously attended for therapy. Therefore, they decided that Hope would engage in out-of-state counseling with me. I found it important, during informed consent and throughout the counseling process, to notify the family about my legal and ethical responsibilities. This also meant I needed to be aware of relevant state laws for the neighboring state, in the event circumstances warranted me to refer to these guidelines and seek consultation.

Hope seemed to feel abandoned by her father, and appeared hesitant to express the impact of his absence on her self-esteem. Her father did not involve himself in her medical treatment. Hope's mother seemed ashamed to admit that her children's father decided to be absent in their lives. This feeling appeared to be consistent with Hope's feelings, as observed through her nonverbal behaviors of avoidance and silence during discussions about her relationship with her father. The mother appeared to feel guilty about the father's lack of participation and tended to overcompensate by being very involved in her children's lives, especially in their medical and mental health treatment. While Hope wanted her mother's involvement, she seemed bothered by her "excessive concern."

DEVELOPMENTAL CONSIDERATIONS

Cognitive Development

Hope repeated the seventh grade due to extended absences resulting from complications and treatment for non-Hodgkin's lymphoma. Her records revealed a learning disorder not otherwise specified diagnosis. Her records also indicated that she scored an average to above average IQ. She achieved at a level consistent with this IQ, except in mathematics ability, which tested below her measured IQ. Teachers described her as creative with an enjoyment for writing.

Hope received extended time testing accommodations for her math difficulties. Additionally, she used home-based instruction when medically necessary. Hope maintained a high "C" grade point average, and utilized the resources available to assist her with improving her academic performance. She worked with a tutor, and took summer classes to make up credits.

Personal, Social, and Emotional Development

Hope's past counseling experiences included being treated for self-injurious behavior. She cut her arms and wrists. Although her previous counselor diagnosed her with depression symptoms, Hope's records indicated that she never made previous suicide attempts. Hope often abstained from eating during times when she experienced episodes of depression. In addition to counseling, a psychiatric nurse addressed concerns related to eating and nutrition. Hope's cancer moved into remission after drug therapy treatment. Her doctor monitored her medical status. She reported no physical complications related to the cancer diagnosis at the time of intake.

She reported feelings of sadness and loneliness because she believed that people did not really understand her, even her family at times. She struggled with identifying positive personal characteristics and displayed a negative self-image. She expressed difficulty maintaining friendships due to her inconsistent attendance at school. She denied self-injurious behaviors or suicidal ideation at the time of the intake appointment.

RELATIONAL CONSIDERATIONS

Hope experienced a strained and distant relationship with her biological father. She reported a good relationship with her younger brother. She also reported that she maintained a positive relationship with her mother and stated that it was "okay," indicating no current stressors in her relationship with her mother. Hope established few friendships, and cited her inconsistent attendance as the reason. She also indicated that many of her peers felt that she used her medical condition to get sympathy. She felt that they did not really understand her medical condition, or its impact on her physical and emotional health.

MULTICULTURAL CONSIDERATIONS

Adolescence is a time when identity development occurs. Hope experienced difficulties with identity and relationships. She expressed confusion surrounding various familial and peer relationships, and struggled emotionally. She needed direction and guidance. Hope described her family structure differently from many of her peers who lived in two-parent homes, or in shared-custody environments. She did not see the "father as the leader" role within her home environment. She did not know her father well, which appeared different from her ideal of what she believed a father should be. She felt different among her peers. She experienced difficulty expressing her feelings, and joked that she received that trait from her father. Although this behavior caused her some distress, she seemed somewhat joyful that in a way this provided a connection to the father she did not know. As a young girl, she did not hold a good image of the role of a father, or the sense of safety and protection she believed parents should provide. She internalized her circumstances and developed a negative self-image as she compared herself and her life to others.

CONCEPTUALIZATION

Hope often internalized what she observed to be negative events in her life. She showed difficulty expressing her feelings, and seemed guilty for having them. She struggled with maintaining healthy familial and peer relationships. Her negative and faulty interpretations of the events and situations in her life (e.g., her low self-image and the impediments of her medical condition) caused feelings of depression and engagement in self-injurious behaviors. Through her previous experiences in counseling, she recognized cutting behaviors to be unhealthy and ineffective in alleviating her pain. She still felt pain after engaging in self-injurious behaviors and appeared to be asking for help in finding a better method for dealing with her negative thoughts and feelings. She seemed to know that she could not do this on her own.

Goals and Target for Client Change

I established the following goals for Hope: (a) to use more healthy modes of self-expression; (b) to demonstrate positive social and assertiveness skills; and (c) to recognize and reframe negative thought processes. Additionally, I provided Hope and her mother information on educational resources to address Hope's academic needs.

Strategies for the Client

I chose a cognitive behavioral approach, in particular, rational emotive behavior therapy (REBT). This approach focuses on the role of thinking and beliefs as the root cause of personal problems. It stresses action and engages in practices that combat irrational, self-defeating ideas that are unhealthy for an individual (Ellis, 2008).

Hope indoctrinated herself with negative thoughts and beliefs about events in her life. These thoughts caused her to become depressed with a pessimistic outlook on life. She engaged in self-harm and withdrawal as a reaction to these feelings, and demonstrated difficulty effectively communicating her thoughts and feelings to others. The REBT techniques of identifying her irrational thoughts and triggers helped in beginning an exploration of Hope's presenting issues, including the origins of the negative thoughts. This facilitated my guiding her through the process of disputing those negative thoughts and replacing them with rational thoughts. The process also involved addressing negative behaviors and replacing them with more positive actions. This modality provided an eclectic facilitation of a variety of techniques that addressed

Hope's cognitive, affective, and behavioral concerns and included teaching her new skills.

Goals and Strategies for Myself

Creating a safe place that encouraged engagement in counseling became the goal that I established for myself. I wanted to remain patient and commit to developing a genuine, therapeutic relationship with Hope. Although I worked from a cognitive behavioral perspective, I recognized the importance of utilizing the person-centered ideals to build the foundation of an encouraging environment to help facilitate change.

COUNSELING PROCESS FLOW

In my observation, I found Hope to be quiet and I discovered that she yielded to her mother to answer questions during the initial meeting. It seemed that her mother appeared much more involved in the previous counseling process than what I planned for in this round of counseling. In an effort to build rapport with Hope and set boundaries with her mother, I reviewed the counseling process with both. I also created a structure for the sessions. I communicated the importance of the mother's involvement in Hope's treatment. However, to facilitate change, I also stressed the need for sessions to be focused on Hope and her development and practice of effective skills.

In addition to parental consent, I obtained Hope's assent. I clearly informed both Hope and her mother of the counseling format that entailed meeting with Hope individually for the weekly 45-minute sessions. This included regular 10-minute end-of-session meetings with her mother to review progress and address any treatment-related issues. Her mother agreed. The initial individual meeting provided an opportunity for Hope to discuss anything that she did not mention previously. For me, this presented an opportunity to begin the process of building a therapeutic relationship with Hope. Afterward, I invited her mother in to review the next steps. This also served as an opportunity to get her mother acquainted with the newly structured counseling process.

Hope met several criteria for an adolescent at risk for suicide attempts. Factors for high-risk concerns included feelings of isolation, depression and hopelessness, difficult familial relationships, academic struggles, cognitive distortions, and previous self-injurious behaviors. In every session, I asked a scaling question and/or conducted a suicide or self-harm assessment with Hope. I documented the assessments and results and provided crisis helpline information in the event she felt suicidal.

I met weekly with Hope over the course of 5 months. I began the first session by getting to know Hope and building rapport. I wanted to understand her difficulties and joys at home, school, and within the various areas of her life. This also served as a means to learn about her thinking patterns and how they might lead to unhealthy behaviors. I focused on getting Hope involved in the counseling process and invested in her treatment planning. These goals reflected feedback from her reports and input on what she committed to work on in counseling. We also discussed triggers and her ability to recognize them. Her first homework assignment evolved from this. I encouraged Hope to track or journal her feelings and write about the situations and happenings that caused her to feel withdrawn and depressed.

During our next few sessions, we began to address the negative thoughts Hope reported. In addition to giving her the space to reflect and express her feelings, we also discussed alternative behaviors. This process involved role-playing and self-monitoring. I often gave Hope homework that included practicing the skills we discussed in sessions. By the fourth session, Hope came in smiling and discussing issues about school, math, and relationships.

Hope indicated that her medical conditions often made her feel sad and left out. Math did not seem to be her best subject. She found it difficult to concentrate due to her presenting issues. Missing school stifled her progress, as she found it difficult to grasp some of the basic concepts. In addition to repeating seventh grade, Hope began working with a tutor and the professional school counselor to assist Hope in credit recovery.

Hope expressed difficulty getting along with the few friends she acquired since returning to school. She felt that her friends thought that she sought attention by exploiting her medical issues. She began practicing appropriate ways of expressing her feelings with friends and recognizing the motives for talking about her cancer. She became receptive to listening to her peers and chose to be honest with them about her feelings and behaviors. Hope felt relieved that her friends seemed not to be angry at her, but also felt that they did not seem to understand the impact of her diagnosis. They felt that Hope complained and did not make connections of her medical and mental status to her behaviors. Their views of the effects of cancer appeared different from what they observed her going through. She began to provide more education and information about her medical condition to her peers. She also began complaining less about her diagnosis, as she realized they mostly viewed this behavior as her reason for seeking sympathy.

By the sixth session, Hope demonstrated improvement in her communication with peers and her eating habits. However, she started to convey some angst toward her mother. During the next few sessions, Hope expressed more difficulty in her relationship with her mother. She seemed angry with her mother, but reluctant to explain. Hope's mother expressed, prior to the start of my session alone with Hope, that Hope seemed really depressed. During the meeting with Hope, she appeared distant. In a therapeutic confrontation regarding the reason behind her feelings toward her mom, Hope disclosed physical abuse by her mother's former boyfriend. The abuse occurred over a period of several months until the mother ended the relationship nearly 8 months prior.

After disclosing this abuse, Hope became very emotional. I gave her space to cry. The abuse revelation added to the previous list of suicide risk factors. Her emotional state and withdrawn behavior also became a cause for concern. She denied, upon questioning, any suicidal ideation or thoughts of harming herself. I informed Hope that I needed to report this abuse. I invited her mother into the session when Hope felt ready. Hope's mother seemed aware that her ex-boyfriend grabbed or pushed Hope, but did not appear to know the extent of previous incidents of being pushed, slapped, and grabbed. Hope also reported one incident of being punched and verbally abused. Her mother's ex-boyfriend often said that Hope "faked" her illness. Hope indicated that she did not tell her mother about the abuse because she did not think that her mother would do anything.

Both Hope and her mother verified that the mother's former boyfriend did not abuse the youngest child. In an effort to follow up on this report, I consulted with the younger brother's therapist. He confirmed that the younger sibling denied witnessing or experiencing any type of abuse. Because Hope lived in a neighboring state, and the abuse occurred in that state, I made the call to children's services in that state. Hope and her mother cooperated throughout the process and her mother apologized profusely to Hope. Hope's mother moved Hope's next appointment up a few days. She became concerned about Hope's withdrawal. In an attempt to not revert back to negative behaviors such as cutting and not eating, Hope decided to come to her counseling session earlier. Additionally, she felt that she needed further help.

Hope appeared anxious when she met with me. I acknowledged the difficult circumstances that she dealt with and commended her for taking action to help herself. I wanted to give her permission to feel what she felt, and to express it. Hope finally expressed in her own words that she became "angry" at her mother for not protecting her. She felt alone. Her demeanor appeared somber during the session. She thought about cutting her arms again. She tearfully reported, "I cannot promise you that I will not try to hurt myself." I facilitated an assessment to evaluate suicidal ideation.

Hope agreed with my suggestion that she seek more supervised care. I brought her mother in, and we arranged more intense treatment for Hope. Hope's mother tearfully agreed to admit her. I explained the process of admission, consulted with her on-site psychiatrist, and contacted the hospital's inpatient program. Hope continued to cry, but admitted that she knew she needed more help. The inpatient staff team escorted Hope to the intake process. I reassured both Hope and her mother that they made the right decision. I attempted to validate their decision by stating that I understood that this experience seemed difficult. Hope's psychiatrist walked with them to the inpatient floor.

During this crisis situation, I became very directive and educational. Hope thought that she came in for counseling that day, but discovered that she needed much more. Since our initial meeting, I consistently conducted suicidal assessments because she presented with several risk factors common in adolescents who attempt and complete suicide. Her tone and demeanor, when she indicated she could not promise she would not hurt herself, convinced me that she needed more intensive intervention. She held on to anger toward her mother and did not verbalize it for an extended period of time. She suppressed other feelings that eventually emerged, thrusting her into a crisis mode.

OUTCOME

With regard to her treatment goals, Hope made progress by using more healthy modes of self-expression; however, she still needed to continue work in this area. She began to engage in more positive social and assertiveness skills. She effectively increased her awareness of negative thinking and altered her thought processes, when needed. She continued to journal.

Hope appeared well and joyful. I believed that the strategies that I used proved to be effective. I still believe that building a solid therapeutic rapport is essential to effective work utilizing cognitive behavioral therapy. I still believe that this approach helped strengthen and empowered the client to change and stand on her own, which is an essential premise of counseling.

I accepted a job offer from out of state. I knew that it would be important for me to inform Hope early of my decision to prepare her for termination and secure the most effective counseling referral. It became a difficult decision; however, I knew I worked on empowering clients to become independent.

After a positive 2-week inpatient treatment, Hope scheduled her next meeting with me shortly after her discharge. The psychiatrist indicated that Hope seemed initially hesitant, but quickly became engaged in her treatment. The physician prescribed her a low dosage of fluoxetine (Prozac). She effectively participated in cognitive behavioral groups and individual counseling. The psychiatrist recommended that Hope continue with her previous counseling treatments and schedule a follow-up medication review and management with one of the psychiatrists within my agency's practice team.

Hope appeared relaxed, happy, and excited to discuss her treatment. She mostly enjoyed being in the group counseling sessions and meeting the other individuals. She reported learning that there are other people going through difficult times. We discussed the work she did and the lessons and practices she took away from the experience. She indicated that she worked on her relationship with her mother and forgave her for not making earlier attempts to protect her from her mother's ex-boyfriend.

Hope appeared grateful and much clearer and focused on moving forward. She also continued to journal and seemed excited to tell me that she received a new journal book. I complemented her again on her courage for getting the help she needed. I recognized her progress and we discussed maintenance and skills needed for her to deal with potential setbacks.

I also recognized the importance of looking forward regarding planning Hope's continued treatment. After accepting the out-of-state position, I identified a colleague I worked with in an alternative school. She provided art therapy. I thought the art therapy would be effective for Hope at this point in her process. I informed Hope and her mother of my leaving in 2 months. She and her mother expressed sadness upon hearing this news. I reminded her of the great progress she made. I indicated that in the remaining six sessions, I wanted to introduce her to the new counselor. I invited the new counselor to one of our sessions to meet Hope. The meeting went really well, and the new counselor informed them about what to expect during art therapy. They all appeared excited about working together. I felt good about the referral and the new opportunities for Hope to continue to develop her self-expression skills.

REFERENCE

Ellis, A. (2008). Rational emotive behavior therapy. In R. Corsini & D. Wedding (Eds.), *Current psychotherapies* (8th ed., pp. 187–222). Belmont, CA: Brooks/Cole.

CHAPTER 14

TO BOOTH OR NOT TO BOOTH

Brenda L. Jones

Upon approaching my retirement as a professional school counselor, I decided to become a licensed professional counselor in clinical mental health. A supervisor at the County Juvenile Detention Center referred Adam, a 17-year-old Hispanic male, to me for counseling. Before being placed in detention, Adam resided with his mother, father, an older adult brother, and a 7-year-old sister. Four other brothers lived elsewhere. This case study highlights the interplay of systemic, developmental, relational, and multicultural influences, and the many risk factors (i.e., low social, emotional, personal, and educational support) that ultimately contributed to Adam's delinquency. The therapeutic interventions used in this case study diminished these risk factors and fostered growth.

SYSTEMIC INFLUENCES

Adam defined himself by his life experiences. He indicated that his behavioral and legal concerns started at approximately age 13. His history of legal troubles included referrals for several public intoxications, theft, and violations of probation, resulting in referrals for expulsion, child in need of supervision (CINS) assessment, and contempt of court. I found limited information in the files on Adam's family. Although Adam valued his relationship with his parents and siblings, and verbalized strong emotional ties, I discovered disconnections in the family dynamics. His parents seemed far removed from his behavioral and legal concerns and did not respond to consultation requests regarding Adam. His family lived in an economically deprived neighborhood where the home living conditions stifled Adam's personal, social, and emotional development. Adam's brothers and friends remained an influence in his life and frequently led him to unhealthy courses of action. One of his brothers happened to be incarcerated. The prison recently released another brother on parole. His two oldest brothers modeled violent tendencies and socialized him into a peer gang and drug culture. Although Adam denied gang involvement, his records noted that he associated with known gang members. This, along with his parents' lack of guidance, negatively impacted Adam's decision making and social behavior.

DEVELOPMENTAL CONSIDERATIONS

Cognitive and Intellectual Development

Adam's file noted no history of placement in special programs in the school system. The file referenced Adam as a regular education student who failed to succeed academically, mostly due to lack of attendance. He reported to be a junior but failed to give the total number of high school credits earned toward graduation. Although 17, he appeared to be in Piaget's concrete operational developmental stage due to his limited problem-solving skills and his inability to consider other possible solutions when crucial choices needed to be made (Piaget, 1967; Wadsworth, 2003).

Personal, Social, and Emotional Development

Adam, a study in contrasts, appeared to hold a good understanding of social norms and appeared to understand the inappropriateness of much of his behavior. However, developmentally, he appeared lacking in experience and understanding in this area. Many times, he lacked skills that connected his choices and behaviors to possible alternatives or consequences. Although it appeared that he could exercise good judgment, it also appeared that he often chose to not do so (or appeared influenced to not do so) when it required compromising his desires or perceived needs. As a result, Adam seemed ill equipped to understand and respond effectively to the myriad of problems he faced. Many of his choices seemed self-sabotaging. He frequently found himself in situations that spiraled him out of control. Consequently, he established a history of truancy, defiance, and, at times, verbal aggression toward teachers, school administrators, and campus police.

Mild to moderate levels of depression, along with moderate to severe levels of anxiety, as evidenced by psychological testing done at the detention center, compounded Adam's personal, social, and emotional development. Previous evaluations revealed substance-related factors that impacted Adam's depressive symptoms. He reported that he tried marijuana at the age of 9, began drinking alcohol and using cocaine at age 13, and began using heroin at age 15.

On the morning of our first counseling session, I remembered being apprehensive about my initial efforts to counsel an incarcerated youth. Through his nonverbal cues, he projected a tough guy image that could potentially set a negative first impression. He strutted toward me, with streetwise-type strides. He showed prominent facial acne scars and multiple tattoos on his neck and arms. Both of his eyebrows projected fragmented diagonally shaped slashes. A tattooed teardrop drooped from the corner of his left eye. His nonverbal cues appeared to project an attitude of "I-dare-you-to-counsel-me." The images he projected fed my apprehensions.

After introductions, we went into the designated room. He appeared to be very guarded and displayed subtle signs of suspicion. The majority of his responses appeared somewhat superficial, not revealing much about his current thoughts, feelings, or concerns. After several failed attempts to establish rapport, I decided that a creative metaphoric intervention might encourage his engagement and disclosure. After he agreed to participate, I explained to him that an intruder in the room interfered with our attempts to engage in counseling. I gave this intruder a name, "Mr. Booth"—an analogy of the old telephone booths once used to make phone calls at public facilities. Callers enclosed themselves in the booth, inhibiting others from entering. I explained to Adam that something similar seemed to be happening in this session, in that "Mr. Booth" surrounded Adam and kept him from engaging in counseling with me. I asked him if he agreed with my assessment and became astonished when he did, considering the tough guy image that he projected earlier. I, then, asked him to pick up "Mr. Booth" and place him in the corner of the room, away from the counseling session. To my amazement, he did just that! When he returned to his seat, I said, "Now I can see you clearer. I see a potentially hurt and vulnerable individual who might need my help." Adam, who displayed a tough guy exterior, began to cry profusely. After crying for a while, I asked him to tell me the full story surrounding his detention, which he did. At that moment, I witnessed the beginning of a newly formed partnership. His participation suggested to me that the tough lines that he carefully crafted seemed not so firmly drawn. He exposed his vulnerabilities. At the end of the first session, I reminded Adam to pick up "Mr. Booth" on his way out, which, also to my surprise, he did. Before doing this, he asked me to verify that he left no evidence of his crying. After I did so, he strutted out of the room as he came in—proudly carrying "Mr. Booth." The metaphoric use of "Mr. Booth" fostered insight for Adam in that it illuminated, through visualization, an awareness of his impact in counseling. It also helped him to think flexibly and to find his voice, which provided a platform for the start of healthy expressions (Belmont, 2013).

RELATIONAL CONSIDERATIONS

To foster progress, I conceptualized Adam's presenting concerns from a contextual frame and better understood him from a relational-cultural perspective. Adam lacked trust in most individuals outside his family and peer systems; consequently, he initially appeared uncomfortable in our first session. His lack of trust caused him to experience inadequate connections with me that would enable him to know that I would provide enough support for him to express himself authentically. In essence, he used "Mr. Booth" as an asset—a defense for survival. He hid the true Adam and displayed inauthentic ways of being. Unknowingly, he created disconnections in the therapeutic relationship as he did many times in other situations (Powell, 2004). A working relationship started to emerge with "Mr. Booth" clearly being the catalyst. "Mr. Booth" needed to be included (not dismissed) in my initial contact with Adam in that Mr. Booth subsisted as a product of many of Adam's life experiences, served many purposes, and provided many benefits for him in and out of the detention center. After this session, "Mr. Booth" did not need to be removed before starting a session. Adam and I easily maintained rapport over the course of subsequent sessions. At first glance, I did not recognize the true potential in Adam. With this activity, Adam created a new perception of himself and I created a more objective perspective about counseling Adam. Although I did not fully gain his trust, this served as the beginning of trust building in this therapeutic relationship.

MULTICULTURAL CONSIDERATIONS

Remaining cognizant of the uniqueness that Adam brought to counseling—his ability to cope and survive in a challenging environment—continued to be an important consideration. Equally important, a continuous examination of my own convictions remained crucial in avoiding inaccurate assumptions about Adam. Many of Adam's beliefs and perspectives derived from specific life experiences, not only from being an ethnic minority male, but also, as he stated, from being a member of a close-knit family system where his identity and self-worth closely aligned with their opinions and approval. Specific family characteristics (living in a neighborhood characterized by poverty, being labeled as a CINS, sibling incarceration, gang and drug involvement, and exposure to violence in various contexts) fostered his socialization and promoted his engagement in problematic behavior. The challenge for me evolved into bringing him to a level of awareness that would be the impetus to promoting change without minimizing his family system that he valued and considered supportive.

CONCEPTUALIZATION

With Adam, I found myself working against ingrained habits resulting from a myriad of negative influences. Adam admitted to having inhibitions in social settings. His lack of trust stemmed from a habit of believing his negative thoughts surrounding impending interpersonal relationships. He also realized that his choices, many times, did not result in good consequences. Although he remained aware of what he needed to do to correct his behavior, he stated that he could not resist the temptations brought on by his substance abuse. Adam's stay at this detention center happened to be temporary. He realized that he could not resolve his concerns alone. Adam agreed to stay in treatment with his on-site substance abuse counselor. Consequently, my goals, interventions, and strategies encompassed continued collaboration with this counselor.

Goals and Targets for Client Change

Adam sometimes stated that "the world was out to get me." Consequently, increasing his awareness of self became my goal to promote connections with his trust and anger issues to his choices and behaviors.

Strategies for the Client

It became important to progress incrementally in a short time frame. Adam possessed great potential for growth, but his skill sets, social and emotional developmental levels, and systemic influences showed potential to hinder interventions and progress. It appeared that many of his struggles stemmed from a lack of awareness of his own personal strength, so I started an empowerment strategy to foster his social, emotional, and cognitive skill building. I wanted to inspire him to be a part of the process by having him become aware of, draw inspiration from, and capitalize on his strengths apart from others who also held influences over him.

Goals and Strategies for Myself

Adam presented complex problems, and a sense of appreciation for the diverse life experiences that he brought to counseling became essential. With this, I diminished the influence of my own personal values and beliefs regarding counseling an incarcerated youth. I became objective in my approach and framed his problems in workable terms. This laid the foundation for us to build a strong counselor–client relationship.

I designed my goals and strategies to provide developmentally and culturally appropriate activities that: (a) elevated Adam's level of awareness; (b) minimized his impulses, thereby enabling him to connect his choices and behavior to an array of possible alternatives; (c) assisted him in clarifying his goals regarding his problem situation; (d) helped him in addressing emotional and behavioral concerns to include increasing his sense of responsibility for his own behavior; (e) enhanced his communication skills by conducting role-play activities that assisted him in acquiring more effective and appropriate ways to express his feelings, while simultaneously assisting him in disputing self-talk that served as a catalyst for his lack of trust and poor interpersonal relationships; (f) fostered academic and career guidance by using my experience as a former professional school counselor; and (g) worked in collaboration with the substance abuse counselor allowing Adam, in an open, honest, and culturally appropriate manner, to serve as an integral partner in the treatment of Adam's personal drug use.

COUNSELING PROCESS FLOW

I assumed an integrated approach to counseling with Adam, in that it gave me a range of possibilities for framing his problems and treatments. It also afforded me the opportunity to display varied counseling styles based on Adam's presenting needs. I found most of Adam's problems to be centered on all-consuming, paralyzing thoughts that continued in his daily life without verification. While disclosing his past experiences to me, he unknowingly demonstrated patterns of thinking that inhibited trust and healthy communication with others. Using skills from person-centered therapy as the core therapeutic foundation, I found aspects of other theoretical models such as rational emotive behavioral therapy (REBT), reality/choice therapy, and gestalt therapy to also be valuable. The active stance of confrontation practiced in gestalt therapy and REBT appeared effective. The cognitive aspects of REBT seemed to complement the affective nature of gestalt.

Infusion of Creativity

Along with these concepts, I enjoyed combining gestalt therapy with the utilization of a counseling approach called *impact therapy*. These approaches combined creative counseling techniques and experiments with my integrative approach. Infusing impact therapy in each session enabled me to keep counseling sessions active with the clients constantly thinking, seeing, and experiencing (Jacobs, 1992). These techniques promoted a more time-efficient session, eliminated unnecessary talk, and increased deeper level disclosure, when appropriate, through the use of props and expressive arts (Jacobs, 1992; Vernon, 2009).

Adam and I met for 10 sessions. The initial session dealt with the client and me getting acquainted and building trust. Person-centered therapy techniques enhanced Adam's ability to tell his story with minimal interruptions and no judgment.

The second session started the abatement of Adam's wall of defense, enhancing two-way communication. Although he related to me in a polite and straightforward manner, nervous laughter became a defense used when he became uncomfortable. Using relational culture techniques, I worked with Adam on self-awareness so that he could begin to bring himself out of a place of chronic disconnection to one of authenticity, support, and enjoyment (Powell, 2004). Prompting him to remember "To Booth or Not to Booth" promoted his engagement. I also realized the importance of transparency in earning his trust and became open to sharing notes taken during our sessions.

I used REBT and choice therapies during the third and fourth sessions to assist Adam in becoming aware of his self-imposed barriers—the negative thoughts about impending consequences. This caused him to worry, which increased his stress levels and resulted in increased anxiety and depression. I also wanted him to become more open-minded, and take responsibility for his behavior. I conceived the acronym PACT, planning against counterproductive thinking, to use as a working model to integrate for Adam an REBT-type framework.

PACT
Adam's thoughts about situations at hand and the impending consequences.
Adam's verification of whether these thoughts appeared true or counterproductive.
Adam's exploration of other viable, productive options and solutions if the thoughts seemed untrue.

PACT enabled Adam to alter his cognitions about situations that he perceived to be threatening. I continued to bring his inhibiting thoughts to the forefront so that they could be challenged. Through verification, he distinguished between thoughts and impending consequences that stood out as true and those that seemed counterproductive, especially when dealing with situations that related to his systemic, relational, and developmental issues. This fostered his ability to choose based on facts. This also increased his ability to assume more ownership and responsibility for his choices and options (Ellis & Harper, 1975).

The fifth and sixth sessions focused on enabling Adam to get in touch with his low self-esteem, which contributed to his social awkwardness and depression. He responded in writing to three items on a personal inventory regarding how he felt about himself, and he later verbalized them to me. This provided more dialogue and disclosure. I used videos to normalize Adam's experiences and to promote engagement during discussions about the effect of his drug use and the drug culture in his community. We also examined the roles that his brothers played in his life experiences. Again, Adam made connections between his beliefs, feelings, and choices.

Adam's trust issues interfered with his self-improvement and relationships with others. Planning became a vital first step in building trusting relationships. We agreed that the seventh session would focus on working with Adam on improving his interpersonal relationship skills so that communication and trust could be established to increase his comfort level when seeking social support from others. As a strategy, I used videos chronicling testimonies from people who faced challenges similar to his. Other modalities used during this session to teach positive interpersonal relationship skills involved the creative use of role-play and visualization. I assigned Adam homework, which required him to talk effectively to detention center staff about a situation that he needed to problem-solve and seek out social support. I asked him to report back to me at the next session. As we approached the end of this session, I broached the topic of termination to ease him into that realization. I made him aware that three more sessions remained.

Self-doubt and uncertainty about his level of education, skills, and preparation for adult independence, in comparison to what he described as his more focused and goal-oriented peers, gave rise to his anxiety. During the eighth and ninth sessions, I wanted Adam to assess his strengths and start building on them. After a thorough discussion of his homework assignment, I introduced educational and career possibilities and goal setting, which really sparked his interest. Through the use of the teaching tool of reality/choice therapy—wants, doing, evaluate, and plan (WDEP)—I provided a platform that assisted Adam in assessing his situations, choices, need-satisfying behaviors, and outcomes so that a more specific, attainable, and productive plan of action could be established (Glasser & Wubbolding, n.d.; Wubbolding, 2000).

The 10th session involved the termination process in which we summarized and reemphasized all of the components of the previous nine sessions, and looked forward to using the many coping and problem-solving strategies learned. Adam and I focused on his repeat offending and he defined the issues that served as some of the reasons for his offenses (including systemic and relational influences). A combination of his drug abuse, low self-worth, and his inability to manage his anger and make good choices also served as major reasons for his offenses.

OUTCOME

The therapeutic relationship between Adam and me solidified. I believed that this young man could change. He responded well to the counseling interventions, which appeared to be conducive to his level of readiness and development. He appeared to be more reflective and open-minded to suggestions from others to improve his situation. He made progress in understanding the power of his beliefs and connecting them to his feelings, choices, and behaviors. The concepts, PACT and "To Booth or Not to Booth," challenged his faulty thinking and beliefs. This assisted him in heightening his awareness and being more present centered. He began to find his personal strengths, minimize his lack of trust and disconnections with others, and became engaged in the process of fostering his own social, emotional, and cognitive growth. Through the use of PACT and REBT, he also started to take responsibility for his actions, mainly making better choices and handling his anger. Through the use of WDEP and postsecondary occupational information, Adam explored his expressed interest in welding.

The detention center transferred Adam to another facility outside his home city. Regretfully, I did not see him again after the transfer. Because of his age, longstanding habits, and lack of family support, Adam requires comprehensive services and interventions at his next detention facility. This is central to his continued rehabilitation. Adam needs to remain in counseling in order to sustain his confidence, self-worth, and ability to make appropriate choices, thereby minimizing his depressive tendencies. I assisted the substance abuse counselor in completing a treatment plan that followed Adam to his next facility. In addition to personal and substance abuse counseling, I recommended that he be given an opportunity to complete his credits for graduation or obtain a General Education Development (GED) diploma and vocational training. Although more work will be needed regarding his chemical dependency, Adam enthusiastically used many of the intervention strategies that the substance abuse counselor and I provided as he worked toward change and toward minimizing his depression.

REFERENCES

Belmont, J. (2013, October 8). The magic of metaphors in counseling [Blog post]. Retrieved from http://www.counseling.org/news/blog/aca-blog/2013/10/08/the-magic-of-metaphors-in-counseling#sthash.Lzz9C5Mc.dpuf

Ellis, A., & Harper, R. A. (1975). *A new guide to rational living*. Englewood Cliffs, NJ: Prentice Hall.

Glasser, W., & Wubbolding, R. E. (n.d.). 10 Reality therapy. Retrieved from http://www.cengage.com/resource_uploads/downloads/0495097144_81298.pdf

Jacobs, E. (1992). *Creative counseling techniques: An illustrated guide*. Odessa, FL: Psychological Assessment Resources.

Piaget, J. (1967). *Six psychological studies*. New York, NY: Random House Publishing.

Powell, K. C. (2004). Developmental psychology of adolescent girls: Conflicts and identity issues. *Education, 125*(1), 77–87.

Vernon, A. (Ed.). (2009). *Counseling children and adolescents* (4th ed.). Denver, CO: Love Publishing.

Wadsworth, B. J. (2003). *Piaget's theory of cognitive and effective development: Foundations of constructivism* (5th ed.). New York, NY: Allyn & Bacon.

Wubbolding, R. (2000). *Reality therapy for the 21st century*. New York, NY: Routledge.

CHAPTER 15

BRICE AND THE BRIGHTLY COLORED SOCKS

Kristopher M. Goodrich

I began working with Brice, a 16-year-old high school student, during the fall semester of his junior year. A colleague, who owned the counseling agency where I worked part time, referred Brice to me. This colleague saw Brice's mother as a client at the time; Brice's mother expressed great concern about Brice and hoped that he would see a counselor. Brice recently came out of the closet to her and her husband, but wished to keep his identity private to others in his life. This included his Hispanic father and stepmother. Brice's mother described Brice as shy and introspective and that he appeared to be even more withdrawn around the time in which she wanted him to be seen. The mother reported speaking to Brice about seeing a counselor, and stated that he appeared open to the opportunity.

SYSTEMIC INFLUENCES

Brice identified as biracial and a product of divorce. He reported living with his White mother, stepfather, and younger half-sibling, and frequently visited with his Hispanic father and stepmother. Brice reported adjusting well to his current family situation. His biological parents divorced during Brice's younger years. He grew up with his stepfather living in the home with him and his mother. Brice's mother encouraged him to come to counseling following his coming out. Brice knew, then, that his mother and her extended family and his stepfather accepted him. He reported, however, that he would never come out to his father's extended family because of their heterosexism. He knew that they would not accept his sexual identity. Brice expressed no concerns about coming out at school because his peer group accepted gay students.

DEVELOPMENTAL CONSIDERATIONS

Cognitive and Intellectual Development

Brice, an academically gifted student with a keen interest in science and math (and the grades to match), informed me during one of our earlier sessions of his interest in pursuing medical school in the future. Although I did not see Brice's academic records, he reported earning nearly straight As in all of his subjects, with his best grades (and greatest fascination) in the subjects of science and math. Brice reported being in advanced placement courses throughout high school and received near perfect SAT and ACT test scores. Brice reported socializing with other students in his advanced placement courses, and did not see himself different academically from other high-achieving students in these courses. He also reported excitement about his upcoming college career; at the time I met Brice, he applied for an advanced placement undergraduate-to-graduate medical school track at the local university where I worked as a faculty member. Based on my conversations with Brice, I placed him in the formal operations stage of Piaget's theory of cognitive development (Piaget, 1983).

Personal, Social, and Emotional Development

On a personal level, Brice reported no medical concerns. Socially, he reported feeling awkward, especially around his peers who appeared as academically advanced as he. He reported feeling different from them socially, which influenced how well he interacted with them. This appeared more related to his anxiety than his sexual orientation, as some of his friends openly identified as gay. Brice initially struggled, out of fear, when I suggested later in our sessions that he "play" with being more vulnerable with his peers and seize opportunities to open up to them. Over time, Brice took opportunities presented to him with his peers to play with his daring side. His number of peer relationships increased, and over time they became deeper. With each interaction, it became easier for him to express himself to others.

From a familial perspective, Brice struggled socially and emotionally to connect with his father's side of the family because of his biracial identity and sexual orientation. Brice felt that he could not disclose his identity to his father or his father's family members due to their Hispanic identity and cultural expectations related to machismo, gender expectations, and traditional Catholic faith. Brice always felt awkward around this side of his family. He felt that he needed to hide his identity and became hypervigilant in their presence.

RELATIONAL CONSIDERATIONS

For our first session, when I walked out into the lobby, I saw a tall and slender young man, slouched over and nervously waiting in his seat. Everything about Brice appeared unremarkable, including his clothing. Each time we met, it seemed, he wore white, black, or beige, with no labels or trendy clothes. His hair (although conservatively styled) fell over his forehead as a protective barrier to hide his face. Brice appeared to me as someone who tried deeply to blend in, perhaps hoping to fade into the wall. This provided the context for our first session together.

Once we developed a rapport, Brice reported feeling awkward around people in general, although he could not pinpoint a reason why. He informed me that he felt this way his whole life, and his shyness appeared long before he began questioning his sexuality. He would later admit that questioning his sexuality would play a role in some interactions in the present day, but a trait-related social anxiety appeared to be a more prominent factor in Brice's interactions with others.

As I learned more about Brice, I discovered that he felt comfortable around his mother's side of the family. This included his mother, stepfather, stepbrother, and his mother's relatives. His father's side, however, felt more strained. Brice reported not having a deep relationship with his biological father, but feeling closer with his stepmother, who facilitated most of his relationship with his father. Even then, Brice and his father only interacted intermittently. Brice reported having good peer relationships, although he admitted that he felt shy around his friends and only disclosed his identity to a couple of his peers. He described himself as a socially awkward person, and often seemed unaware of how to better interact with his peers.

MULTICULTURAL CONSIDERATIONS

Brice's identity as a biracial, Hispanic-identified gay adolescent in the Southwest surfaced as the prominent multicultural consideration in our counseling relationship. Brice's understanding of traditional Hispanic culture, and his father's family's attitude toward gay persons, influenced his hesitance to disclose to them. Brice saw the culture built around machismo and traditional gender norms, and knew his father's side of the family seemed strongly influenced by their Catholic faith. He also heard them make heterosexist remarks at past family gatherings. This made him fearful of coming out to them and influenced his willingness to put in the amount of work needed to solidify these relationships.

Brice reported that beyond his family, his biracial identity did not influence him much. Relationally, he felt more connected and supported by his mother's White family; however, living in the Southwest, he seemed surrounded by other biracial Hispanics. The majority of his peer group identified as Hispanic or biracial, so he did not feel a cultural conflict in school. He seemed to know other gay persons from Hispanic backgrounds, which made him feel more comfortable with his peer group than with his father's side of the family. No other multicultural considerations appeared to influence the counseling relationship, other than generational differences between counselor and client that sometimes required the client to explain youth culture terms or popular cultural activities unknown by the counselor.

CONCEPTUALIZATION

From the point in which I first met Brice, I assumed that anxiety would be a presenting concern. I based this on his initial sheepishness in the lobby, his mother's report to my supervisor, and his twitchy nature in session. I saw that he struggled with uneasiness. Although anxiety over his coming out appeared to be an initial presenting concern, his anxiety appeared much more generalized to interacting with persons outside of his disclosure. After my first couple of sessions with Brice, I diagnosed him with social anxiety, which appeared to be a more appropriate diagnosis. Setting a comfortable environment for him so that he felt free to express himself in session became one of my first goals. I softened my voice, took a more supportive (slouching) posture in an effort to mimic him, and attempted to make my body more open, as I tended to cross my legs when sitting with clients. I used my gentle nature to help him open up, which he slowly did in session.

I also let Brice know immediately that, although I obtained a release of information from his mother, I did not plan to seek her advice or counsel without his permission unless required by a disclosure warranting a mandatory (legal) report. I sensed from the referral that his mother appeared to be a strong figure, and that Brice seemed more deferential. I saw this as an opportunity to join with Brice and ensure that he felt open to speak in counseling. I wanted to give him the impression that the sessions appeared more oriented around his needs instead of those expressed by others. The law in the state that we lived in stipulated 14 to be the age of consent for counseling services. This law provided me flexibility while interacting with his mother regarding counseling. Thankfully, his mother never made any attempts to intrude on our work together.

Time-Efficient Methods

I selected as a primary goal to connect with Brice, as the therapeutic relationship between counselor and client best predicts positive clinical outcome regardless of the theoretical approach used by the counselor (Ardito & Rabellino, 2011; Bordin, 1979). Early on, his anxiety in session appeared palatable and needed to be addressed in order for us to effectively work together. I used scaling questions to better understand, from Brice's perspective, how he experienced the anxiety as well as his subsequent goals related to this. He initially reported his anxiety as a high 8 or 9, but set a goal for himself to rank a 2 or 3 by the end of our sessions. In reviewing what this meant for Brice, he stated that he knew anxiety would always be present in him, but he wanted to maintain a lower and more manageable level. We clearly discussed what the anxiety level of 8 or 9 looked like for him in the moment (e.g., intense fear that hindered his action, loss of concentration, strong heartbeat, sweating, and fast breathing). We, then, discussed what a 2 or 3 might look like for him (e.g., manageable breathing, ability to concentrate, steady heart beat that could be controlled). Brice's descriptions, as well as our long-term plan, appeared reasonable. Cognitive behavioral homework assisted Brice in reaching these goals. I introduced Brice to concepts of mindfulness to assist him in reaching his long-term goal. I utilized breathing exercises to teach him, through psychoeducation, a coping strategy to soothe his anxiety. I also asked him to utilize these skills as homework. This also helped us to facilitate his later independence from me, as we looked to later terminate.

In addition to the scaling and mindfulness activities, I asked Brice to keep a log of messages he told himself when he recognized that he appeared anxious. This seemed helpful not only to learn how to combat his negative and self-critiquing messages, but also served as fodder for the different cognitive distortions (Beck, 1972) that we attended to in session. By switching between the cognitive messages he told himself as well as attending to his bodily experiences as he heard those messages, I assisted Brice in better connecting to his body. He also began to understand the need to make a change. Previously, he saw little need or importance to change the negative messages he told himself. When he began to connect the physical elements of anxiety, stress, and fear to his lived experience of heightened breathing, fast pulse, and heaviness in his stomach, he realized the desperate need to hold a more positive self-concept and to practice it. For the first time, he understood the connection between the mind and the body, which he earlier saw as completely separate aspects of himself. Once he began to see the integration between the two, he seemed able to mirror this in other areas of his life; namely, he saw the need to integrate different aspects of his personality and life that he previously wanted to keep separate (e.g., sexual orientation and his interactions with both sides of his family).

Infusion of Creativity

As Brice began to make progress with the homework, I noticed a change in his clothing. The time of year warmed up, and Brice revealed more about his activities outside of counseling. He shared that he joined a local gym that hosted CrossFit training, and that he deeply appreciated the different types of exercises and challenges that the activities presented him. He enjoyed being at this gym even though there appeared to be fewer people his age to socialize with. Brice often came to counseling as the last client of my day following his CrossFit experiences. He still wore black and white, although this time he wore his shirt and shorts. For the first time, I saw a pop of color—his socks. At first, I found it humorous—brightly colored socks with large messages written on them. One displayed the word "BACON." Others displayed characters. All appeared loaded in personality that seemed foreign to Brice. Although it took me a while to understand this, his socks became the one area that allowed him freedom to express himself in spite of the fact that he often hid them under larger clothes or folded down for others to see. In wearing his shorts and socks, he showed me a different side of himself—his otherwise subdued personality.

I started asking Brice about his socks in session. At first, he seemed embarrassed or shocked that I noticed them. Over time, he became more comfortable and appeared excited to show me his different pairs each week. We both agreed that his socks portrayed the daring side of his personality that he often did not feel comfortable sharing with others. I filed this thought away for our future work together.

In one session when he discussed a situation with his peers where he felt he seemed too quiet but wanted to engage more with them, I asked him how his socks would respond to that situation. Brice first looked at me perplexed, "Socks can't talk!" Then I saw him smile. He knew what I attempted to convey: How would the daring side of Brice respond if given an opportunity? Brice knew the answer, but felt scared about how he would be perceived if he said what he wanted to say. Using this, I asked Brice to engage in a role-play with me. I set up the situation so that I played the role of Brice's peers, and Brice took on the persona represented in his socks. Together we worked through the scenario that Brice previously expressed fear and apprehension about (e.g., when he seemed too quiet with his peers). Brice took on the daring role that scared him so much. Although it seemed initially hard for Brice to take on this role, with a little coaching from me he began to feel some comfort in expressing himself. Following the completion of this activity, we processed how it felt for Brice to own his daring persona. For him, it felt great; however, he remained scared about actually doing this with others. I reminded Brice that everything that Brice said and experienced in our role-play represented elements that he already possessed. He responded as himself as he played the voice of his socks. We agreed to continue the process of role-plays to increase his comfort in communicating more frequently with others. We did not fully process Brice's coming out, although he felt comfortable coming out to his peers at school once relationships developed and became deeper. In fact, he actually did this without ever raising the issue of coming out to peers in session with me, but still felt uncomfortable sharing this information with his Hispanic father and stepmother. Using the types of role-plays that we completed with his peers, I asked Brice to take these experiences and apply them to his father—if his socks could talk, what would they say? This experience appeared a little harder for Brice because of the cultural elements embedded within this disclosure. After screening for safety in which Brice thought he would be physically safe in sharing this identity with his father and seemed financially secure through his relationship with his mother, we explored what Brice's goals would be in regard to disclosing with his father. I explained to Brice that not everyone felt the need to come out; and those who do can choose to whom, where, and when those experiences might occur. I further stressed that reserving some time before he disclosed (or never disclose) to his family would not impact his identity or experience. Brice considered this for a moment, but then set a goal to go through with the experience. We, then, utilized the many sessions that followed to practice different ways that Brice could come out. The first few sessions focused on his disclosure to his father, and then later we practiced disclosure to his stepmother. Brice expressed wanting to utilize his stepmother for support when he disclosed to his father, as his stepmother seemed to be a more comfortable person to disclose to. Brice made the decision to disclose at the end of our time together. After his disclosure, his father and stepmother appeared receptive. Following the completion of that experience along with two follow-up sessions, Brice felt secure enough to end the counseling relationship with me and attempt, independently, the skills he learned in counseling.

Theoretical Approach

To accomplish our therapeutic goals, I utilized a mixture of cognitive behavioral and humanistic strategies along with mindfulness with Brice. I used this combination of theoretical approaches to successfully address some of Brice's presenting concerns (e.g., anxiety) and to assist him in his motivation to learn and complete homework. The mix of strategies also appeared useful for Brice as he enjoyed the cognitive behavioral strategies that reminded him of his areas of strength (e.g., academic homework) along with the humanistic work, which pushed him toward the areas he knew he wished to grow (e.g., in areas that focused on his affect, social interactions, and self-regulations).

COUNSELING PROCESS FLOW

Our sessions lasted about 8 months. Although we began our sessions weekly (after the first couple of months of working together), we reduced them to every other week based on Brice's improvement, as well as on other engagements (e.g., social activities). After we decided to terminate our counseling relationship, we scheduled a couple of sessions with a month in between contact to ensure that Brice seemed able to make a smooth transition from counseling. Brice appeared to work well with this schedule; and when time came to terminate, he appeared comfortable with that transition in our relationship.

OUTCOME

At termination, Brice reported having a positive self-concept, a stronger connection to his peers in school, and a neutral, but honest, relationship with his father. I believed that the mixture of cognitive behavioral therapy, humanistic principles, and mindfulness seemed helpful to Brice, as it worked for him at two different levels—in areas where he felt comfort and strength (homework and psychoeducation) and in areas of his weakness (mind/body connection and social aspect, and humanistic counseling). He reported lower levels of anxiety and greater social connections following counseling, even though I felt that he remained a little scared to venture out. I wondered if more self-empowerment strategies would be needed before he terminated, but he initiated the termination. When I inquired about this, he seemed decisive about being ready to end counseling. I agreed to honor and respect his wishes to terminate, which, to me, represented Brice's self-empowerment.

Two years after our last session, Brice scheduled a follow-up appointment with me. Brice finished his first semester in college, obtained a high grade point average (GPA; all As and one A– in his courses), appeared socially connected, and seemed excited about the possibility of medical school in the future. Motivated by his mother, Brice wanted to meet with me to discuss changing his surname (from his father's) to his mother's. When I inquired about the change, he noted that although he still maintained a relationship with his father, he never felt deeply connected to his father's side of the family. Brice reported that he still felt a deeper connection with his mother and her side of the family, and wanted to find a way to better demonstrate this congruence he felt with them to the outside world. This is why he wanted to change his last name to his mother's maiden name. I could tell in session that Brice's mind appeared already made up, but he came to counseling to appease his mother who thought that this move appeared to be drastic. After exploring the pros and cons in session, we came to the conclusion that as an adult, he could identify however he wanted. We, again, used our role-playing skills to better understand how he would raise the idea of the change to his father. He reported feeling satisfied with the outcome. He also asked that we schedule a follow-up appointment in 2 months just to show that he maintained wellness following the completion of the first full year in college. I also added that we should explore working on more self-empowerment strategies. Brice reported throughout our relationship that he struggled with standing up to his mother at times, while trying to also be appropriate and respectful. He wanted to be an adult and live his own life without too much interference from his mother. We agreed that these would be appropriate goals for this session, and I look forward to soon having it with him.

REFERENCES

Ardito, R. B., & Rabellino, D. (2011). Therapeutic alliance and outcome of psychotherapy: Historical excursus, measurements, and prospects for research. *Frontiers in Psychology, 2*, 270. http://dx.doi.org/10.3389/fpsyg.2011.00270

Beck, A. T. (1972). *Depression: Causes and treatment*. Philadelphia, PA: University of Pennsylvania Press.

Bordin, E. (1979). The generalizability of the psychoanalytic concept of the working alliance. *Psychotherapy: Theory, Research and Practice, 16*, 252–260.

Piaget, J. (1983). Piaget's theory. In P. Mussen (Ed.), *Handbook of child psychology* (4th ed., Vol. 1). New York, NY: Wiley.

CHAPTER 16

THE MYSTERY OF HISTORY

Angie D. Wilson
Glenda S. Johnson

I met Kenneth, a 15-year-old boy, while providing counseling services as a contract counselor at a residential treatment center (RTC) in a large metropolitan area. The RTC contacted me because they experienced an influx of adolescent clients with legal problems due to sexual offenses. They agreed to provide sex offender counseling to this client, and did not have staff experienced in treating sexual offenders. Therefore, the therapeutic alliance with Kenneth began as a mandated one, and in order to remain in "good standing" at the RTC, the program required him to meet with me for weekly counseling sessions. Our sessions often took place on the playground of the RTC or we would walk to a park located on the grounds of the RTC.

Prior to his placement at the RTC, Kenneth lived with members of his extended family (his aunt, uncle, and cousin). His aunt and uncle agreed to take care of him and provide a stable family environment because his biological mother struggled with substance abuse and unstable romantic relationships during Kenneth's formative years. Child protective services (CPS) placed Kenneth in the RTC because he acted out sexually against his younger female cousin, and his aunt and uncle requested he no longer live with them. While none of the other members of the family offered a safe place for Kenneth to live, his biological mother expressed excitement about the possibility of working with CPS to provide a safe environment for him. After working with Kenneth for approximately 5 months, his caseworker from CPS recommended that I begin to integrate his biological mother, Debbie, into the sessions. These sessions focused on parent consultations to prepare

Kenneth to move in with Debbie and her husband, Richard. Eventually, Kenneth moved into the home with Debbie and Richard and, as a stipulation of the CSP agreement, Kenneth continued his sessions with me on a monthly basis.

During our first counseling session at my private counseling office, Debbie voiced her concerns about Kenneth's lack of friends, attention deficit hyperactivity disorder (ADHD), and poor grades. Debbie mentioned that Kenneth was sexually abused when he was 11 years old. However, Kenneth never confirmed the abuse, and CPS records and reports indicated no past history of abuse. Debbie also mentioned that Kenneth "was kidnapped" by his aunt and uncle, but her account of the kidnapping differed from the CPS report and the caseworker's account of the family's situation. With all of this being said, there were certainly familial issues present, and Kenneth struggled with the family conflict between his aunt and uncle and his mother.

I counseled with Kenneth for 3 months during his stay at the RTC and for 4 months after his integration into his mother's home; however, I recommended weekly sessions and for Debbie to seek counseling. Toward the end of our time together, Kenneth and Debbie presented a plan for him to have an overnight stay with his aunt, uncle, and cousin (the victim of his sexual acting out). I recommended we collaborate to create a safety plan and inform the aunt, uncle, and cousin. Counselors use safety plans to create safe environments for the person who committed inappropriate sexual acts, survivors of the sexual acts forced by the perpetrator, and potential victims (Center for Sex Offender Management, 2015). Rules related to boundaries, bathrooms, safe words, and communication are standard aspects of safety plans. Consequently, I asked Kenneth and Debbie to begin making a safety plan for us to discuss at our next session. If completed, the safety plan homework assignment would have allowed me to gain insight into Kenneth's and Debbie's thoughts regarding appropriate versus inappropriate visit protocols. Furthermore, the opportunity for a discussion about family reunification procedures would have been appropriate at that time. In order for Kenneth to have contact with his cousin, I would have recommended family reunification procedures that include several family counseling sessions, for the survivor to be engaged in prolonged counseling, agreement from all family members involved, supervised public visits, and eventually visits in a private residence. However, it is highly unlikely that I would have recommended or endorsed an overnight visit(s) due to potential revictimization. Kenneth and Debbie missed the next session, and after calling to reschedule on several occasions, we eventually met. During this session, Kenneth and Debbie decided to terminate counseling; Kenneth shared that he visited his aunt, uncle, and cousin and did not see the need for counseling or a safety plan as discussed at our previous session. Debbie agreed with Kenneth that counseling was not helping and that this would be their last session due to the fact that Kenneth would be meeting with the professional school counselor. Debbie believed that two counselors overwhelmed Kenneth in his current situation. At that last session, I provided recommendations for other counselors who worked with children having problems with sexual reactivity and sexual offending along with psychiatric referrals. I coordinated Kenneth's discharge with his CPS worker as well. At that time, Debbie shared that Kenneth had not been on his medications for 3 months and adapted fine without them.

It is important to note that if Debbie and Kenneth failed to terminate the counseling relationship at that time, I would have begun the termination process and referred them to another counselor due to the fact that aspects of the therapeutic agreement were violated (i.e. contact with the survivor of the sexual offense without a safety plan). Furthermore, I contacted Kenneth's assigned CPS case manager after our last session to report the overnight stay and violation of counseling rules. It was important for me to communicate my concerns about the safety of Kenneth's cousin and my concerns about Kenneth's growth in counseling. It is my hope that the CPS case manager worked with Kenneth and Debbie to find another counselor who could meet his specific needs while protecting Kenneth's cousin and any other potential victims Kenneth may have contact with.

SYSTEMIC INFLUENCES

Toward the end of our time together in counseling, I noticed that Kenneth and Debbie became enmeshed. Debbie did not support my recommended interventions, such as creating a safety plan for visiting the home where the victim resided and attending counseling once per week. Neither Kenneth nor Debbie wanted to address Kenneth's sexual behavioral problems, sexual acting out, or sexual reactivity. Subsequently, my suspicion is that Debbie would not approve of group counseling on a weekly basis as it was difficult enough to get her to agree to counseling once per month. The family system was an integral aspect of Kenneth's counseling and the lack of support from his mother played a huge role in his decision to disengage in the counseling process. Furthermore, access to the professional school counselor might have also been helpful. After several requests, Debbie did not grant me permission to communicate with the professional school counselor(s). The school counselor might have been able to assist Kenneth with problems at school but it is important to note that sexual behavior problems are outside of the scope of school counselors. Therefore, a referral to a community mental health counselor specializing in sexual issues is more appropriate.

Active communication with the professional school counselor might have been helpful in Kenneth's situation. Some interventions and things the professional school counselor might have considered are as follows: coordinating a behavioral intervention team for Kenneth as well as all stakeholders (i.e., district director of safe and secure schools, administration, parents, teachers, campus resource officer, behavior intervention specialist, the student, and the primary professional school counselor). During the team meeting, an intervention plan could have been developed to assist the entire team with communicating and monitoring Kenneth's progress. In addition to a plan, the various members of the team could discuss their roles. Dates, checkpoints, and the effectiveness of the overall behavior intervention program are ideal to measure Kenneth's behavior (Cheung & Brandes, 2011). The primary professional school counselor would have probably utilized a solution-focused brief therapy (SFBT) theoretical approach and provided individual counseling on a weekly basis with the initial counseling goal of establishing a positive, supportive relationship with Kenneth. Utilizing motivational interviewing to increase Kenneth's grades would have been used by the professional school counselor due to its preliminary effectiveness in increasing student's in-class participation and overall academic performance, especially in the area of math (Strait et al., 2012).

During the behavior intervention team meeting, a point sheet could have been created to assist Kenneth in (a) monitoring his own behavior, thereby exercising self-control in focused areas (i.e., respecting boundaries with others); (b) increasing his motivation to participate and engage in all aspects of the school day; and (c) keeping the communication open and ongoing between home and school (i.e., parents' daily signatures). Professional school counselors implement comprehensive school counseling programs and utilize data to answer the question, "How are students different because of the school counseling program?" Therefore, they collect data to measure the effectiveness of the current interventions. These data include the point sheets, attendance, grades, discipline records, and a student questionnaire. This collection of data would have been presented to the behavior intervention team at their monthly meetings. It would have been important for the behavior intervention team to view the data to ascertain if additional research-based interventions and best practices needed to be considered. Based on the results of the data, interventions would continue, be modified, or be dropped, and new interventions would be added, if necessary.

Overall, Kenneth made many improvements while in the RTC; in fact, he made improvements that met the approval of his CPS caseworker and the RTC staff. However, the progress he made seemed to wane, and he regressed significantly after his departure from the RTC. It is important to note that adapting to a new environment for an adolescent is difficult and some regression and behavioral changes may occur. It is difficult to predict what might have happened in Kenneth's case, and I often wonder if he received the help he needed. I hope for the best for him and his family.

DEVELOPMENTAL CONSIDERATIONS

It is important for counselors to determine whether to label an adolescent a juvenile sexual offender or determine if he or she may be sexually acting out or experiencing sexual reactivity. Kenneth's mother mentioned that he had been sexually abused when he was 11 years old; however, he never confirmed or denied the abuse. Although Kenneth exhibited some characteristics of a juvenile with sexual behavior problems, he also exhibited symptoms of sexual reactivity. It is possible that Kenneth engaged in sexual offending and sexual reactivity simultaneously. It is important to note that sexual exploration is developmentally appropriate at the age of 14 when the sexually acting out occurred. However, because his cousin was 10 years old at the time of the sexual exploration, his aunt, uncle, and CPS viewed his behavior as a possible molestation. At the time, Kenneth had not been convicted of a sexual offense against his cousin and there were not criminal proceedings underway. I agree that, at 14 years old, Kenneth understood appropriate and inappropriate touching and boundaries, and he violated boundaries with his younger cousin, thus committing a predatory offense. Due to the sexual nature of Kenneth's previous behaviors, being aware of his sexual development was a key goal during our counseling sessions, and I employed developmentally appropriate interventions to help foster understanding of healthy sexual development and appreciate appropriate boundaries and consent. Understanding healthy sexual behaviors may have assisted Kenneth with making more appropriate choices for sexual exploration in the future. As I mentioned before, Kenneth faced no conviction of a sexual offense at the time he participated in counseling. Indeed, he may have sexually acted out but he was guarded in sharing information due to the fact that counseling was mandated and because of the limits of confidentiality surrounding sexual abuse against children.

RELATIONAL CONSIDERATIONS

During his time in the RTC, Kenneth focused on his counseling work and appeared to be authentic and forthcoming in sessions. Upon leaving the RTC, our relationship shifted. I believe his environment and relationship with Debbie influenced Kenneth's lack of motivation in counseling. I reminded myself of the changes Kenneth experienced. Specifically, within a short period of time, he experienced disconnection from his family and with his peers and staff at the RTC. In addition to those losses, he entered into a new relationship with Debbie and Richard. These changes must have been overwhelming for Kenneth. Establishing a healthy relationship with both Kenneth and Debbie was important to me; therefore, I did not directly challenge the discrepancies in her stories and her lack of support of Kenneth's counseling.

MULTICULTURAL CONSIDERATIONS

I was aware of the age, gender, and race differences between Kenneth and me; I was a Black woman and he was a White adolescent male. Due to the nature of the counseling referral, our counseling sessions focused on sexual concerns and sexual issues. On a few occasions, I asked Kenneth about his comfort level discussing sex and sexuality and if he might feel more comfortable with another counselor. Given my awareness of the possibility of past sexual abuse and our gender differences, I was careful not to push him into discussing things that he did not want to discuss.

COUNSELING GOALS, INTERVENTIONS, AND RATIONALE

Kenneth's counseling goals shifted as he continued the counseling process and his time at the RTC came to an end. When asked what goals he desired from counseling while in the RTC, he stated, "I just want to do better so I can get out of here [RTC]." Kenneth shared that doing better could be described as "Listening to adults who are in charge and not being inappropriate with younger children." My goals for Kenneth focused on fostering a healthy therapeutic alliance, providing consistent support, and developing appropriate ideas about sexual contact and development. I communicated with staff, counselors, psychologists, and social workers on a monthly basis in the form of a multidisciplinary team (MDT) meeting during Kenneth's stay at the RTC. Staff members and counselors at the RTC provided information on Kenneth and his interactions with peers during the school day during the MDT meetings and the meetings allowed for us to work together for Kenneth's betterment.

After Kenneth left the RTC and began living with Debbie and Richard, the goals shifted to focusing on his behaviors and feelings at home. Upon his reintegration into his mother's home, counseling goals for Kenneth included adjusting to his new home environment, understanding the rules and boundaries of the home, increasing his interpersonal relationships with his mother and stepfather, and continuing psychoeducation regarding sexual consent and personal boundaries.

Creative Counseling Interventions and Techniques

Table 16.1 provides a summary of Kenneth's individual treatment plan, which includes creative interventions to engage him and foster interest in the counseling process and counseling sessions.

CONCEPTUALIZATION

Relational and developmental perspectives provide a framework to conceptualize Kenneth's story and progress through treatment.

COUNSELING PROCESS FLOW

I based my work with Kenneth on an Adlerian perspective; however, the RTC recommended that I utilize a cognitive behavioral approach. I provided weekly counseling services to Kenneth for 3 months at the RTC. After he left the RTC and integrated into the home with his mother and stepfather, I counseled with him for 4 months, seeing him once each month. I found it important to foster a healthy therapeutic alliance and saw this as pivotal in our counseling relationship. In addition to forming a productive relationship with Kenneth, I worked to gain his trust by providing a safe environment for him to be authentic and share his story.

During the assessment phase, Kenneth and I explored his family history, beliefs, and recollections of some events prior to his arrival at the RTC. Kenneth appeared engaged and shared his story through expressive arts and talk therapy. He developed some insights about his behavior and those insights helped him transition home with Debbie and Richard. However, during the move home, he began to regress, and while we continued working on the therapeutic alliance, I felt like we lost our connection once he moved home.

TABLE 16.1 Treatment Plan

Goal	Objectives	Interventions	Rationale
Create an inviting therapeutic alliance with the client and assist him in being open to the possibility of counseling.	1. Develop an understanding of counseling, establish a genuine therapeutic relationship, and align goals of client and counselor. 2. Assist the client in identifying issues within daily life that he is not happy with in order for counseling to align with his goals.	1. Create a safe environment and explain the parameters of the counseling relationship. Inquire about the client's desires for counseling. 2. Assist the client with formulating and prioritizing personal goals and tasks through conversation and expressive arts.	1. Creating a safe environment is key for counseling to take place. The therapeutic alliance is an important aspect of counseling as it is difficult for clients to share personal information and feel connected during the session if a healthy therapeutic relationship and environment has not been established. 2. Assisting the client with formulating his own goals is important because the client's desires need to be recognized. Having preconceived notions about what should happen during counseling is counterproductive and may hinder therapeutic growth and the therapeutic alliance.
Complete tasks at RTC with the eventual outcome of being released from the RTC. "I just want to do better so I can get out of here [RTC]."	1. Develop communication skills with peers and others. 2. Learn about appropriate sexual boundaries and healthy sexual relationships. 3. Establish healthy relationship with biological mother and stepfather.	1. Communicate with counselors about recent events and responses to issues within the milieu (i.e., drawings, journaling, poetry, and song writing). 2. Complete psychoeducational models related to healthy sexuality, sexual behaviors, and consent, along with communicating	1. Expressive arts are ways for clients to communicate events, situations, and feelings. Understanding how Kenneth feels about his interactions in the milieu is important when considering how he responds to issues and interacts with others. 2. The healthy sexuality

(continued)

TABLE 16.1 Treatment Plan *(continued)*

Goal	Objectives	Interventions	Rationale
		in therapy about recollections of events and scenarios/role-plays related to difficult situations. 3. Integrate parents into counseling sessions and have face-to-face visits with parents on the weekends at RTC. Weekend visits with parents allowed upon approval from the RTC staff and CPS caseworker.	psychoeducational module is key in assisting the client with understanding appropriate and inappropriate touching, consent, boundaries, and age-appropriate sexual exploration. It may assist the client with understanding and conceptualizing inappropriate experiences with him as the survivor. 3. A progressive integration into a new home environment with new people is important to assist client with change.
Improve coping skills and problem-solving skills related to being in a new environment (home with parents). Overall, decreasing the daily stressors in the client's life.	1. Identify factors that escalate anxiety and stress, and contribute to difficulty coping. 2. Facilitate development of stress management techniques.	1. Inspire the client to think of situations that increase stress, agitation, or anxiety. Educate regarding the relationship between emotions and unwanted behaviors (ABC Model). 2. Teach the client deep breathing techniques, progressive muscle relaxation, and visual imagery. Encourage the client to utilize expressive arts between sessions to journal thoughts, feelings, and emotions.	1. The client will be able to express how emotions and unwanted behaviors are related. 2. The client will be able to respond to the techniques being taught and to replicate the techniques outside of the counseling session.

RTC, relational-cultural theory.

OUTCOME

I often wonder about Kenneth and if he received the help he needed. His progress at the RTC was notable, yet I wonder if his motivation came from a desire to learn about healthy and unhealthy relationships or if he just wanted to leave the center. I feel confident that Kenneth knew the difference between appropriate and inappropriate touching and boundaries, and that he began working on his relationships with his mother and stepfather. However, in hindsight, I would have insisted upon more frequent counseling sessions after he was released from the RTC. On many occasions, I asked Debbie for weekly sessions with Kenneth but she stated it was not financially feasible. Also, my professional experience working with sexual offenders leads me to believe that group counseling might have been effective with Kenneth. However, the family and treatment team never truly agreed that he was a sexual offender.

REFERENCES

Center for Sex Offender Management. (2015). Effective management of juvenile sexual offenders in the community. Retrieved from http://csom.org/train/juvenile/index.html

Cheung, M., & Brandes, B. J. (2011). Enhancing treatment outcomes for male adolescents with sexual behavior problems: Interactions and interventions. *Journal of Family Violence, 26*, 387–401. http://dx.doi.org/10.1007/s10896-011-9373-5

Strait, G. S., Smith, B. S., McQuillin, S., Terry, J., Swan, S., & Malone, P. S. (2012). A randomized trial of motivational interviewing to improve middle school students' academic performance. *Journal of Community Psychology, 40*(8), 1032–1039. http://dx.doi.org/10.1002/jcop.21511

CHAPTER 17

NATALIE'S NEW VISION

Ernest Cox, Jr.

Natalie was a 17-year-old Hispanic female. She was an 11th grade student who was on pace to graduate at the conclusion of her next school year. Natalie appeared to be a bright, confident, and articulate young woman. She had one sibling, a sister, who was 3 years younger. Natalie reported enjoying a good relationship with her sister. Natalie and her sister live with their biological mother and her mother's "boyfriend of the month." Natalie reported a good relationship with her biological father, though she rarely visited him.

In spite of challenges at home, Natalie has continued to perform well academically. She was an A to B student and active in school, and expressed interest in attending college. Natalie held a part-time job at a fast-food restaurant. She made the decision to work in order to contribute to the family finances and maintain financial autonomy. Although she enjoyed academic and early career successes, Natalie discussed some personal–social issues that hindered her home life. She shared about her history of moving very quickly in and out of sexual relationships. These behaviors led to conflicts with her mother. Natalie acknowledged that she liked the attention boys gave her and stated that if her mother gave her attention, she would not need to have boyfriends. She also communicated that she had "relationship issues" with everyone—her boyfriend, her mother, her mother's boyfriend, and her biological father. Additionally, Natalie shared that she had a history of physical altercations with her mother. She felt that both she and her mother dealt with "anger and communication issues." Therefore, our counseling sessions largely focused on anger, communication, and relationship themes.

SYSTEMIC INFLUENCES

The Family System

Natalie's mother contacted the professional school counselor and expressed concerns regarding her daughter's sexual promiscuity. Natalie's mother described the constant state of turmoil at home. She disclosed Natalie often spoke combatively and had a habit of embellishing stories. She also shared that Natalie threatened to run away from home on multiple occasions, but never followed through. Lastly, she wanted their life to change. She wanted a relationship with her children.

The Peer System

Natalie surrounded herself with a small tight knit group of friends. She did not let many people get close because she feared that people would see the dysfunction in her family. Natalie was the oldest of her peer group and always had her eyes on the future. Thus, her goals centered on building relationships with her mother and addressing the painful drama from her life.

The School System

A concerned teacher initially referred Natalie to counseling. The teacher did not know about Natalie's issues at home. She referred Natalie to the counselor because she saw "risky" physical behaviors in the hallways and noticed Natalie seemed troubled in class. Because of these observations, Natalie's teacher accessed the school counseling resources available to her. Professional school counselors address the needs of students, parents, and staff. Professional school counselors hold certification and/or a teaching license as well as a minimum of a master's degree in school counseling. Professional school counselors focus on addressing the developmental needs of all students in academic, career, personal, and social domains (American School Counselor Association [ASCA], 2014). Professional school counselors support the growth of students by helping to remove barriers that interfere with their success.

DEVELOPMENTAL CONSIDERATIONS

Natalie was 17 years old. She was nearing the end of her adolescent years and in many respects entering her early adult years. Natalie maintained a part-time job, was on pace to graduate from high school and enter college, and had narrowed her career interest. She was financially self-sufficient and the primary caregiver for her younger sister. Natalie seemed capable of examining her experiences, appeared optimistic, and followed through with her ideas. She worked to solidify her personal identity and cultivate relationships with others.

RELATIONAL CONSIDERATIONS

Natalie entered counseling because she felt disconnected from her mother. In our first session, she identified her habit of building a wall around herself as a defensive mechanism. Despite this tendency, she still valued her relationships with her sister, her close friends, and her boyfriend.

MULTICULTURAL CONSIDERATIONS

Natalie is a 17-year-old Hispanic female. Her family qualified for free and reduced lunch in schools. The family was a lower-upper class, matriarchal, single-parent household.

CONCEPTUALIZATION

As a director of guidance and counseling, there are occasions when my support is required in the form of consultation, collaboration, or the provision of counseling services to students. In this case, I provided counseling services to a student at the request of the campus counselor and administrator. We provided counseling services through the comprehensive school counseling program model, which centered on individual planning and responsive services. The purpose of responsive services is to intervene on behalf of a student whose immediate personal concerns put his or her personal, social, and/or academic development at risk. The purpose of individual planning is to guide students as they plan, monitor, and manage their own educational, career, personal, and social development.

In my initial conversation with Natalie, she shared that her life was full of relationship drama. She described drama in her relationship with her mother, her mother's boyfriend, and her own relationships. Natalie acknowledged that her home issues caused social challenges at school. Her goal centered on finding a way to live a life free of drama, to reestablish a relationship with her mother, and to find independence.

Infusion of Creativity

I practice from a narrative therapy approach with a solution-oriented focus to highlight potential solutions and clients' strengths. I incorporate interventions from a number of theoretical orientations including transactional analysis (TA), reality therapy, Adlerian theory, and cognitive behavioral therapy. I utilize TA, specifically egograms and the drama triangle, in order to visually depict roles and cross transactions. I use reality therapy to focus on decision making by following the WDEP model (want, doing, evaluate, and plan). I infuse these therapeutic interventions using impact therapy, an approach founded by Ed Jacobs. Impact therapy is a theory-driven, multisensory approach to counseling that recognizes that client change comes not only from verbal but visual and kinesthetic exchanges. Impact therapy is a multisensory approach to counseling that recognizes the client, and the brain, like novelty (Jacobs, 1992). Impact therapy is applicable in the school setting as it serves as a form of brief therapy and helps an individual be active and engaged in the change process.

Time-Efficient Methods

Individual counseling in schools shares some similarities with mental health and other forms of counseling. Like mental health counselors, professional school counselors receive training to work with individuals, families, and groups to facilitate awareness and personal and social growth. However, limitations on time and a large caseload of students represent a major difference between school counseling and counseling within other settings. Professional school counselors find themselves seeking and using time-efficient methods. Many schools place a high demand and focus on the academic development of students. School administrators ask that individual counseling services fall within a 30- to 45-minute time frame. Therefore, counselors in school must work from a brief therapy model in order to quickly and efficiently respond to students' needs.

COUNSELING PROCESS FLOW

Natalie and I elected to meet in the mornings, because this was the time when Natalie transitioned from home life to school life. She communicated that her home life impacted how she functioned during the remainder of the day. We did not preestablish a set number of counseling sessions. We agreed to meet once weekly until she felt the frequency needed to change.

Session 1

In our first session, we reviewed the limits of confidentiality, completed an intake, began to build rapport, and gathered biopsychosocial information. During the first session, Natalie exhibited openness and receptivity to the counseling process. She voiced she felt ready for change in her life and her relational strife. Natalie shared her story and how she understood her family structure. She complained her mother seemed to always highlight the dysfunction in the family.

The root of Natalie's current conflict centered on her mother's relationship with her new boyfriend. In a recent argument with her mother, Natalie brought up issues she faced with her mother's boyfriend. Natalie's mother responded defensively, and the argument escalated. Natalie threatened to run away from home. She admitted that she used this threat often but never followed through. Natalie recalled that family conflicts occurred infrequently. She estimated they engaged in "big fights" once or twice a week. Occasionally, she threatened to run away from home, but shared that these were hollow threats. She would never actually run away because she was too close to graduating and going off to college.

As the session progressed, Natalie said, "My friends and sister are impressed at the tolerance level I have for my mom." She explained this by saying that it frustrated her to have a mother who wants to act like a child. Consequently, she felt the burden to act like an adult. She suspected her mother experienced low self-esteem and often made bad decisions. Natalie expressed her love for her mother but felt intolerant of her mother's behavior. reaching her current point of frustration. She often called her mom to task and expressed her concerns about their relationship. She acknowledged that conversations escalated to verbal and physical altercations. Natalie wanted her mom to understand her feelings. Instead, she said that her mother expressed that Natalie "was mouthing off" and acted disrespectfully toward her and her boyfriend. In the past, the conflicts between Natalie, her mother, and her mother's boyfriend became so intense that they resulted in professional filing reports to the department of family and protective services.

Currently, Natalie stated she felt safe and secure. Her family had a history of communication difficulties, which she hoped to change on her end. She was candid throughout the session; although she spoke of relationship conflicts, she also shared glimpses of when things were working well. In our first session, Natalie identified strengths as independence and caregiving, and described exceptions where her family functioned collaboratively. At the end of our first meeting, we planned for Natalie to gather data and pay attention to times when her family got along.

Session 2

During our second session, I infused multisensory counseling techniques. At the beginning of this session, I inquired to see how things had been better. Natalie said that things were okay; they had not been better or worse. Over the past few days, she spent time looking for times when everyone got along. She found that these times were few and far between. Natalie felt like she acted as the parent in the family all week long. She really wanted to threaten to run away this week but did not because it would have been counterproductive and would have led to a bigger fight. Natalie continued to feel frustrated by her mother. Her frustration centered on a comment that her mother made during a fight. She said her boyfriend meant more to her than her children.

In response, I felt that it was beneficial to introduce multisensory techniques into the session to help Natalie see the story from a different perspective. I introduced TA, specifically Berne's three ego states (parent, adult, and child). I asked Natalie what she believed the roles were of the parent, adult, and child. Natalie had a general understanding of the role each ego state represented. We discussed that people can potentially act as either the parent, adult, or child. When two people interact, a transactional response occurs. I found a white board and asked Natalie to draw three different circles on the left side of the board mirrored by three circles on the right. She did this and then labeled each circle as parent, adult, or child. I asked Natalie to make a statement that was typical in her interaction with her mom. Natalie said, "Mom, do you know what your plans are for the evening and what time you might be home?" I asked Natalie to indicate the ego this communicated. She felt she made an adult statement. Next, I asked her to give me an example of how her mom would respond. Natalie stated that her mother would say, "You are always getting in my business." Natalie identified that this statement could be typical of how a child responds. Natalie immediately shared that this model made sense. She shared the idea of adult-to-adult conversations appealed to her as a relational goal. She noted that everyone in her family responded from the child ego state. Natalie believed that she and her mother found ways to take things out of context rather than listening to each other, attending to the delivery and manner of communication, and observing the body language that accompanied the words.

The session quickly progressed. Natalie said things made sense in her mind and she started to see what could be done differently. I decided to stick with TA and introduce Karpman's drama triangle. We used the white boards again. Natalie followed along, drawing a triangle and placing the names indicating the roles of the victim, rescuer, and persecutor in each corner of the triangle. Natalie drew lines between each label, representing that a person could move between roles. I asked Natalie to choose the two other people with whom she experienced conflict. Natalie identified her mother and her mother's boyfriend. I asked her to assign each person a role of the victim, persecutor, or rescuer. Natalie said her mother played the victim, she was the rescuer, and mother's boyfriend was the persecutor. Next, we discussed the interaction and dialogue that occurred within the drama triangle. Natalie related the drama triangle to her life. She reflected and shared that she may have multiple roles in the triangle. Natalie stated, "I don't want to be in this triangle, I don't want the drama, I want out."

Natalie verbalized that the hands on explanations helped her better understand that it was her mother's interaction style. She learned they both chose to interact counterproductively. She wanted to create a plan to move away from the drama and rebuild her relationship with her mother.

To focus on goal setting, I conceptualized Natalie's situation using WDEP since we had the "W" and the "D." At the end of the session, I asked Natalie to make another attempt at doing some homework and reporting back next session. I asked Natalie if she felt comfortable writing notes to her mom. Natalie said she wrote notes to her mom in the past. I asked her to consider using a journal to write notes to her mother again. Natalie liked the idea and thought her mom would like it too. She planned to ask her mother to participate by responding to questions or asking what questions she had. The goal of writing focused on beginning a dialogue and limiting the potential for verbal altercations.

Session 3

Natalie missed our third session. She cancelled, but left a note. The note simply stated, "Can't make session today, things are going surprisingly well. See you next week."

Session 4

Our fourth session, which ended up being our last session, seemed different. Natalie came in to the session more energetic than normal. I checked in to see how things had been different. She shared that things were going well. Her relationship with her mom improved. Natalie said she got along with her mother's boyfriend and began focusing on her senior year.

I shared with Natalie that I noticed a tremendous change over the past 2 weeks. Natalie mentioned she worked really hard with her mother to build their relationship. She said journaling was exactly what she and her mother needed. Journal communication provided an opportunity for them to express thoughts and feelings. Natalie said her mother hesitated to participate at first. However, as she engaged in the activity, she opened up and expressed how much she cared for her children. Natalie used the journal and wrote about things she learned, including the drama triangle. She drew diagrams for her mom and explained what she had learned. Natalie told me that journaling allowed her to communicate her feelings. She told her mother that she was done with drama and wanted her mother to be done with it also. They used the journal to open up communication with each other, to build trust, and to start piecing their relationship back together. She felt that she had a new outlook and the confidence to do things differently in life.

OUTCOME

From time to time, I see Natalie in the hallways on her campus. She regularly approaches me, says hello, and gives me a quick update on how things are going. Natalie will soon graduate from high school with good grades. Her teachers report that she engages in school and works diligently in class. Natalie maintains positive peer relationships at school. She also reports that her home life is going well. She continues to have a great relationship with her sister and her mother's boyfriend. She is proud of the fact that they learned to interact with each other. Natalie is most proud of her relationship with her mother. To this day, they continue to journal with each other and speak respectfully to one another regardless of the topic.

REFERENCES

American School Counselor Association (ASCA). (2014). *The ASCA National Model: A framework for school counseling programs.* Alexandria, VA: Author.

Jacobs, E. (1992). *Creative counseling techniques: An illustrated guide.* Lutz, FL: Psychological Assessment Resources.

CHAPTER 18

THE WINDING ROAD THROUGH ADDICTION AND FAMILY LOSS

Shane Haberstroh
Thelma Duffey

As I (Shane) drove through the countryside on my way to facilitate a family retreat in a residential addiction treatment center, I wondered what the weekend would bring. I usually began these weekends with feelings of hope, anticipation, and deep respect for the families attending the program and their process of recovery. I also felt a tinge of apprehension. We would spend 20 hours together over 3 days, participating in a multifamily group experience, working in brief family counseling sessions, and developing family aftercare plans. The clients in the treatment center ranged in age from young adolescents to older adults, and the diversity of the clients and family constellations enriched our interactions and dialogue. Walking into the treatment center each weekend, I expected some common themes to emerge among the families' stories, and I also anticipated the unexpected to unfold. I hoped I could somehow navigate those unexpected moments creatively, with relational intention, and in a manner that helped the families gain clarity and relief.

In this chapter, we discuss the counseling process with Chris, an older adolescent, and his family as they negotiated their boundaries, communication styles, and relational connections. We review how they learned to differentiate between enabling behaviors and loving support. Chris's parents, Janey and Ben, and his 12-year-old sister, Lisa, flew in from a neighboring state to attend the family retreat. Chris's family seemed cautiously optimistic about seeing him, but voiced some skepticism about his treatment progress. They wanted him to stay in treatment an extra week; however, Chris met the criteria for discharge the following week. He seemed eager to return home. His family expressed fears about him potentially relapsing, and anger about his falling grades, legal issues, and disrespect for the family during his active addiction.

SYSTEMIC INFLUENCES

Chris lived within many different worlds. Within his familial, peer, institutional, and educational systems, Chris learned to evade difficult moments, escape into oblivion, and disarm people with a charming smile. Or he distanced others through bouts of rage. Within his family system, each member detached in his or her own way and avoided the pain lurking behind any real conversation. The family settled into familiar routines, patterns of communicating, and expected reactions to Chris's addiction and their unspoken grief. They focused much blame and anger onto Chris, who responded accordingly. He was an easy target, a ready conduit for their pain, and he played his role well. This routine, while familiar, drained the life from Chris's family, reinforcing their desperation.

The educational and legal systems funneled Chris through their due process and legal mechanisms. Because of his parents' status, Chris enjoyed some privilege. His father worked as an attorney and his mother was an anesthesiologist. His parents paid his rent, legal and probation fees, tickets, tuition, and provided him an allowance while he attended school. They felt stuck, exasperated, and worried about what would happen if they cut off all support; if they gave Chris tough love. They felt guilty. They also loved one another and missed the family they once had.

Legally, Chris faced two counts of probation violation and his probation officer recommended that Chris either enter treatment or complete his sentence in county jail. These threats seemed abstract to Chris. However, he chose treatment. People suffering from addiction often face the choice between seeking treatment and facing incarceration (NIDA, 2012). The legal and institutional systems threaten clients' loss of freedom and expect concrete change to occur in treatment. These dire consequences can frighten families and friends of those who are addicted, yet those suffering from addiction often seem oblivious to these impending consequences.

Finally, peer systems profoundly influence adolescents' behaviors and maturation (Rosner, 2013). Drug-using peers reinforce each other's addictive behaviors, trigger relapses, and support minimization and denial of their addiction (Rosner, 2013). Many 12-step recovery programs and treatment centers recognize that peer interactions play a powerful role in both relapse and recovery (Galanter, Kaskutas, Lagressa, American Society of Addiction Medicine, & Research Society on Alcoholism [U.S.], 2008). Treatment and recovery programs offer new rituals and relational expectations, and promote acceptance, authenticity, and accountability. Chris sensed the hope and power in treatment by watching others change, acting with courage, and supporting others during times of deep pain. He also felt the pull and connection to his roommates who still used drugs regularly.

DEVELOPMENTAL CONSIDERATIONS

Chris recently turned 19 years old, lived with three roommates, and attended a local state university. He did not suffer from any serious developmental delays; however, he began drinking at age 12, started smoking marijuana regularly at age 14, and began smoking heroin at age 16. This early regular substance use impaired Chris's executive functioning and mood regulation (Center for Substance Abuse Treatment, 2013; National Institute on Drug Abuse [NIDA], 2007). Furthermore, Chris's father reported a history of heavy drug use in his past, and his grandfather died from cirrhosis of the liver due to alcoholism. These factors played an important role in Chris's development, because the genetic predisposition for addiction hinders natural brain development (NIDA, 2007). As a result of structural and neurochemical differences in the limbic system and prefrontal cortex, those predisposed to addiction often struggle with impulsivity, recklessness, and mood and other co-occurring mental health issues (Haberstroh & Duffey, 2014).

Men appear to be more at risk than women for developing addiction (Haberstroh & Duffey, 2014; NIDA, 2007), and this was the case for Chris. He suffered from both substance dependence and major depression, and these issues progressively impaired his potential development. He failed his first semester of college, received two alcohol-related driving under the influence (DUI) charges, and the university expelled him from his dorm for destroying his room while intoxicated. His pattern of reckless and impulsive behaviors and disregard of the consequences of his drug and alcohol use characterized his delayed maturity. In treatment, he tended to minimize his addiction and suggested he could drink more responsibly in the future. He contended adamantly that heroin was the real problem, not alcohol or "weed," and stated that his heroin use was not "that bad. It's not like I shoot it!" While Chris tested well above average on IQ tests and, when sober, excelled at academic achievement tests, his developmental issues centered around his social and relational functioning.

RELATIONAL CONSIDERATIONS

Chris enjoyed camaraderie in the treatment center with a small group of other adolescent clients. Despite his reported bouts of depression, he appeared affable and well liked among his peers. However, when his small group focused on serious conversations, grief, and exploration of the terrible tolls of addiction, Chris became quiet or tried to lighten the mood through humor. His small group counselor pointed this out to him several times. Chris often shrugged at this feedback. Authenticity and accountability eluded him, because a silent grief consumed him. Three years ago, the family system shattered when Chris's older brother, Tom, died in a car accident. From early childhood to his teens, Chris deeply admired Tom. Tom reciprocated and advocated for Chris at home, protected him from bullies in the neighborhood, and treated Chris with respect and honesty. Tom also taught Chris how to get high and mentored him into the "party world." When Tom died, the family seemed to implode and quietly disconnect from each other. Each member turned to his or her own private grief and their silence echoed in their disconnection. Chris felt truly alone, finding a numb comfort in drugs. His relationship with heroin seemed stronger than the ties with friends and family. For Chris to feel his grief and face the facts of his life meant enduring a pain that seemed insurmountable.

MULTICULTURAL CONSIDERATIONS

Chris came from an upper middle class Caucasian family. He lived within a privileged community and interacted in a culture of like-minded and culturally similar peers. In some ways, these factors limited the natural consequences and feedback needed to help Chris change his behaviors, or gain insight into his addiction. Given that the treatment center included people from many diverse backgrounds, Chris heard stories of tremendous loss, racism, and abuse. These stories began to enlighten Chris about the role of culture in abuse of power, and he began to see the role of privilege in his life. Finally, gendered expectations played a role in Chris's treatment and recovery. Some men face unique challenges in addiction treatment related to expressing and identifying emotions, connecting with new sober peers, and identifying the relational consequences of their actions (Haberstroh & Duffey, 2014). Chris often found himself at a loss for words when asked to describe his feelings.

CONCEPTUALIZATION

Many factors contributed to a conceptualization of Chris's addiction and treatment progress. His addiction progressed to the point where he met many of the criteria for alcohol, cannabis, and heroin dependence. Motivationally, Chris seemed to contemplate what real recovery could mean for him, but displayed ambivalence toward engaging in work around expressing his grief, facing his issues with honest and humble accountability, and admitting the true depth of his addiction. I suspected that if Chris became vulnerable and honest, and others authentically connected with him during those moments, he would connect with himself, his hopes, and his pain. The path would not be an easy one. I hoped that the power of the group, shared connections, and structure of the family retreat would provide a forum for Chris and his family to reconnect and gain an honest appreciation of the addiction and the responsibilities of recovery. My goals for my work with Chris and his family focused on attending to spontaneous moments of vulnerability, encouraging honest discussions, and beginning to rebuild a sense of realistic hope for the future.

COUNSELING PROCESS FLOW

We developed the family retreat program to provide education about the principles of addiction and recovery in an interactive and experiential format. The families engaged in activities to create cohesion, identify effective communication styles, and learn about addiction, enabling, treatment principles, and aftercare planning. I (Shane) met with the families in large groups, small communication process groups, and brief family counseling sessions. Several turning points emerged for Chris and his family during the weekend.

Our discussion about the interplay between genetic, neurobiological, and environmental factors, as well as choice, humanized Chris in his family's eyes. We discussed at length about how researchers understood addiction as a progressive brain disease. From this discussion, we concluded that addicts show demonstrably different brain structures and functioning than nonaddicts and genetic differences predict addiction and these preexisting neurological differences predispose people to addiction. We also discussed that this meant Chris and others who face addiction must be more accountable for their behaviors. Much like those who suffer from diabetes follow stricter diets, those suffering from addiction succeed when they adhere to specific recovery principles. The principles of abstinence, honesty, connection with sober peers, and vulnerability guide the initial work for those in recovery.

Chris and his family learned about family roles, the influence of homeostasis in family systems, family rules, and patterns of communication. We discussed boundaries and enabling. One of the most powerful moments for Chris and his family emerged from a small group activity centered on authentic and honest communication. We discussed using "I statements," and identifying feelings, as well as listening to each family member in a mutually empathic way. The interactive communication activity focused on allowing family members to speak honestly and be fully heard by each other. To prepare for the activity, each member wrote three behaviors they disliked that Chris used, and three behaviors or attributes they liked about him. Chris did the same for each family member, and began to feel guilt about his past when he admitted reluctance identifying aspects he did not like about his little sister. He found one, and sat quietly staring at his worksheet after he wrote it.

The family shared their work with one another and I (Shane) facilitated their discussion. I found when families took the time to write their concerns and feelings down on paper, they shared honest and vulnerable statements that they often left unsaid at home. Chris and his family did just this. They looked at each other and shared their pain, love, memories, and fears. As the facilitator, I encouraged each member to empathize and hear one another by reflecting what they heard each other say. For example, Chris's little sister sat across from him, eyes rimmed with tears, and said, "I don't like it when you drink and get high and disappear, and we don't hear from you. I'm scared you're going to die like Tom, and I feel alone and mad." Chris looked at the floor, and I invited him to look directly at his sister. He fought the urge to cry, and lost. He found something in himself then. He accessed his courage and respect for his little sister who always seemed to love him no matter what he did. He looked at her tearfully and said, "You're scared and alone when I party and don't come home. You're scared I'm going to die like Tom. I'm sorry, so sorry." At that moment he felt his grief and realized that his behaviors truly hurt those who cared for him.

Infusion of Creativity

After the family expressed their feelings, concerns, memories, and love, I noticed they sat closer together and seemed much more relaxed and connected. Chris's father sat with his arm around Chris's shoulder and his mother leaned into his father. Chris held his little sister's hand.

I found that most of the time when families risked authenticity, it created space for connection and relief. Next, we moved to an experiential activity to demonstrate the power of family roles in dysfunctional systems.

Using experiential family sculpture techniques, I asked volunteers from the multifamily group to play the roles of the family hero, scapegoat, mascot, lost child, enabler, and addict. We identified one sentence for each member to repeat, and I arranged each participant in a manner that visually illustrated his or her role within the family.

1. The chief enabler stood behind the addict with both hands on his shoulders. She repeated the phrase: "I've got it under control, everything's okay."
2. The hero stood to the right of the enabler and placed a hand on her shoulder as a demonstration of support and shared *parentified* responsibility. She repeated the phrase: "I got straight As again. I'm always here to help."
3. I asked the scapegoat to stand just outside the door to the group room and repeat loudly: "I hate you! I'm out of here!"
4. The lost child sat in the corner of the room quietly.
5. The mascot roamed the room and encouraged everyone to "just lighten up and have fun!"
6. Finally, the addict stated, "I want to drink. I just want to drink."

The participants repeated their phrases in unison for a couple of minutes. We paused and discussed that while the family appeared chaotic from the outside, within the family system, each member seemed stuck in a monotonous routine. We concluded the activity by asking the person who played the addict to leave the role-play. The rest of the family maintained their roles and poses. We processed how it felt to be in those roles and members shared they felt angry, lonely, scared, tired, stuck, and unheard. We discussed how family members also benefit from treatment, recovery, and support because addiction corrupts family systems. Finally, I asked the person playing the role of the addict to return to the family system. He returned to the exact spot he left and leaned back against the hands of the chief enabler. Accordingly, we discussed the need for systemic changes.

OUTCOME

As Chris and his family prepared for the next steps in Chris's treatment, we focused on aftercare planning, living arrangements, social support, and outpatient counseling to focus on family issues, grief,

addiction, and mental health recovery. As we discussed living arrangements, Chris adamantly refused to attend a halfway house. Instead, he
wanted to return to his apartment and be with his friends. He argued
that they only drank and partied on the weekend, and that he learned
about the dangers of addiction and would not use again. He wanted
his parents to continue to pay his bills and provide him an allowance. I
voiced my concerns that the temptations of his old lifestyle and relationships with drug-using peers increased his chance of relapse. Chris's
parents struggled with potentially enabling his relapse. In our conversations, he admitted using his allowance and rent money for drugs. Chris's
parents did not want Chris to be homeless and they did not want their
son to die of an overdose. They faced their own fears and grief over
watching their son decompensate, and wanted to do everything in their
power to help him. They realized they contributed financially to his
drug use and decline. My goal in these conversations focused on helping the family develop a realistic plan that supported recovery for
everyone in the family. Because Chris failed his spring semester, and
was suspended from school, his parents agreed to support him in his
first 2 weeks in a halfway house. We then developed a longer term
financial support plan contingent upon Chris staying sober, attending
school, contributing to his own education through work or volunteer
activities, and engaging in aftercare counseling. His parents refused to
subsidize his addiction any longer.

I learned that Chris relapsed on alcohol, and soon began smoking
heroin again. This time, he declined quickly. He disappeared for 6 months,
lived on the streets, contracted hepatitis, and the university dismissed
him for academic failure. Chris returned to treatment shaken, scared,
and alone. These experiences humbled him, and in his crisis he learned
that his recovery and his family were precious to him. As we sat together
in another family retreat, one of his young adult peers adamantly shared
that "meth" was his "problem" and we "couldn't tell him he couldn't
have a beer!" Chris glanced at me from across the room, nodded, and
shared his experience, strength, and hope with his peers.

REFERENCES

Center for Substance Abuse Treatment. (2013). *Addressing the specific behavioral
health needs of men: Treatment improvement protocol series, No. 56* (DHHS
Publication No. SMA 13–4736). Rockville, MD: Substance Abuse and
Mental Health Services Administration.

Galanter, M., Kaskutas, L. A., Lagressa, D., American Society of Addiction
Medicine, & Research Society on Alcoholism (U.S.). (2008). *Research on*

alcoholics anonymous and spirituality in addiction: The twelve-step program model, spiritually oriented recovery, twelve-step membership, effectiveness and outcome research. New York, NY: Springer-Verlag.

Haberstroh, S., & Duffey, T. (2014). Counseling with addicted men. In M. Englar-Carlson, M. Evans, & T. Duffey (Eds.), *A counselor's guide to working with men* (pp. 263–283). Alexandria, VA: American Counseling Association.

National Institute on Drug Abuse (NIDA). (2007). Drugs, brain, and behavior: The science of addiction. Retrieved from http://www.drugabuse.gov/publications/drugs-brains-behavior-science-addiction/preface

National Institute on Drug Abuse (NIDA). (2012). *Principles of drug addiction treatment: A research based guide* (3rd ed.). Retrieved from http://www.drugabuse.gov/sites/default/files/podat_1.pdf

Rosner, R. (2013). *Clinical handbook of adolescent addiction.* Chichester, West Sussex, UK: Wiley-Blackwell.

CHAPTER 19

IMPRISONED IDENTITIES

Thomas Anthony Chávez

Early in my professional training, I proclaimed my desire to work with
adolescents. When I shared this choice with others, they often questioned, "But, why? That is such a tough age!" Simply mentioning the
terms "adolescent" or "teenager" elicited friends' and colleagues' memories of harrowing teen years and awkward adolescent experiences. In
these conversations, people also shared stereotypes of adolescents as
hormonal, sex-crazed, lazy, confused, moody, irresponsible, manipulative, shut down, troubled, and socially inept. Sometimes they associated
adolescence with criminal behavior or antisocial characteristics, and
implicated parents as unknowingly or even intentionally contributing
to their children's dysfunction and antisocial behaviors.

Certainly, some families face unique circumstances that contribute
to persistent behavioral problems among their children. Oftentimes
these problems are extensive enough to require intervention with both
parents and children. Some adolescents with social and behavioral
concerns may enter counseling and find it productive and rewarding.
Other times, teens may need multiple and intensive or long-term interventions, such as hospitalization or residential treatment. Unfortunately,
when behavioral problems persist despite supportive services, youth
often become involved with the legal and juvenile justice systems.

In my work with justice-involved youth, I noted many commonali-
ties among the adolescents I served. First, I could not help but to notice
the overrepresentation of youth of color. Second, many adolescents
talked about being or identifying as a "thug" or similar label. Third,
most had a lifelong experience being "in the system" of child and adolescent services, which included mental health, foster care, and detention.

Fourth, each adolescent had a parent, both parents, or other family members who had been or were currently involved with mental health and criminal justice systems. Therefore, many of my young clients did not live with their biological parents. Finally, it was not uncommon that my adolescent clients lived in poor and violent neighborhoods. These concerns were no different for 15-year-old "Markus."

I first met Markus at a high security juvenile treatment center. He was tall, slim, and of African American descent. In addition, he was dressed in full correctional attire and mechanical restraints. Although seemingly anxious and taking time to respond, Markus acted with respect toward me. Admittedly, I did not expect this behavior. With limited range of motion due to his restrained wrists, he reached out with a handshake and adamantly called me "sir" as expected of all the young inmates, or in his term "jailbaits." I returned my handshake with brevity because the institution expected minimal physical contact be made with the inmates to mitigate others sharing contraband with the inmates.

A staff member escorted Markus and me from his cell to a large room with Plexiglas windows. Security personnel observed us through the windows and via cameras that were securely built into the high corners of the walls. The room was furnished by sofas that were gravity bound, purposely designed to be heavy enough so that angry inmates could not pick them up to throw at someone. The support staff closed the door behind them, leaving Markus and me to "work on his issues." Markus seemed to not be bothered by me or the surroundings. I, however, internally planned an escape route "just in case." My goal in this first meeting, nevertheless, was to get to know Markus and understand his "problems," which I had already reviewed in his two-volume medical chart.

SYSTEMIC INFLUENCES

Family and fathers play a critical role in many African American communities and life; however, social–historical factors, such as racism, contribute to the multiple challenges they face (McAdoo & McAdoo, 1998) as witnessed in the case of Markus's family system. Markus felt unsure where he stood with his father. On the one hand, he understood that the behaviors his father displayed (abusive toward his mother and gang involvement) were not healthy and created much strain for the family. On the other hand, if Markus gave up on his father, he would lose his model protector of the family. As his father was in and out of prison, Markus seemed to take on this protective role. He was very explicit about wanting to protect his mother and siblings. However, he did not have to do it by himself, as his paternal uncle literally and symbolically replaced Markus's father's role. This all changed when Markus's uncle was murdered. Markus no longer could depend on his protective male being there. The need to protect his family, possibly from the violence he witnessed in his community, became a larger burden for him. While knives fascinated him from a young age, this attraction became even more pronounced after his father's incarceration and uncle's death. Markus also depended on his gang to protect him in his community as well.

Markus often wondered if his behavior was an inevitable part of him and his family, stating that chaos and violence were simply "who I am." If he severed his relationship with his father then, in a sense, he would be severing a part of himself. His connection to his father seemed to be the legacy of being like him and he would hold onto that no matter the expense.

DEVELOPMENTAL CONSIDERATIONS

Markus was, again surprisingly, willing to openly share about himself and his perspective and reasons for his criminal behavior. He explained to me that his "anger problem" persisted from early childhood. In fact, many young inmates dealt with "anger problems" or "anger management" most of their lives and they often attributed anger as the cause for criminal involvement, along with explanations of their "crazy family life." Markus recalled that he lived with his mother and four siblings (one younger sister and three older brothers) in his early to late childhood before living with his paternal grandmother. Markus's mother and father never married and he admired his father despite witnessing him abuse his mother. Furthermore, Markus's father remained continuously involved in gang and criminal behavior and was in and out of prison throughout Markus's life. Markus added that his paternal uncle, too, had been involved in similar behaviors, before a rival gang murdered him. Nevertheless, Markus still spoke highly of both his father and uncle, somewhat idolizing them.

Markus's brothers, he explained, engaged in criminal behavior. In fact, his oldest brother had been incarcerated many times throughout Markus's life. Markus recalled wanting a bike at age 13. His father told him that they could not afford one and "anger took over" Markus's body, resulting in Markus becoming aggressive toward his father. Markus's brother tried to intervene, but Markus stabbed his brother with a kitchen knife. Markus exclaimed that he always had "a fascination with knives." This was the time of Markus's first contact with the children's court system.

School/Education

Markus attended public schools for most of his life. As a consequence of a past incarceration, the courts referred him to an intensive "school" that provided multiple treatment services. Incidentally, he recalled that at this time he was 13 years old and this year marked both his father's return to prison and his uncle's murder. He continued to narrate his school life in terms of his negative behavior. Academically, Markus experienced much "restlessness and problems with concentration" throughout elementary school. By age 11 he began to "hang with the wrong crowd." He had "outbursts" to the point of throwing desks over, threatening school personnel, and fighting with his peers. Like most of the young inmates, although still far from graduating from high school, Markus wanted to work toward a general equivalency diploma. He, however, feared being given a diploma with the institution's name on it would mark him "crazy" for the world to see.

Medical Information

While Markus's current physical health was generally good, his psychiatric evaluations revealed diagnoses of attention deficit hyperactivity disorder (ADHD), oppositional defiant disorder, bipolar disorder, intermittent explosive disorder, various learning disorders, and borderline intellectual functioning. Accordingly, his chart and treatment protocols included many prescriptions to manage his issues. At our first meeting, Markus took medication for depression and ADHD, which he expressed helped him "concentrate better." Finally, at age 13, Markus began to experiment with alcohol and marijuana use. His alcohol use became more frequent, as he had the goal of becoming inebriated each time he drank.

RELATIONAL CONSIDERATIONS

Outside the setting of the highly structured program of the juvenile treatment center, Markus may have looked to others like any other adolescent in the general population. He appeared personable, humorous, compliant, and well liked by peers and staff. He did have occasional tiffs with his peers and did fight with one of his peers in his corridor. Otherwise, Markus partook in all milieu programing without any problems. His general sociability and overall behavior seemed quite different from what others documented in his medical chart. I wondered if I was simply naïve and working with a possibly budding "sociopath," which I was led to believe by the medical and legal jargon overwhelmingly evident in his chart.

MULTICULTURAL CONSIDERATIONS

While Markus shared about himself and his family system, I considered factors Markus did not articulate. A general social justice framework allowed me to understand Markus from a critical perspective (Crethar, Torres-Rivera, & Nash, 2008). African and Latino Americans are overrepresented in the American justice system (NAACP, 2016) and, as such, terms such as "thug" can often be associated with these populations. This partially explained why Markus and some of his peers seemed to accept and internalize this negative label. I wondered if this constrained other possible identities or ways of being in the world. Similarly, his multiple labels of pathology and crime reflected the relationships between discourses, expectations, and identity. For example, many times the support staff used the language of "risk" or "manipulative behavior" in their conversations. In addition, many staff members advised the young inmates to "take responsibility" for their life and behaviors whenever they "made excuses" discussing their lives. This brought up many thoughts for me. First, I contended many stigmas regarding adolescence, mental illness, and criminal behavior existed *within* institutions that are there to otherwise "rehabilitate" youth (Heflinger & Hinshaw, 2010). Second, staff felt innocuous behaviors, such as a handshake, carried malicious intent. Finally, the treatment professionals expected that the young inmates take full responsibility for the past and future behavioral change. That is, they enforced an individualistic perspective. This perspective assumes problems lie *within* the individual only, reducing incarcerated youth to broken psyches and mere *behaviors*. This model neglects the role of context, relationships, and identity in an adolescent's world, despite these factors being critical during adolescence.

Within the context of society and the cultural institution of incarcerated males, Markus struggled with understanding his sexuality. He considered the possibility of being gay, coping with yet another stigmatized identity. Furthermore, sexuality in the prison system can be a highly sensitive issue relating to masculinity and ideals of toughness, which creates a "prison within prison" (Evans & Wallace, 2008). In the case of Markus, he eventually identified as bisexual, which placed him at risk of being in a "prison within a prison within a prison." Issues of masculinity consequently become a barrier to treatment among men in prison (Kupers, 2005) and it appeared that this was so for Markus.

CONCEPTUALIZATION

As a new counselor in training, who was I to provide him counseling any different or better from services received in the past? I mean, he was labeled as "resistant to treatment," as one counselor had boldly marked in one of his "progress" notes. It was no doubt that Markus struggled with depression, but even more so, he experienced much grief and trauma from a young age. Thus far, he indicated to me that he lived in poverty, in a violent neighborhood, witnessed his mother's abuse by his father, dealt with "ambiguous loss" (Boss, 2000) of his parents, and had not processed the death of his uncle. In a later session, Markus also disclosed to me that he had been "molested" by a peer at the intensive school setting where he had been placed. Markus disclosed to me in the context of "being molested" that he wondered if he was gay. He went on to say that he secretly dated a male peer his age when he was 13 years old. He was trying to make sense of his identity.

Considering many other professionals labeled and diagnosed Markus with various pathologies, I questioned the value any assessments might add. If I continued to work from a framework of pathology, would I not arrive at the same or similar results? I had to begin my conceptualization of Markus from the point of understanding the context of his life circumstances and the systems that influenced him. I wanted to find Markus's strengths in the midst of his behaviors that were, without a doubt, problematic in his personal, family, and social life. He willingly disclosed information, almost to a fault. This did not seem like a "resistant" client. I felt compelled to avoid completing one more pathological assessment, but instead bring in another explanatory model to explain Markus's life and treatment. I knew this could be risky, considering how the intersected cultures of criminology and medicine tended to pathologize inmates.

COUNSELING PROCESS FLOW

It is quite common among youth in "the system" of mental health, foster care, and juvenile justice to have many fleeting relationships. This includes relationships with family members, community members, and therapeutic personnel as this population moves between various service agencies. Consequently, they experienced heightened issues of trust. It was critical that I establish the therapeutic relationship with Markus, but this was more about my own work. I had to truly explore my personal biases as influenced by larger society with my clinical supervisor. There was no doubt that some stereotypes were deeply embedded within me, despite my great desire to work with adolescents in general. This growing awareness would allow me to understand Markus as more than just an object with "bad behavior" or the simple consequence of "bad parenting."

Due to phone conversations with Markus's grandmother, who had custody of him at the time, I was well aware of the fact that I would not be able to work with Markus's mother or father. His father was in prison and his mother's whereabouts were unknown. I felt challenged working with Markus's grandmother because the only contact I had with her was via telephone. She lived at least 3 hours away and did not have reliable transportation. In addition, the facility restricted phone use and inmates earned extra calls according to the existing strict behavioral program.

Because Markus was well versed in cognitive behavioral interventions, I took his interpersonal strengths into consideration and based most of our therapeutic interactions on interpersonal process and therapy (Mufson, Dorta, Moreau, & Weissman, 2011; Teyber & McClure, 2010). Interpersonal process facilitates the establishment of a therapeutic relationship, which I found not as challenging as I expected in Markus's case. Most importantly, I let my guard down about being "manipulated" by a "resistant to treatment, budding sociopath." Interestingly, Markus did not expect to be able to talk about his "excuses," or rather, his previous experiences of trauma, in which incarcerated youth often experience and rarely receive treatment, especially among youth of color (Spinney et al., 2016). This opened up "space" for new ways of interacting with supportive personnel and thus creating "corrective emotional experiences" (Teyber & McClure, 2010).

Infusion of Creativity

We took time to honor his father and uncle despite their behavior. I encouraged Markus to draw about the things he felt his father and uncle did well. We were quite limited because of the high restrictions of materials for fear of using items as weapons, as well as limitations in confidentiality due to being observed at all times by support personnel. In a sense, Markus's drawings served as a minimal two-dimensional commemorative. We also became creative and used the paper to sculpt three-dimensional figures that similarly represented Markus's wishes for his commemorative. Furthermore, this project allowed him to slowly let go of responsibility for the family chaos and fears about needs for protection. This space also allowed Markus to understand his behavior *and* himself in context, honoring his unique life circumstances and recognizing social injustices such as poverty, neighborhood violence, and stigmatization. It was critical to transform his role perspectives on aspects of his life and in society.

Markus was obviously physically incarcerated, but most important to me was how various aspects of his identity seemed to be "incarcerated" or locked in a "prison within a prison, within a prison." Being imprisoned physically did not concern Markus as much as one might think because it provided him some protection from the turmoil in his family and community. However, his psychological imprisonment seemed to impede his adolescent identity development.

According to Markus, rigid thinking framed the treatment philosophy at the facility, or as he analogously expressed, "[E]ither you're expected to be perfect or nothing, there is nothing in-between." These statements reflected the singular focus on behavior. The staff expected inmates to "be more normal than normal." Making a mistake or violating a minor rule meant that staff deemed the inmates worthless. With this in mind, I asked Markus to talk about his anger instead of perfectly "managing" his "anger problem." We discussed anger in the context of his life circumstances and did not simply conceptualize it as a biologically inherited part of who he "truly" was.

He grew more confident in his identity. In our discussions, he expressed having romantic feelings for another male inmate in the treatment center. We explored the safety of "coming out" as bisexual in the heterosexual and gay community and in the hypermasculine environment of the institution (Evans & Wallace, 2008). We discussed the relationship with his father, who had been part of hypermasculine environments himself, and talked about the potential homophobia he might encounter in the African American communities (Ward, 2005) to which he belonged. Nevertheless, Markus wanted to be truthful about who he was with his family. Markus's grandmother had been his most trusted and consistent family member and he decided to come out to her over a phone call. Fortunately, his grandmother expressed love and support and further discussed with me what this might mean for her and Markus's life.

OUTCOME

While I was able to monitor Markus's outcome during our time in the juvenile treatment center, he still needed to complete a 2-year sentence.

Considering the progress he made in the program, the treatment team made the decision to move him to a less restrictive setting. I am not sure what happened to Markus once he moved. I felt that I was another fleeting relationship. I, to this day, worry about whether our discussions provided enough information and skills that would translate to the world, or as the young inmates called it, "the outs." I wondered if he would be able to manage the multiple negative representations of being a "normal" adolescent. I wondered if he would be able to manage the "spoiled identities" (Goffman, 1963) of criminality, mental illness, and having two incarcerated family members. I wondered if he would be able to reintegrate into the community and whether he would return to the prison system as an adult. Overall, Markus and I collaboratively worked toward physical liberation, but more so toward liberation of his multiple incarcerated identities bound by his behavior, family concerns, and society as a whole.

REFERENCES

Boss, P. (2009). *Ambiguous loss: Learning to live with unresolved grief.* Cambridge, MA: Harvard University Press.

Crethar, H. C., Rivera, E. T., & Nash, S. (2008). In search of common threads: Linking multicultural, feminist, and social justice counseling paradigms. *Journal of Counseling & Development, 86*(3), 269–278.

Evans, T., & Wallace, P. (2008). A Prison within a Prison? The Masculinity Narratives of Male Prisoners. *Men and Masculinities, 10*(4), 484–507.

Goffman, E. (1963). *Stigma: Notes on the management of spoiled identity.* New York, NY: Simon & Schuster.

Heflinger, C. A., & Hinshaw, S. P. (2010). Stigma in child and adolescent mental health services research: Understanding professional and institutional stigmatization of youth with mental health problems and their families. *Administration and Policy in Mental Health and Mental Health Services Research, 37*(1–2), 61–70. http://dx.doi.org/10.1007/s10488-010-0294-z

Kupers, T. A. (2005). Toxic masculinity as a barrier to mental health treatment in prison. *Journal of Clinical Psychology, 61*(6), 713–724. http://dx.doi.org/10.1002/jclp.20105

McAdoo, H., & McAdoo, J. (1998). The dynamics of African American fathers' family roles. *Michigan Family Review, 3*(1). Retrieved from http://quod.lib.umich.edu/m/mfr/4919087.0003.102?rgn=main;view=fulltext

Mufson, L., Dorta, K. P., Moreau, D., & Weissman, M. M. (2011). *Interpersonal psychotherapy for depressed adolescents.* New York, NY: Guilford Press.

NAACP. (2016). *NAACP Criminal Justice Fact Sheet.* Retrieved from http://www.naacp.org/pages/criminal-justice-fact-sheet

Spinney, E., Yeide, M., Feyerherm, W., Cohen, M., Stephenson, R., & Thomas, C. (2016). Racial disparities in referrals to mental health and substance abuse services from the juvenile justice system: A review of the literature.

Journal of Crime and Justice, 39(1), 153–173. http://dx.doi.org/10.1080/0735 648X.2015. 1133492

Teyber, E., & McClure, F. (2010). *Interpersonal process in therapy: An integrative model.* Boston, MA: Cengage Learning.

Ward, E. G. (2005). Homophobia, hypermasculinity and the US Black church. *Culture, Health & Sexuality, 7*(5), 493–504. http://dx.doi.org/10.1080/13691050500151248

CHAPTER 20

GROWING A GENTLE GIANT

Thelma Duffey
Shane Haberstroh
Stacy Waterman

Fifteen-year-old Armando walked into his first counseling session wearing a sheepish smile and friendly demeanor. Armando participated as a member of the Peer Mentoring Program (PMP) at his junior high school, where we provided counseling services. The program focused on helping at-risk youth negotiate school life and develop life skills, such as communication, conflict resolution, and values clarification. Armando's reading scores and academic performance, coupled with family dynamics that placed him at risk for academic, social, and behavioral failure, perfectly positioned him to be a PMP candidate. Two of Armando's brothers lived in a juvenile detention home because they engaged in violent acts, and his close cousin received a life sentence in prison for murder. Several of Armando's teachers shared concerns about Armando slipping through the cracks, and nominated him for inclusion in the yearlong pilot program. While the program directors encouraged student participation, students had the ultimate option to participate. Armando's mother signed a consent form and he registered for the PMP.

SYSTEMIC INFLUENCES

In spite of some destructive and challenging systemic influences within Armando's environment, a number of healing and productive influences supported him, as well. For one, the school received federal funding to serve migrant children through a Title I Program. Second, the school district implemented the PMP that gave Armando an opportunity to participate in counseling and other personal growth activities. Finally, Armando's parents' love, concern, and gratitude for any opportunities afforded to their children influenced his experience. The community also served as a support through several community- and school-based projects, including a partnership with the local Young Men's Christian Association (YMCA). Opportunities for creativity, deepened connection, and student success sat at the core of many of these projects.

DEVELOPMENTAL CONSIDERATIONS

Imagine being 15 years old and reading at a fourth grade reading level. Imagine further that most of your peers are also 15 years old and reading at a third or fourth grade reading level. How will your fourth grade reading skills help you master eighth grade social studies, science, or literature courses? And, what might it be like to stare at the pages in the text books and know you are responsible for learning something you cannot read? Armando faced this challenge every day. Although bright, he encountered academic delays in large part because of language, systemic, and environmental factors. And although his reading level fell below that of the average student his age nationwide, his scores paralleled those of the average student at his school. Given the role that academics can play in a person's ability to transcend and move beyond unwanted circumstances, and Armando's hope to live in the larger world of opportunity, these surfaced as important barriers for Armando to negotiate and overcome.

Some students faced with these kinds of academic barriers act out in the classroom. They may feel embarrassed, bored, or hopeless to master their work. In those cases, people often misbehave or skip school. Or they may attend school but daydream or fail to participate. Armando would sit quietly at his desk and attempt to make sense of information written for someone from another context, and with another skillset. And still, he persevered.

In addition, Armando displayed some definite emotional strengths—loyal, friendly, well-principled, and quiet; he marched to his own drumbeat. This helped him avoid some dangerous situations. Unfortunately, it also made him somewhat invisible at home and at school. Therefore, it behooved him to find his voice and place in a system filled with large needs that could overtake the attention of interested but overstretched staff. Relational-cultural theory (RCT) is a developmental theory that speaks to the need for voice, and the role that connection can play in fostering growth (Duffey, 2007; Jordan, 2001). Participating in the PMP afforded Armando an opportunity to identify his voice and deepen connections with faculty, counselors, and peers. Through the program, he took part in individual counseling and group activities designed to promote relational health and resiliency.

RELATIONAL CONSIDERATIONS

By understanding the relational dynamics within a culture, we can better understand a person's relational complexities. Understanding Armando's landscape supported my understanding of his experiences. For example, Armando's large and extended family focused on loyalty. They prized family connection, which played a central part in family life. School life had its challenges, as well as its systems of support. Friendly with his peers, Armando experienced little competition among groups. The largest threat to his relationships and his ability to enjoy them involved the sometimes seductive nature of family feuds and gang violence that permeated his world.

Children in Armando's circle occasionally faced vulnerabilities in situations they did not create or wish to be a part of. To use RCT as a model, adolescents in Armando's position could value connection while also employing any number of disconnecting strategies (Jordan, 2001). That is, although adolescents like Armando may want to enjoy connection with others, they may find their sense of belonging by using destructive group behaviors, such as bullying, and violence. These often falsely empower people to use an "us against them" way of being in the world. Thankfully, Armando did not choose this path of belonging, and our work involved helping him navigate productive avenues that could yield the greatest profit for this gentle spirit living in an ungentle world.

MULTICULTURAL CONSIDERATIONS

The third oldest child in a family of 13 children, Armando lived with his parents and siblings in a small home close to the school. His parents worked as migrant farmers and traveled north, with children in tow, during part of the year to work in the fields. Through the years, Armando often began the school year later than some of his peers and left for work before the semester ended. Armando had a small cohort of peers who followed a similar school schedule and faced similar challenges. These challenges involved socioeconomic, educational, and cultural factors. The high side of Armando's cultural background involved the close-knit Hispanic family life that many people in his daily life enjoyed. Children grew up with extended family and neighborhood matriarchs who looked out for the young and invested politically to bring positive change to a challenging environment. The down side of Armando's neighborhood's culture, however, involved drugs, gang violence, family feuds, and occasional break-ins and burglaries.

While these challenges permeated Armando's world, he came to school with a focus on learning, getting along with his peers, and doing well in school. When several of his brothers struggled to different degrees with gang-related activities, these naturally affected Armando. During those times he became quiet, attempted to talk about his situation, and sought help. This is how I (Thelma) first learned about Armando and his world; in knowing him, I gained a deeper understanding of myself.

I learned that Armando loved his family, felt shame and sorrow about some of his siblings' experiences, and wanted a positive future. I also learned that even well-meaning systems can become so large that the child who does not present special challenges can be overlooked and become vulnerable to environmental risks, such as violence. Finally, I learned that there is great fulfillment in working with adolescents like Armando—through advocacy, creativity, and relationship. These are lessons that helped us work through some of the developmental, multicultural, relational, and systemic challenges that arose during our time together.

Infusion of Creativity

Think for a minute about the excitement that young boys and girls living in a somewhat insulated environment might feel as they load a bus from their school and take a tour downtown. Accompanied by their program counselors and volunteer faculty and staff, the bus embarks at a big building where they meet up with a coordinated staff at the YMCA who greets the bus with popular music that could make almost anyone cheer. Armando's school district offered this creative activity to students through the PMP—an activity that inspired the way I (Thelma) ultimately worked with Armando and his peers in our individual and group work. Music is a universal language for many people of any age, and for adolescents, this is even more the case.

Armando and his peers entered the "Y" auditorium where they learned more about the "Exercise to Music" project designed for the PMP group, where students from throughout the school district lined up and exercised to their favorite music. They enjoyed the energy, attention, and bonding that activities like these can provide. I did notice that

Armando initially stood back and observed the large group. However, he soon jumped in and joined in what proved to be an outstanding intervention.

The "Exercise to Music" activity inspired Armando to find energy in exercise, to feel fellowship with others, and to find the "fun" in participating in something productive. Music provided a contagious and connecting factor, and the kind delivery of information from the YMCA staff made it more so. I left the YMCA inspired to discuss other ongoing group activities with the school principal. These also inspired me to use music as a counseling intervention in our individual counseling sessions.

CONCEPTUALIZATION

In working with children and adolescents like Armando, it is important to consider ways of empowering them, while also providing a structure of support, psychoeducation, and opportunities for peer involvement using their creativity and imaginations. I conceptualized Armando's situation as that of a young boy developmentally sandwiched between two worlds—the world of the child, where there is a semblance of safety and security, and the more adult world that many students in Armando's school district experienced following junior high school. I considered some of the challenges that Armando faced, such as the language, academic, and environmental factors, but also focused on using Armando's strengths and the creative outlets available to us when conceptualizing ways to work through some of them. Knowing Armando's love for music, and appreciating the value of storytelling in counseling, I invited Armando to share his experiences and identify future goals by using popular music to tell his story.

COUNSELING PROCESS FLOW

Music as a Counseling Tool

Armando responded powerfully to the YMCA's "Exercise to Music" experience. I learned there that music not only motivated Armando to become engaged with others, it also inspired a sense of joy within him. It provided him with an opportunity to "feel" the music, to use it to express himself, and to help him connect with his experiences.

I used Armando's love for drawing as part of our process by inviting him to draw comic strip figures to tell his stories, and subsequently added music to the comic strips. We wondered, "If this strip had a song to go along with it, what would it be?" Armando enjoyed finding just the right song to punctuate his art and narrative. Knowing that Armando thrived when using his creativity, I also employed an intervention I later referred to as "A Musical Chronology and the Emerging Life Song," which gave him a structure to share his story and process his feelings. It gave me an opportunity to take his emotional pulse, and it gave the two of us a creative forum to set our counseling goals (Duffey, 2005).

A Musical Chronology and the Emerging Life Song

This intervention is based on the idea that many people can listen to a song on the radio or on television and become instantly reconnected to a memory or experience. Music has a way of connecting people to memories and invoking a mood that reflects these memories. Given the challenges that people can have expressing themselves in counseling, and the sometimes inadequate nature of sharing words, music can be an ideal catalyst in counseling.

Simply put, A Musical Chronology involves four steps (Duffey, 2005):

- Step 1: Clients reflect on and compile a song list of music that helps them share memories.
- Step 2: Clients use the music to process their memories of important life events.
- Step 3: Clients identify a song or songs that reflect their current thoughts, feelings, and beliefs. This serves as their emotional baseline.
- Step 4: Clients select a song that conveys their hopes for the future, which represents their desired counseling goals.

The rock bands KISS and AC/DC influenced Armando's storytelling and served as mood-setters for our work. With the music in the background, Armando spoke excitedly about something funny his brothers did, and then showed a glint of sorrow because he missed them. He shared tales of family fun, loneliness and isolation, and, sometimes, hopelessness. Sometimes, he talked about how he wanted to grow up and have a good job and a family. Armando's music helped give words to his hopes and punctuate his stressors and frustrations. Eventually, I began using this process in a group format, and found that the sharing of music helped Armando and other students normalize their experiences with one another and discover points of connection in their experiences.

OUTCOME

Life continued in its usual way for Armando and many of his peers. While weekends continued to offer backyard barbecues and family get-togethers, day-to-day life also brought occasional situations involving gang violence and other hurtful and often traumatic stressors. Armando, however, displayed a form of resilience in the face of those pressures that kept him from engaging in destructive relationships and supported him during difficult times. During these times, Armando would enter my room with few words to express himself, and we would use some form of creativity, such as art or music, to help him begin. Once he began, Armando had much to share. Much like my connection with the other cohort members, Armando and I shared a strong alliance. This naturally supported us in our work. It also presented some challenges. I felt a strong need to "make things better." Part of my own process involved doing all I could to lend support and advocate for Armando and the other children I worked with, while accepting the limitations of my role and range of influence. I did what I could, and then worked to accept the things that were not mine to influence.

When Armando described his frustrations with reading, and his desire to succeed, I often consulted with his teachers on ways to use his motivation and creativity in the classroom. And when he described feeling sad for his parents, who loved him and his siblings very much but could not easily manage the circumstances they experienced as a family with the court system, we talked about what a strength it is to have the love of family—and how powerful a parent's love can actually be. We also talked about how confusing it can feel for a child whose family experiences violence—and love—and loyalty. And we would reflect on how helpless it can sometimes feel for the child who wants everyone to get along and be happy. This characterized Armando's experience, and accepting the limitations of his own range of influence, while also connecting to the power of his potential for transcendence and a happy life—his ultimate challenge.

I worked with Armando on an "as needed" basis following the PMP for the year, in what I can only describe as a most fulfilling experience. Although sometimes tentative, he sought help, tried to state his needs, and made himself open to feedback from his support system and from me.

Armando successfully moved into the ninth grade and entered high school. I, too, made a major move that year to a new town for family reasons. It is amazing what an impact children and adolescents can have on our lives. I missed Armando and his peers deeply. I thought about them often, and always wished them well. Years later, much to my surprise and excitement, I heard from Armando on social media. Life continued to present some challenges for him, but he found ways to work with them. Gainfully employed and married with children, Armando lived out his childhood dream. As counselors and educators, we are not always privy to the later lives of the children and adolescents we are privileged to work with, and I considered myself very fortunate to receive this update from this young man. Armando continued to be a gentle spirit—and from what I could tell, transitioned into quite the role model by assuming a new role and becoming his own son's "gentle giant."

REFERENCES

Duffey, T. (2005). A musical chronology and the emerging life song. *Journal of Creativity in Mental Health, 1,* 141–147. doi:10.1300/J456v01n01_09

Duffey, T. (2007). Promoting relational competencies in counselor education through creativity and relational-cultural theory. *Journal of Creativity in Mental Health, 2*(1), 47–59. doi:10.1300/J456v02n01_05

Jordan, J. V. (2001). A relational-cultural model: Healing through mutual empathy. *Bulletin of the Menninger Clinic, 65*(1), 92–103. http://dx.doi.org.libweb.lib.utsa.edu/abs101521bumc6519218707

CHAPTER 21

GROWING UP LILY

Donna A. Tonrey

My approach to counseling is typically grounded in a systemic perspective and I use a directive approach, especially when family issues are involved. However, in this particular case, I believed it best to use an individual, nondirective approach: Carl Rogers's client-centered therapy (Rogers, 2003). I planned to be nondirective, practice empathy, reflect and clarify, and set the stage for the client to find a solution for her problems. I begin with this explanation to illustrate that I chose an approach different from my customary method to best meet the interests of my client. The dynamic between the client and her mother, as well as my meeting with the mother individually, influenced my decision to make a suitable adjustment in approach. I believe this adjustment significantly impacted the outcome.

Lily is a 15-year-old Caucasian female from a middle-income family. Her parents are divorced and she has one sibling, a 17-year-old sister. The family identifies with the dominant culture of the United States. They are Protestant, although not religiously active. Lily presented as well-groomed and with appropriate affect. She appeared to be in good physical health and had never been in counseling. Lily's mother reported that Lily met all developmental milestones in the normal time frames.

SYSTEMIC INFLUENCES

I often invite parents to join in on part of a session, and occasionally an entire session. This is consistent with my desire to approach family situations systemically. However, Lily's mother communicated her lack of interest in joining in on any of the sessions, noting the counseling was solely for Lily. Since Lily appeared open to working individually in sessions, I chose to counsel her using a client-centered approach. Even when working with clients individually, counselors can often look at the client's situation systemically. As a result, we conceptualized her situation by looking at the family dynamics.

DEVELOPMENTAL CONSIDERATIONS

At 15, Lily possessed the characteristics inherent to Piaget's formal operational stage of cognitive development. Most individuals in this stage understand the concept of cause and effect, use logic to solve day-to-day problems, and can present a reasonable argument (Vernon, 2009). Lily willingly came into counseling at the suggestion of her mother, who stated that Lily needed to address her feelings regarding her parents' recent divorce following an 18-year marriage. Additionally, Lily's mother reported that Lily did not work hard enough at her schoolwork, given her low grades. She also reported Lily's poor attitude at home. Mother defined the poor attitude as Lily being verbally disrespectful and unwilling to talk with her regarding the divorce.

RELATIONAL CONSIDERATIONS

The therapeutic challenge consisted of helping Lily process the difficult feelings she experienced toward her mother, and remain connected, or loyal, to their relationship. Since her mother showed no interest in being a part of the therapeutic process, I endeavored to help Lily learn ways of being disloyal to the dysfunction rather than to the relationship. I provided Lily with the opportunity to reflect on and process her thoughts and feelings in a safe therapeutic environment. This would also help her learn to address her mother in a manner that would not lead to the typical arguments.

Lily hoped her mother would join in on the sessions, but accepted that she chose not to. She shared no interest in her father joining in on any sessions. Part of Lily's work involved understanding her parents as human beings, imperfect but deserving of respect, and herself as a child without the power to change them or their behavior. Instead, Lily's work involved learning how to manage her thoughts, feelings, and behaviors, and to see that others also wrestle with their own thoughts, feelings, and concerns. Although her parents did not show emotional availability in ways she would like, Lily's work involved seeing and accepting the ways in which they met and did not meet her emotional needs. It also involved learning to act in her best interests and manage her own mental health needs. Given that people learn to act in these ways in relationship with others, I wanted to provide Lily with a therapeutic relationship that supported her growth and maturity. By doing so, Lily could learn to trust herself as she experienced another person as trustworthy in relation to her.

Lily attended counseling weekly for about a year, and then every other week for another year. After that time, she participated in monthly sessions. Together, we focused on Lily taking responsibility for her thoughts and feelings, and acting on them in an appropriate manner, regardless of how she perceived the behaviors of those around her. This exercise often required considerable effort.

Lily talked openly about family issues. She reflected on her own experiences and enjoyed being heard and understood. She addressed issues with great insight. As an example, Lily reflected on her thoughts and feelings regarding her mother's materialism. Lily shared that her mother may be using the boyfriend for financial security. After taking a closer look, Lily understood that her mother spent many years being insecure financially. Lily's father would spend most of his weekends at the bar, spending money that their family needed for essentials. Both of Lily's parents worked; however, together they did not earn enough to cover her father's drinking binges. Once Lily began to understand some of her mother's possible insecurities and reality, she separated these from their relationship, which allowed Lily to engage with her mother in a respectful manner. Over time, Lily developed the ability to look for some of the positive interactions between her mother and her boyfriend, which helped Lily gain some objectivity toward that relationship.

As Lily developed a better relationship with her mother, other issues emerged. Lily met a boy with family issues, and she felt confident she could help him because her life continued to improve. This became very complicated. I personally knew this boy and his issues. I am a clinical supervisor, and I supervised the therapist working with this boy in counseling. What Lily presented in session resonated with his counselor's report. This boy actively used drugs, was sexually promiscuous, and was considered by the system to be ungovernable. I knew that I needed to maintain empathetic understanding with Lily, preserve confidentially regarding this boy's situation, and remain congruent in facilitating the therapeutic work. These are the complexities that can arise for supervisors working in small communities, and it is our job to handle each case ethically.

Goals and Targets for Client Change

I assisted Lily in examining her feelings toward this boy. She exhibited enough insight to recognize that he struggled significantly, and in meaningfully larger ways than anything she dealt with in her family. It was important that I protect our trust, knowing that if I lost her trust and she left counseling, this could end destructively. She seemed naïve with regard to her confidence that she could solve this boy's problems.

In the next session, Lily informed me that she had sex with this boy, also 15 years old. We explored her feelings about having sex; she processed it and examined what she thought and felt. She realized that he coerced her into the decision, and that she did not feel ready for a sexual relationship. At this point, I felt relieved for Lily and hopeful about her progress in counseling. Lily began to recognize the importance of acting in her own best interests. She also recognized that this boy's issues seeped into her world and created difficulties for her. We processed through this dilemma for several sessions. I wanted to offer Lily a safe therapeutic environment, while being reflective, displaying empathic understanding, and accepting Lily without judgment.

Lily's relationship with her mother improved. She consciously behaved more respectfully, became more accepting of her mother's boyfriend, and began to establish a relationship with him. Her schoolwork, however, showed no improvement. Once she decided she would no longer see the boy, and her home life improved, Lily began to examine her schoolwork. Simply said, she lacked interest in any of the subjects and could not see any use for the work. She expressed no interest in going to college. No one in her family completed a college education, and she knew she would not be the first. She resolved to withdraw from school. Once Lily turned 16 years old, she was convinced that her mother would sign off on the paperwork for her to withdraw, she seemed inspired. This created a dilemma for me: I did not want to offer my opinion, and yet, I felt confident that her leaving school would be a bad decision. How could I continue to be nondirective, offer Lily empathetic understanding and clarification, protect the therapeutic relationship, and encourage her to look at the serious consequences of withdrawing from school?

MULTICULTURAL CONSIDERATIONS

Although my cultural background looked similar to Lily's, our family cultures varied in that I was raised with, and continued to hold, a high regard for education. I needed to be sure that my bias did not cloud the discussion with Lily about her desire to quit school. I assisted Lily as she developed her own opinion on this decision. I asked her to, just for the moment, envision herself as 38 years old with a 16-year-old daughter. I encouraged her to think about what that might look like: Where are they living? What is the home like? Is she married, and, if so, is the father involved in parenting? Lily pictured life as a 38-year-old woman. I then asked her to imagine that her 16-year-old daughter came home and informed her that she wanted to quit school. Lily looked directly at me and immediately said, "That is not fair." I asked her what she meant. "Of course I would want my daughter to graduate from high school," she said. "Oh," I said. "That is interesting. You would want it for your daughter, but not for yourself?" Lily got the point, but she could not commit to staying in school. She did commit to continuing the conversation, and we did so over the next year. The conversation continued and the decision remained hers.

CONCEPTUALIZATION

Lily came into counseling because she did not get along with her mother, and she also harbored anger toward her father, who drank heavily. She stated her mother's materialism annoyed her. Her mother recently began a new relationship with a wealthy man, and Lily thought her mother dated him solely based on his wealth. Lily expressed no desire for her parents to get back together, and she wanted her home life to be "normal" where everyone "got along" without fighting or drinking. Now, her mother expected her to adjust to this new man in their lives, when she simply wanted the family to consist of her mother, her sister, and herself, at least for a while. I felt for her, as no one allowed her time to process the divorce before her mother introduced a new boyfriend.

COUNSELING PROCESS FLOW

In between the time Lily tried to save the boy she met and contemplated quitting high school, she presented another serious situation. In one of our sessions, Lily informed me that she used cocaine; I felt nothing short of shock. I knew she met some new kids and ran with them. Lily expressed some concern about their drinking because she did not drink. She continued to be angry about her father's drinking, and regardless of whether her friends drank, she did not participate. Lily clearly did not equate using drugs to drinking alcohol. I decided to review the restrictions on confidentiality with her, and told her that if she indicated that she would hurt herself or others, I could not keep that confidential. Lily immediately asked if I planned to tell her mother.

I told her I did not know. If she continued the drug use, then yes, I would inform her mother. Lily then talked about what occurred when she used cocaine with her friends, saying, "It just happened." She also stated that she did not intend to "try it" again.

What a difficult situation. Lily approached her last semester of high school. She struggled to remain in school, and she abused cocaine. I remained confident that Lily trusted the therapeutic relationship and the counseling process. However, I also did not want to be naïve, and wanted to ensure I did not miss a blind spot.

Lily understood that if I thought she used cocaine again, I would inform her mother. I began each session by asking if she used any drugs, and she consistently reported she did not. Our work continued with Lily processing the various areas of her life: her feelings about school; her improving relationship with her mother and her mother's boyfriend; and her connection with her sister. Lily still did not visit her father on a regular basis. She would see him on holidays, and he would get drunk every time. Given the situation, I saw no reason for us to work on developing a relationship with him beyond what existed. At the time, she reported he became inebriated whenever she spent time with him.

Lily showed signs of progress in counseling. However, in our next session she informed me she used cocaine again. Although I did not feel Lily's behavior warranted a diagnosis of substance use disorder, the fact that her father appeared to be suffering from alcoholism increased her risk of such issues. We previously discussed this, and yet she used cocaine again. I reminded her of our deal; I would need to tell her mother. At this point, Lily pleaded with me not to tell. Given my concerns for her safety, I could not agree to this. I asked her to explain the circumstances and her reasoning for trying cocaine again. She explained that recently she went out with her friends, saw everyone using cocaine, and decided to try it again. Immediately afterward, she thought about being a 38-year-old mother with a 16-year-old daughter. She thought to herself, "I can't do this again."

I agreed to wait before informing her mother until I consulted with a colleague. I explained that her best interests and safety came first. Although I believed she meant what she said, I lacked information to make a decision. I told her that once I consulted with a colleague, I would make my decision.

Goals and Strategies for Myself

I met with a colleague and we reviewed the case information. My colleague asked my thoughts regarding the best course of action. I felt conflicted. If I made the wrong decision, I could potentially damage all the progress Lily made, and interfere with any future progress. With the help of the colleague, I decided I would not inform Lily's mother. However, I also made a commitment to myself that if Lily used cocaine again, then I would inform her mother, knowing that not keeping my word could damage our work.

Lily appeared to be feeling some trepidation as she entered our next session. I explained my concerns about her using cocaine, and my lack of trust that she would refrain from using again. I relayed that I met with my colleague, as I said I would. Lily responded by saying she broke off all ties with that group of friends and did not intend to see them again. She further stated that she understood if I felt compelled to tell her mother. However, she asked if I could extend her some time to build our trust and prove that she meant what she said. I agreed again, with the same condition, that we would begin each session with a check-in.

For the next 6 months, I began each session with check-in questions, and Lily did not report using again. She talked about social activities with her old friends, and she started dating someone who respected her. Lily spent a good amount of time with her best friend, and they often planned fun activities. I had no reason to doubt Lily. As we approached our final sessions, Lily continued to come into counseling prepared to discuss her thoughts and feelings regarding her life.

OUTCOME

Lily was an exceptional adolescent. At 15 years of age, she learned to take responsibility for her own thoughts, feelings, and actions. Lily did not want to become a parentified child, and she did not attempt to be in charge of her mother or the family system. Instead, Lily saw the family more objectively. She could own that she wished her family operated like other families, yet she accepted it. At the end of each session, I gave Lily a suggestion of what to reflect on given our discussion, and she completed the task every time. She never hesitated to ask questions. She recognized her growth and embraced it, knowing it meant she had to be responsible for herself. Lily also recognized that her father needed help, but lacked willingness. Lily resolved her anger toward him; however, she would not continue to be exposed to his drinking. Lily also accepted her mother as a good person, a good caretaker, and that she loved Lily. Lily accepted it for what it was, and understood that she received her mother's best efforts.

Lily graduated from high school with a modest grade point average and took pride in herself for doing so. When I began our work together, I reflected on how I wanted to help this young lady mature, remain connected to her mother, release the anger associated with her father, avoid trouble and bad decisions, and graduate high school. I attempted to provide Lily with a trusting environment in which she could explore her thoughts, feelings, actions, and decisions without feeling judgment or disapproval, and she possessed the motivation to do so.

Two years after Lily's counseling ended, she left a voice mail message stating that I would never believe the reason for her call. Lily enrolled in a real estate course and contemplated seeking a license. She said, "Can you believe it? I am enrolling in a class to learn something new. I just had to let you know, because I never thought I would be calling you to let you know that I was taking a course, and here I am." Lily giggled throughout the entire message. She appeared to be very proud of her decision and she wanted to share it with me.

REFERENCES

Rogers, C. (2003). *Client-therapy: Its current practice, implications, and theory.* London, UK: Constable.

Vernon, A. (2009). *Counseling children & adolescents* (4th ed.). Denver, CO: Love Publishers.

CHAPTER 22

LABELS LIMIT AND RELATIONSHIPS HEAL

Tammy L. Wilborn

As a professional counselor, I have worked with diverse clients ranging in age, development, identity, therapeutic needs, and clinical settings. I have learned how incredibly powerful it is to sit across from clients and listen to their stories. These stories are as diverse in meaning as the clients themselves. Ultimately, clients' stories seem to reflect common existential dilemmas: Am I good enough? Does who I am and what I say matter? And if and when I tell you my story, can you help me? As a counselor educator and supervisor, I use stories as instructional tools to bring counseling to life in the classroom and facilitate understanding of practical counseling implications. As a qualitative researcher, I recognize the importance of voice, and therefore I believe stories are necessary tools for meaning-making and knowledge construction (Creswell, 2013; Moustakas, 1994).

The story of my clinical experience with Chris, a 15-year-old White male youth in a residential facility, is one that I have shared with many of my students. The case of Chris will reflect a counseling philosophy that contends when counselors *show up* for their clients and serve responsibly, they can facilitate conditions for clients to grow, heal, and ultimately change.

I first met Chris in 2004. He lived in the cottage where I worked as a residential counselor serving male youth, ages 14 to 18. The residential program was part of a large nonprofit agency that provided a continuum of care (i.e., adoption, foster care, group home, residential, hardware-secured residential, and transitional living) for male and female youth with emotional, psychological, and behavioral disturbances. As a residential counselor, I was a member of a multidisciplinary treatment team that included the youth, direct care staff, caregivers, psychiatrists, nurses, recreational therapists, educational staff, and state custodians. As a relatively new counselor, this was a wonderful environment to work in because I gained multiple perspectives that helped me facilitate both the process and content aspects in my counseling sessions.

I mentioned earlier that the program I worked in was a residential program that was part of a continuum of care. The treatment team regularly conferred about children transitioning through programs to identify concerns and other relevant details. Chris transferred from the program's hardware-secured residential facility to my cottage, which was a lower level 24-hour supervised residential program. Prior to Chris's transition, I met with Dr. Amos to discuss Chris. Dr. Amos was a Black female psychiatrist who worked as a full-time psychiatrist, authorizing the medical orders for admission into the residential programs, and providing ongoing medication management for the youth. To me, her role was powerful and influential. I respected Dr. Amos because she was a Black female doctor and she had power. She was *smart, kind,* and *important*. But, I also respected Dr. Amos because she respected my role as a counselor. She supported the work I did and encouraged me when I felt hopeless to make any real difference with young clients who had many challenges that seemed to work against them intrapersonally, interpersonally, and institutionally.

On this day, we greeted each other with our usual greeting and started our small talk as we had come to do many times before. After a few minutes, I noticed the familiar pattern of changes in Dr. Amos's tone and facial expression that usually indicated we needed to *get back to business*. "You know you're getting a new resident this week from level 4, right?" she asked. "Yes, we've been talking about him in our meetings," I replied. She said, "Tammy, I'm going to be honest with you. This kid Chris is pretty scary. He's got severe depression and substance abuse issues with a history of repeated suicide attempts. Read his chart. He's made some progress and is ready to step down to level 3 to your cottage. . . . " As I listened to Dr. Amos, it seemed that Chris did sound pretty scary, but he was not atypical of the youth with whom I usually counseled. After all, residents lived at the center because they demonstrated high-risk behaviors that warranted 24-hour supervised residential care. Chris sounded pretty normal at this point. "Tammy, the bottom line is this: Chris is either going to be a serial killer or he's not. The difference will depend on you." What? With my new degree in hand, I was fully equipped to *save* the world. I was not, however, prepared to fix a serial killer. "Dr. Amos, why me?" She said, "Because you can do it."

SYSTEMIC INFLUENCES

The Family System

Chris's maternal and paternal family background indicated a history of mental illness. Family members believed Chris's estranged father suffered from schizophrenia, which contributed to his absence for significant portions of Chris's life. These absences left Chris in the frequent care of his paternal grandmother. Chris's mother experienced chronic bouts of depression and reportedly had an extensive legal history. Reports indicated that Chris's mother had a history of child protective services (CPS) allegations of child neglect and abuse. Additionally, the State terminated Chris's mother's parental rights and awarded guardianship to the paternal grandmother. At the time of my work with Chris, his mother was incarcerated for a double murder charge. This information characterized some of the family-of-origin factors that contributed to the pervasive problems facing Chris.

The Peer System

At the peer level, it was clear that the few friends that Chris did have were not prosocial influences. These negative peer influences supported Chris's substance use. I read reports that Chris and his friends abused a variety of illicit drugs, with marijuana being his drug of choice. He and his friends also used over-the-counter medications such as cough syrup and pain relievers to get high.

The School System

In school, Chris's infrequent attendance impaired his academic performance and he failed several grades. Chris's behavior was another challenge for him in school. He had many disciplinary actions for defiance and disrespect. His last *offense* at school led to expulsion. He brought a bird's head (that he cut off) in a jar and placed it in the teachers' lounge. Later exploration of this event would yield his belief that he *"was helping"* these animals by killing them to end their *suffering*. My conceptualization of these various factors helped me to see that my work focused not on fixing a serial killer but restoring hope for this young boy.

DEVELOPMENTAL CONSIDERATIONS

Early traumas and a family history of mental illness led to Chris experiencing multiple treatment episodes. Chris had an extensive history of inpatient and outpatient treatment for depression, substance use, suicide ideation, and animal cruelty. Additional details regarding attainment of early developmental milestones were unavailable.

RELATIONAL CONSIDERATIONS

Childhood traumatic experiences affected Chris's ability to establish and maintain healthy relationships, which was evident both in his personal relationships and the therapeutic relationship. Chris had limited social interaction with others and was essentially socially withdrawn. He also appeared unfulfilled and hopeless about his life. This hopelessness fueled chronic depressive episodes and multiple suicide attempts. During his last suicide attempt, he set himself on fire. This led to an acute psychiatric hospitalization and ultimately residential treatment where I became his counselor. The impact of early childhood traumatic experiences was evident in his ability to establish a connection with me in counseling. He appeared guarded, withdrawn, and mistrustful—characteristics commonly associated with children who experience trauma (Cohen, Mannarino, & Deblinger, 2006).

MULTICULTURAL CONSIDERATIONS

After weeks of sessions, I could not seem to find a way to connect with Chris. I met with Dr. Amos once a month, who seemed satisfied with his response to the mood stabilizer she prescribed. She also recounted that he spoke little in their sessions as well, and encouraged me to keep trying. I conferred with my clinical supervisor twice a month to discuss my treatment plan and the challenges I had in sessions. She offered recommendations for new interventions, which met with little success. After weeks of limited progress, I wondered if there was something about me that blocked our progress. Specifically, I wondered if being a Black female counselor and working with him, a White male youth, was an issue. I decided to explore this cultural difference in session. I shared, "Chris, I've been meeting with you for several weeks and I still feel like we aren't connecting. Sometimes there might be things about the counselor that blocks the client from opening up. I'm wondering if a bit of that is in our relationship?" He asked, "What do you mean?" "Well, I'm wondering if the fact that I'm Black and female is an issue for you and the reason you're not talking in session?" He looked up and said, "No, not really." I waited to see if he would follow with anything more. He did not. I stated, "Chris, I noticed that you said not really. I recognize that the question can be a bit uncomfortable but if this is an issue for you, then we can talk about how we might still be able to work together." He looked up and said, "I've never worked with a Black counselor before, but you seem alright." And with that, he was done. The session ended. I was determined that there was a way in. A part of me knew that a part of him expected me to give up as others had before me. I wondered if he also hoped I would prove him wrong.

CONCEPTUALIZATION

One of my favorite professors, Peggy Ceballos, shared that, "We were all once babies." This statement reminded me that despite the fact that I will encounter challenging clients who may be difficult to understand, like, and ultimately help, I remember that these clients were babies at one time in their life. With this mantra in mind, I can empathize with and ultimately serve these clients, seeing the possibilities for hope in their lives and the counseling process. Taking a systems approach to conceptualize Chris's treatment needs highlighted how various systemic factors intersected in ways that created a trajectory of hopelessness, apathy, and self-destruction.

Goals and Targets for Client Change

From an existential perspective, the meaning that we attribute to circumstances influences our thinking and our behavior (Frankl, 1984; Moustakas, 1994; Yalom, 1980). Existential counselors facilitate clients' awareness that they are free and responsible to change the meaning they attribute to life. They help clients learn they are capable of choosing the life they want. From this perspective, anxiety is a function of clients' failure to exercise their freedom and often leads them to seek counseling.

One curative factor in work with children and adolescents who have experienced trauma is to challenge thinking errors that adversely impact meaning-making. For example, one goal of working with children with abuse histories (i.e., physical and sexual) is to challenge the belief that the abuse was their fault. Equally important, counselors help children see that despite the fact that they were not responsible for the abuse, they are in control of their current thoughts and behaviors, and can develop healthy skills to cope with trauma triggers. In practice, this framework aligned well with the clinical framework of the residential program. The residential program followed cognitive and behavioral modalities that emphasized understanding the function of the youths' behaviors and discovering the underlying cognitive distortions to facilitate change. In Chris's case, my goal was to figure out how to get Chris to stop and address the pervasive messages in his mind that "he did not matter" and ultimately that his "life was not worth living."

COUNSELING PROCESS FLOW

In our first session, we met in one of the counseling offices at the on-campus school. I took the short scenic walk down to the school to get fresh air and get mentally ready to meet with this prospective serial killer. I checked in with the front-desk receptionist and let her know that I needed to see the new resident, Chris. After a short time, Chris arrived, accompanied by the direct care school staff. I walked with Chris to one of the counseling rooms and encouraged him to sit in the chair away from the door. I had learned from working in residential to situate myself closest to the door in the event a client became verbally and physically abusive in session and I needed to escape. As I sat across from Chris for the first time, one thing was evident to me: He seemed to have the cold stare of a killer. I could see why Dr. Amos, someone whose professional opinion I trusted, would say something that seemed so negative about a client. Chris appeared frightening. He had poor hygiene. He made limited eye contact and rarely spoke. It became clear to me that he was not going to talk. So I did what many inexperienced counselors do. I filled the silence with my voice. I explained my role as his counselor as well as the counseling process. I explained that I would see him once a week for individual counseling, twice a week for group counseling, and once a month in family therapy. "I wanna go home," he said. "When am I gonna go home?" he asked. The answer to that question was a bit complicated. I knew he would eventually be discharged to his paternal grandmother's care, but I also knew she did not want him back anytime soon. "That, Chris, will depend on what you do in here," I said. He looked down and remained silent for the remainder of the session. We were done. We would continue in this pattern for weeks: me trying to engage Chris and Chris not talking or talking very little in session, and eventually repeating that he wanted to go home. I would remind him that his discharge depended on him.

I was concerned about not connecting with Chris, and the treatment team expressed concerns about Chris's behaviors in the cottage. Staff members reported that Chris withdrew more into himself. He was the target of ridicule from peers because he was new and he had poor hygiene. The staff expressed additional concerns about Chris because he carried around a notebook that contained graphic images of death and mutilation of women. They were alarmed that these images suggested imminent risk to me. I discussed with them that regardless of the content in his notebook, I respected his right to express himself.

Infusion of Creativity

One day, Chris showed up to session with his notebook, holding it like an anchor. I did my regular check-in to see whether there was anything he wanted to talk about and he said his usual no. I decided to focus on his notebook. I asked him what was in the notebook and he shared that it was just a book that he kept some "stuff" in. "Poems, drawings, I don't know—random stuff," he said. I asked if he felt comfortable sharing his notebook in session. He asked if I was sure. I assured him that I was. He reluctantly opened it and displayed a collage of magazine clippings of female body parts with blood and hate messages on or near the images. The images were definitely concerning to me. Rather than rejecting these images or shame Chris, I decided to get interested in his story. As Chris talked about the images, he began to open up. He shared that the images "probably" had something to do with his mom but he was not sure. We explored that metaphor, and as the session came to a close, I asked Chris if he could bring his notebook to the next session. He agreed and did. We talked some more about the contents. A few sessions later, he allowed me to take his notebook after I shared that I learned so much about him through his art and poetry, and I wanted to spend more time with his work. I hope this showed him that his voice mattered—he mattered. The following week I shared that his poem "Hans" significantly stood out to me and I wondered if we could discuss it. He shared that "Hans" was his favorite poem because he wrote it after his last suicide attempt. My window of opportunity had arrived.

Time-Efficient Methods

The theoretical foundation of the residential program followed a brief counseling model meant to stabilize residents within 3 to 6 months. However, the severity of the treatment issues also determined a client's length of stay. As such, Chris stayed in treatment for 10 months. Over the course of those 10 months, Chris literally came *alive*. He became more engaged and vulnerable in sessions, sharing with me how early experiences of abuse led to his feelings of worthlessness and apathy. I incorporated cognitive behavioral techniques to process how the abuse was not his fault, and that the depression and suicidal ideation seemed connected to internalized messages of worthlessness and hopelessness. When I explored if his suicide attempts were attempts to die or to escape pain, Chris acknowledged that he was tired of trying to unsuc-cessfully numb the pain with drugs. He wanted the pain to stop even if it meant taking his life. During the final months of his stay, Chris began to find a reason to live and his transformation was obvious. Outside of sessions, his hygiene improved and he even began to wear his hair back so that his face could be seen. He became the resident jokester and guitarist, and on any given evening could be found playing his guitar for the cottage residents. Chris's progress was also evident to his grand-mother, who eventually allowed him to come home for weekend passes. After several successful home passes, Chris went home to live with his grandmother.

OUTCOME

After approximately 2 years as a residential counselor, I needed a change so I transferred to a new position as a foster care counselor. I was at my desk one day when I received a phone call. It was Chris. "Hey Ms. Lewis, this is Chris. Do you remember me?" He had gotten my office number from a former staff member who worked at the cottage. "Of course I remember you Chris! How are you!" "I'm fine. I'm sitting on the porch watching the leaves fall." I knew what he meant. "Chris are you high?" He laughed. "Yeah, I told you that I would stop that other stuff, but I wasn't never giving up smoking weed." I chuckled as I distinctly recalled how emphatic he was in that session. "Yes Chris, I remember. If that's all you're doing, then you should be proud of yourself. You've come a long way." He shared that he was working and taking psychol-ogy courses at a community college. He continued, "Ms. Lewis—I'm calling to tell you thank you." "For what?" I asked. "Because I'm happy. You helped me to be happy." I thanked him and reminded him that he made the decision to live and then trusted me to be along for that part of his journey. He was not buying it. "Thank you Ms. Lewis. That's all I wanted to tell you." And he was gone.

I have often reflected on and shared my experience working with Chris throughout my career and now more recently as a counselor edu-cator. Chris's story in my opinion could be a story about how much I got it *wrong*, but it could also be about my persistence to get it *right*. For me, getting it right meant creating a therapeutic environment that con-veyed to this child that he mattered; that his life mattered, even if it only mattered to me. Chris's story reflected the beauty of counseling as a gift that counselors must use responsibly. We never know who we will end up *saving* on our journey *serving*.

REFERENCES

Cohen, J. A., Mannarino, A. P., & Deblinger, E. (2006). *Treating trauma and traumatic grief in children and adolescents*. New York, NY: Guilford Press.

Creswell, J. W. (2013). *Qualitative inquiry & research design: Choosing among the five approaches* (3rd ed.). Thousand Oaks, CA: Sage Publications.

Frankl, V. E. (1984). *Man's search for meaning: An introduction to logotherapy*. New York, NY: Simon & Schuster.

Moustakas, C. (1994). *Phenomenological research methods*. Thousand Oaks, CA: Sage Publications.

Yalom, I. D. (1980). *Existential psychotherapy*. New York, NY: Basic Books.

CHAPTER 23

BUCKING THE SYSTEM

Lisa L. Beijan

The client in this case study is Sarah, a Caucasian high school student from Fort Worth, Texas. Sarah started counseling at 17 years of age, the summer before her senior year. She lived with her biological parents in a middle-class neighborhood and attended public high school. Her one sibling, an older sister, attended college.

Sarah attended a highly ranked public high school where she took advanced placement courses and excelled as a student in the top 10 percent of her graduating class. An accomplished musician like her sister, Sarah performed in the school orchestra, where she held second chair. Sarah felt highly critical of her scholastic abilities despite doing well in advanced courses. Fearful of performing poorly in music and academics, she maintained unrealistic standards of perfectionism, and would become anxious when she perceived herself to fall short.

Sarah described her family as close-knit with minimal conflict and stated they shared a focus on education and achievement. Her father taught mathematics at a university, and her mother taught high school English. Sarah's sister attended a prestigious music school in New York on a scholarship. Sarah stated feeling supported and accepted by her family, but recognized pressure from them to do well in school and music, which I believe contributed to her feelings of anxiety.

SYSTEMIC INFLUENCES

Sarah attended a high school well known for its music program. This afforded Sarah many opportunities, but it also increased Sarah's pressure to consistently perform at a high level. Both her orchestra director and her private violin lesson instructor were respected in the music industry. They enjoyed a reputation for developing talented, high-achieving high school musicians who often received prestigious performance scholarships to highly ranked music schools. Sarah knew both her director and her violin instructor expected her to pursue professional performance. This created added pressure for Sarah, who became tired of the competitive pressures and doubted whether she wanted to pursue a career in such a high-pressure field. Sarah planned interviews and auditions at several schools recommended by her director and instructor. She also arranged interviews with two smaller and less prestigious schools.

DEVELOPMENTAL CONSIDERATIONS

Sarah came to counseling because of her anxiety about school, music, family, and relationships. Having just completed her junior year, Sarah faced significant developmental tasks and doubted she possessed the resources to adequately address them. Erikson (1968) described the psychosocial crisis of adolescence as ego identity versus role confusion. This is a time when the adolescent explores possibilities to form his or her identity. As a person prone to pleasing others, Sarah struggled to build a unique identity. Sarah's mom, nervous about her impending empty nest, complicated matters. Sarah and her mom experienced conflict over the same issues—violin practice time, getting up in the morning, and completing chores.

RELATIONAL CONSIDERATIONS

Sarah would become defensive or refuse to engage with her mother during these conflicts. Sarah's mom contributed money toward Sarah's private music lessons, competition fees, and travel expenses, and felt she could reasonably expect Sarah to "do her part" by practicing when she requested. This caused Sarah frustration because she thought her mother's expectations of practice time depended on how much time her sister practiced, and Sarah saw this as an unfair comparison.

Sarah's primary social relationship, her boyfriend of 1 year, recently left to attend college out of state. She spent time with three close friends at school, and did not feel a need for a large group of friends. Yet, Sarah said she felt dissatisfied with the quality of her friendships, often feeling misunderstood. She placed a high value on the opinions of others and developed a hyperawareness of how others viewed her, making it difficult for her to relax and be present in social situations.

Based on my initial interactions with Sarah, she appeared to be an introvert with adequate social skills. Her hyperawareness of others' opinions of her, her avoidance of criticism, her unrealistic expectations of herself, and her fear of not performing well contributed to an almost constant state of anxiety. Sarah's fear of making mistakes and disappointing authority figures made it difficult for her to make decisions. Sarah's increased awareness of the discrepancy between her own goals and the goals others had for her added to this fear. She wanted to please everyone around her, but grew tired of her perceived pressure to perform.

MULTICULTURAL CONSIDERATIONS

Sarah came from a White, well-educated middle-class family. Her cultural environment promoted a quest for achievement and encouraged success, status, and high performance. Sarah's own self-critical nature and the overachieving culture to which she belonged reinforced her anxiety.

CONCEPTUALIZATION

Goals and Targets for Client Change

Sarah and I developed our goals for her counseling process collaboratively. In working with adolescents, I believe it is important for the client to define the goals for counseling apart from the parents' concerns, so while we took her mom's feedback into consideration, we established goals based on Sarah's most important concerns. Our initial goals included:

1. Learning cognitive and behavioral coping strategies to help manage symptoms of anxiety
2. Improving communication with her mom about Sarah's need to have thoughts and feelings of her own
3. Developing appropriate assertiveness
4. Learning cognitive skills to manage unrealistic self-expectations

Goals and Strategies for Myself

Developmental Perspective

I set goals for myself as Sarah's counselor. One of my challenges in working with adolescents is allowing time to build the relationship. Parents want fast results, and I want my client to experience symptom relief as soon as possible, but trust building with adolescents can be a slow process. Teenagers often see adults as evaluative or instructing, and they expect new adults they meet to fit into those expected roles. My initial goal included the development of a different type of relationship where Sarah felt affirmed instead of corrected. I sought to provide this experience as early in the therapeutic process as possible.

Cognitive Perspective

My other goal at the onset of counseling consisted of effectively adapting cognitive behavioral strategies to Sarah's individual developmental level. One of my areas of interest is neurobiology, which has important applications when understanding the cognitive development of adolescence. The teenage brain is constantly "under construction," with bursts of new neural production resulting in a dramatic increase in neural connections, followed by periods of neural "pruning" when those connections are decreased for improved efficiency (Siegal, 2013). The most change occurs in the prefrontal cortex, the area of the brain responsible for decision making, planning, problem solving, and understanding consequences. This constant neural construction and revision means that the adolescent prefrontal cortex is easily overwhelmed in the face of problem solving, decision making, and stress management (Badenoch, 2008). A task that may seem simple to an adult can feel impossible to a teenager with constantly changing neural connections. Keeping this in mind, I wanted to challenge Sarah without overwhelming her with skills beyond her reach. By embracing and honoring Sarah's adolescent brain development, I became better able to support her and help her develop the new skills she needed (Siegel, 2013).

COUNSELING PROCESS FLOW

For the sake of brevity, some of the topics discussed in counseling sessions have been omitted. All session material relevant to the main themes of the counseling process are included.

Intake

Sarah and her mother attended the initial counseling intake session. Sarah experienced increasing amounts of fearfulness and anxiety and requested counseling. Her parents supported Sarah attending counseling, and Sarah's mother agreed to participate in whatever way would be most helpful for Sarah's treatment. Due to Sarah's minor status at the onset of services, the three of us discussed confidentiality to clarify expectations. Sarah and her mother both agreed to the confidentiality of Sarah's counseling (within the standard limitations to confidentiality). I told them an exception existed if Sarah's safety or immediate well-being were at risk. Sarah agreed to invite her mother to attend a family counseling session if necessary, and her mother agreed to attend sessions when doing so would be helpful.

Relational Considerations—General

Sarah's mom described Sarah as a perfectionist who had difficulty making mistakes or accepting criticism from others, yet she was hyperaware of pleasing the authority figures in her life. Sarah's mother described her as "ultrasensitive and defensive" at times, especially when responding to correction. Sarah's pattern of expressing a mix of denial, anger, and defensiveness or breaking down into tears and hurt feelings frustrated her mother.

Sarah spoke very little during the initial part of the intake session, and expressed feeling nervous about talking. She seemed to relax slightly following our discussion of confidentiality. Sarah shared that some of her defensiveness came from her frustration of being "micromanaged." Sarah and her mom's primary areas of disagreement revolved around violin practice time and morning time schedules. Despite Sarah's excellent grades and track record of responsible behavior, her mom still managed the details of Sarah's schedule. While this frustrated Sarah, she acknowledged a reluctance to give up the "perks" of her mother's help, such as having her mom make her lunch or drive her to school on the mornings she ran late. Sarah described feeling constant internal pressure to please others and perform well.

Sessions 1 to 10

Strategies for the Client

I met with Sarah for 23 sessions over a 12-month period. Two of the sessions included Sarah's mom—the intake session and one additional family session. I spent the first few sessions focused on building a relationship with Sarah and establishing a trusting therapeutic connection. During those sessions, Sarah shared about her feelings of pressure related to orchestra, especially when she felt she did not measure up to her director's expectations of her. Sarah and I worked on the basic cognitive behavioral skill of identifying feelings, thoughts, and beliefs around this issue. We did so to start the process of recognizing the maladaptive beliefs contributing to Sarah's anxiety (Beck & Weishaar, 2014).

Another issue Sarah addressed in her early sessions concerned her relationship with her mom. In spite of the summer vacation schedule, Sarah kept busy with orchestra activities, rehearsals, and mentoring, and she did not feel motivated to practice when she got home. Her mom grew increasingly frustrated because of the amount of money she paid for lessons, contest fees, and travel for auditions. They engaged in heated and defensive conflicts, and Sarah saw her mom pulling away from her and treating her in a passive-aggressive manner. I made behavioral suggestions, such as using a code word with her mom to let her know Sarah needed to take a break from an argument. We also practiced ways of communicating so she could address her concerns when she perceived her mom pulling away from her.

The fifth counseling session involved a joint session with Sarah and her mom. Sarah processed her frustration of feeling overly controlled by her mom, sometimes based on expectations coming from her mom's experience with Sarah's sister. Her mother discussed her need for Sarah to be accountable for practice time given the considerable financial costs. I reflected back what the other said to help them understand each other. I also used some psychoeducation to help Sarah care for more of her needs as she moved into adulthood. My goal consisted of encouraging her mother's willingness to allow Sarah to make mistakes and learn from them. I discussed Sarah's willingness to do her part by taking more ownership for her responsibilities. I also encouraged Sarah and her mom to shift from their current pattern of nagging and arguing to one of choices and consequences. Sarah's mom admitted she experienced difficulty in allowing Sarah to experience consequences when she felt she could protect Sarah from them.

Infusion of Creativity

Sarah continued to process the anxiety she experienced when multiple stresses started piling up in her life. We saw this clearly in session. Sarah got a speeding ticket, which made her late for class, and she lost a piece of her instrument. Since she actively experienced anxiety in our session, I took the opportunity to help Sarah practice some basic skills. We practiced paced breathing, a breathing exercise available as a phone app (Paced Breathing, 2015), to help Sarah calm her physiological symptoms of anxiety. I joined her by closing my eyes, got into a comfortable position in my chair, and exaggerated my breathing. This helped reduce her feelings of self-consciousness and the fear of looking "silly." Following the breathing exercise, I asked Sarah to use play dough to sculpt how she felt. These two activities helped Sarah feel calmer and less overwhelmed. The play dough gave her a visual picture of her experience. At this point in the session, we talked about the thoughts contributing to her anxiety, such as "This is horrible. I'm never going to catch up. Everyone is going to be mad at me." We also looked at Sarah's behaviors contributing to her stress—procrastination, not allowing enough travel time, rushing through cleaning and maintaining her violin, and avoidance. Sarah agreed she needed to be honest with her mom about her stress. In this way, she could ask for help.

Sessions 11 to 20

Relational Considerations—Authority Figures/ Systemic Influences—School

In Sessions 11 through 20, Sarah continued the process of choosing a college. She dealt with core issues of people pleasing, locus of control, and fear of failure. She processed her relationship with her private lessons instructor. Her interactions with her instructor shifted as we worked on reducing people pleasing and increasing assertive communication, and her instructor responded negatively to these changes. As long as Sarah would do what he wanted, they avoided conflict. As Sarah's feelings of freedom to disagree increased and her ability to voice her needs emerged, she saw a different side of her instructor's personality. He cancelled lessons and gave her minimal feedback. He spoke negatively about her to other students and stopped offering her opportunities for auditions and competitions. Sarah talked to other students and learned some of them experienced similar situations with this instructor. This resulted in a turning point for Sarah. She recognized his behavior did not concern her, and she lacked the power to fix it. She also realized he made mistakes and his opinion did not determine her choices.

The awareness Sarah developed about her instructor directly impacted her process of college interviews and auditions. She realized she planned most of her college visits to music schools with competitive performance programs; schools her instructors and music mentors wanted her to attend. As Sarah developed her ability to discern her own opinions, wants, and needs, she doubted her initial plan to pursue a performance degree. She lacked passion in that way. Although she felt passion for music, she disliked the intense competition of performance. Sarah started to consider attending smaller liberal arts schools with music education programs. I encouraged Sarah to "listen to her gut" during college visits and notice her experience of the campus as a whole. As she did this, Sarah realized she felt less anxious and more at ease at the smaller schools and could picture herself as a part of student life there. In contrast, she felt more anxiety at larger schools and did not see herself fitting in.

Relational Considerations—Boyfriend/Strategies for the Client

We addressed Sarah's relationship with her boyfriend next. He was a year older and becoming increasingly involved in friendships and activities at college. This made it harder to spend time with Sarah, triggering her feelings of insecurity. He missed several Skype dates due to his busy schedule and spent time with friends in his room when they did talk. Sarah expressed confusion about what to do because they did not speak clearly and directly to one another. We practiced these skills in session, role-playing different scenarios until Sarah gained confidence in her ability to use them with her boyfriend. She communicated her needs to her boyfriend, and thankfully he appeared receptive and willing to meet her needs. This introduced another turning point for Sarah because she realized not everyone would respond in the same negative manner as her private lessons instructor. Experiencing her boyfriend's positive response showed Sarah the impact of assertive communication in healthy relationships.

The next major issue Sarah and I addressed in counseling included choosing a college. A highly regarded music school offered her a substantial scholarship, and she knew other musicians would think she was crazy if she did not accept it. Her favorite small liberal arts college accepted her, and offered a partial scholarship and a work-study position. Sarah chose the smaller school, but avoided telling anyone. Her instructor and her director knew about the music school scholarship and assumed she would accept it. Sarah feared their reactions when they found out she turned it down. Rationally, she knew she could not avoid telling them indefinitely, but every time she tried to broach the topic she froze up. We addressed her fears in several sessions, working on identifying and modifying Sarah's inner dialog to reduce her sense of panic. We discussed the worst-case scenarios and role-played her responses, coming up with respectful replies for her teachers and mentors, while honoring her right to choose her own path. Eventually, Sarah told them about her decision, and she reported things went better than expected.

Termination Sessions

Sarah and I used our final three sessions to focus on her feelings about graduating, leaving home, and moving to college. She spent time in session processing her mixed emotions of excitement, fear, sadness, and anticipation. Sarah did not feel a need to continue counseling after she moved to college unless she became unable to manage her issues on her own. We talked about the specific warning signs she could look for to indicate a need for help, and how to go about finding a counselor if she needed one. In our final session, we summarized Sarah's growth during her counseling process and she identified areas she wanted to continue to work on—internal locus of control, assertive communication, realistic expectations of self, and not overvaluing the opinions of others.

OUTCOME

I consider my work with Sarah a success because she learned to value her own perspective and communicate her wants and needs effectively. She developed skills for managing anxiety, lessened her dependence on the opinions of others, and strengthened her internal locus of control. Sarah embraced most of the strategies I used in our sessions. The most effective strategy involved role-playing, because Sarah needed concrete interventions, and it helped her build confidence in her ability to implement what we practiced. Behavioral interventions like paced breathing also helped because of their simplicity and ease of use. Sarah found basic identification of thoughts and beliefs to be effective, but more advanced cognitive exploration exceeded Sarah's developmental level and she found it confusing. In hindsight, I wish I had used more expressive arts activities in my counseling with Sarah. At the time I worked with Sarah, I did not have as much expressive arts experience as I do now, and I can see how more of those types of activities may have helped Sarah conceptualize her struggles more completely. Considering Sarah's receptiveness to our work together, I expect her to do well in college. We experienced difficulty at the beginning of the counseling relationship due to Sarah's quiet nature and difficulty trusting. However, once we formed a connection, she opened up to doing the work of counseling, which made it rewarding for me.

REFERENCES

Badenoch, B. (2008). *Being a brain-wise therapist: A practical guide to interpersonal neurobiology.* New York, NY: W. W. Norton.

Beck, A. T., & Weishaar, M. E. (2014). Cognitive therapy. In D. Wedding & R. Maniacci (Eds.), *Current psychotherapies* (10th ed., pp. 231–261). Belmont, CA: Brooks/Cole.

Erikson, E. H. (1968). *Identity: Youth and crisis.* New York, NY: W. W. Norton.

Paced Breathing. (2015). Trex LLC (Version 2.1) [Mobile application software]. Retrieved from https://play.google.com/store/apps/details?id=com.apps.paced.breathing&hl=en

Siegel, D. J. (2013). *Brainstorm: The power and purpose of the teenage brain.* New York, NY: Penguin.

CHAPTER 24

KILLIAN'S KILLER LOVE AFFAIR

Norèal F. Armstrong

Killian, a 16-year-old male, attended a Texas high school. His older brother abused drugs, but tried to stay clean. After a physical altercation with their dad, his brother moved out of the house. I came to know Killian as his group counselor at an Intensive Outpatient Program (IOP) for substance abuse in Texas. Killian later joined my individual caseload. Killian displayed charisma, sarcasm, and honesty. He stood 5 ft. 5 in., 135 lbs., with dirty blonde hair that looked like a mix between the Shaggy character from Scooby-Doo and Justin Bieber around 2009. Killian enjoyed and related to rap music, missed his brother being home, ate a lot of snacks, and drank more coffee in a 2-hour period than most adults I knew. Killian appeared old for his age; old because of his experiences, not the years he lived. Killian's addiction to heroin gripped him tightly.

SYSTEMIC INFLUENCES

From a systemic perspective, I believed Killian's problem to be that he grew up in a family with a strong history of substance abuse. His family provided the basic need of shelter, but safety and belongingness lacked in the home. Killian shared stories about his dad and brother getting into arguments and things becoming physical between them. He reflected on a few instances while in treatment when his dad commented, "You should just come have a smoke with me." Many of Killian's school relationships revolved around drug use and did not provide any substantial support or insight into who he could be.

Combining this knowledge, I began to realize Killian failed to develop an identity outside of being a heroin addict. He lacked autonomy and self-awareness.

Differentiation within a family system allows for family connection without loss of individual autonomy (Walsh, 2016), and the Bowen model asserted that the degree of anxiety and differentiation in a family accounted for the variability in how a family functions (Walsh, 2013). When Killian entered our program, his family experienced high levels of anxiety, and he encountered little opportunity to develop his autonomy. He identified as an addict because every week, at the start of each group and A.A. meeting, he stated, "Hi, I'm Killian and I am a heroin addict." Working from a 12-step (Alcoholics Anonymous, 2001) perspective, Killian followed a model helpful to many people in recovery. He learned this language in the IOP program, and would undoubtedly use it if he continued in recovery. At the same time, he wanted to see himself beyond his addict status, and to grow his understanding of himself through his relationships with others (Jordan, 2008).

DEVELOPMENTAL CONSIDERATIONS

Adolescents in Killian's age group are in the formal operation stage of development. They generally want to be seen as individuals and often seek to establish a unique identity (Vernon, 2009). I believed if I could help Killian see past the addiction, he could uncover his true self without the drug, and imagine a future without heroin ruling his thoughts, feelings, and behaviors.

RELATIONAL CONSIDERATIONS

Killian's parents appeared to be in his life, but not really a part of it. Killian's mom desperately tried to get him help, but often felt unprepared for what came next. Killian's father actively used drugs as well, which made quitting difficult for Killian. I suggested that his dad attend our adult IOP and other facilities for treatment. However, Killian and his mom told me that his dad did not want to come. Killian struggled in school, where he focused on girls and risky behaviors. Killian did not get into trouble at school and did the bare minimum with his class work. He did not report any medical concerns, other than being small in weight because of his addiction. Socially, Killian seemed to be well liked by his peers. In our groups, he would not hesitate to share about his experiences with addiction. On the surface, he appeared to be the "life of the party," but as I got to know him in his individual sessions, he appeared less self-assured and withdrawn. Having a sense of self is necessary to build relationships and connect with others (Jordan, 2008). Killian's lack of self-assurance led to strained relationships and disconnections with his family. The family history of substance abuse did not provide an environment suitable for Killian to develop in healthy ways in his growth-fostering relationships. We talked about this in session and I mentioned feeling as if he wanted to be what his peers expected of him, and not his true self. Killian slightly agreed; thus began my task of discovering his identity. As stated earlier, when asked, he would initially say, "I am a heroin addict."

MULTICULTURAL CONSIDERATIONS

Culturally, Killian and I differed most in age and use of substances. Although I remember being an adolescent, many things are different for teens today than in my time. Topics and situations that Killian spoke of or experienced did not exist in my adolescence. Regarding substances, I am one of a few counselors I know who work with substance abuse, yet cannot personally identify with that experience. We also differed in gender and race. As a Black female counseling Killian, a White male, we developed great rapport because of our openness to learn about each other apart from typical stereotypes. We shared genuinely with one another. Our age, gender, race, substance culture, and family background, although different, did not hinder the counseling process. I let Killian know I wanted to help him cope without using drugs. I believe we crossed our cultural barriers, in part, because I respected Killian as an autonomous individual and allowed him to discover his true self.

CONCEPTUALIZATION

I learned significant information about the addicted brain, the 12 steps, and the effects of substance abuse through serving people suffering with addiction over the past 7 years. I learned that incorporating the program of Alcoholics Anonymous (A.A.) as a foundation can be beneficial for clients in their steps toward recovery and maintained sobriety. However, I also believe from a developmental perspective that consistently identifying as an addict can be detrimental to adolescents' social and emotional status and development. I saw it in Killian.

COUNSELING PROCESS FLOW

Goals and Target for Client Change

Once we addressed the more immediate life and death needs related to his addiction, and in combination with his addiction recovery work, we identified additional counseling goals. These included identifying triggers, learning and applying coping skills, setting goals for achieving better grades and relationships in school, and my personal goal for him, identifying as someone other than a heroin addict. Killian also expressed interest in attending college. While working with Killian, I established goals for myself.

Goals and Strategies for Myself

I wanted to correctly use narrative therapy to assist Killian in connecting to a new "narrative." I wanted to get his parents involved in the program's family night, and to provide Killian with multiple resources to help with school success and college planning. I wanted to provide a path to forge a positive connection. Before working with Killian, I consulted with an IOP colleague who worked with Killian in the group setting. We discussed what goals I thought would be good for Killian, and my colleague agreed. We also discussed counseling techniques I thought would be best to use. I decided to use narrative therapy and solution-focused techniques.

In the previous year, I became very interested in narrative therapy. I began reading more literature, attending workshops, and incorporating it into my sessions with clients. Listening to Killian talk about being an addict, he spoke as if he could not control his actions and feelings while using drugs. Heroin had him under a spell. Killian, skilled in telling vivid accounts of his lived experiences, created a scene you felt a part of. I believed that using narrative therapy would provide a natural outlet to express himself and re-author (White & Epston, 1990) who he is. I also believed solution-focused techniques would assist Killian to identify situations in which he did not use heroin or engage in risky behaviors. Time was of the essence: only 5 weeks remained for us to work together before his discharge date.

The Counseling Relationship

Our counseling relationship developed easily. We established trust early and we both agreed to be honest about our actions. Killian knew what I would and would not share with his mom, and I believe that he would be honest about his actions and behaviors.

Strategies for the Client

After seeing Killian interact in group and with me in session, I felt using narrative and solution-focused techniques would be beneficial. Narrative therapy seeks to find unique outcomes that cannot be accommodated within the dominant story of a person's life (White & Epston, 1990). In Killian's case, his dominant story is the life of a heroin addict. Narrative therapy also works well when considering how people relate, connect, and disconnect from one another. Identification of the unique outcomes in Killian's life can be facilitated by the externalization of the "problem-saturated" story in his life and relationships (White & Epston, 1990). Killian often relied on metaphors and graphic scenes to explain how he felt or what he did. I ultimately wanted Killian to remember his addictive challenges while also seeing himself as more than a heroin addict.

Killian and I met for three sessions before I decided to try the narrative technique of externalization with him. In the session leading up to his externalization of the problem, Killian mentioned that he felt bad about previous life choices. When I asked him to describe it further, he stated, "It's like I am in a graveyard and the bodies aren't fully buried; there's a hand sticking up here, a leg there." I asked what those skeletons represented for him and he shared that he witnessed unfortunate and scary things happen to people, but he always escaped harm. Killian expressed guilt for taking part in activities where others sustained injury; yet, he remained unscathed—at least physically. Killian expressed a desire to uncover each skeleton and deal with it. He wanted to do the work. As I ended the session that day, I shared with Killian the purpose of narrative therapy. I explained we would start the following week. Killian seemed interested in the process.

When our next session arrived, Killian came in with a fresh cup of scalding hot octane (coffee) and snacks, plopped on my couch, and got comfy. I started the session by asking him about his week. "Fine, same ole, same ole," he replied. Before we started, I explained that externalizing the problem consists of interrupting the story he tells about himself. Once he separated from his story, he could experience the capacity to intervene on his own behalf and change the story (White & Epston, 1990). Killian stated that he understood and wanted to participate. I began by asking Killian to imagine his addiction to heroin as an entity outside of himself. I asked, "If it were a real being, what would you call it?" "My Lover," he stated without hesitation. "My Lover." "Hmmm, that is interesting," I replied. "Tell me how you decided on "My Lover." Killian turned his head in my direction and said, "Because she makes all the pain go away." I found it interesting that Killian named his addiction "My Lover" because he engaged in multiple sexual experiences and moved quickly from girl to girl. Killian expected the girls he dated to be there for him at his beck and call; yet, he often did not return the favor. He shared in group and in an individual session that if one girl did not respond when he wanted, he would just move on to the next one. Wanting to know more about his story, I probed deeper.

I asked Killian, "What pain?"

"The pain I feel inside."

"What has caused this pain?" I inquired.

"Things that happen at home, things I've done, things . . . "

"Things that are in the graveyard you were telling me about?"

"Yes. When she is around I don't think about those things or feel bad about anything."

"She helps to numb your feelings."

"I know she is bad, but it feels so good."

Killian continued to explain how it physically felt good when he used heroin. He spoke of how the cares of his world would just fade away. As the session ended, I asked Killian to think about instances when he resisted his "Lover," and to be prepared to share those in our next session.

By Session 5, only 3 weeks remained in the program. Killian actively participated in group and shared in our sessions. However, I did not see much improvement in his thoughts and actions regarding a sober lifestyle. From a developmental, relational, and systemic perspective, Killian needed the support of his family and peers. I decided to call Killian's mom to see if his dad wanted to come in for a session, or join our adult IOP. Unfortunately, his father would not come. Therefore, I continued working with Killian, hoping that he would receive support from our IOP, his mom, and a few peers at A.A.

As we began our fifth session, Killian sauntered in, turned off his music, and positioned himself comfortably on the couch. I started the session by asking Killian how he felt about the A.A. meetings he attended. He reported that he could only relate to a few of the people there. He wished more people closer to his age attended. Killian went right back to our conversation about his "Lover," and wanted to tell me more about his ability to resist her. The externalization technique allowed him to see himself separate from his addiction. Killian shared that he never really defeated her, but that some days he resisted her and did not let her tactics bother him. When I asked him how he resisted her, he shared that he tried to spend time listening to music, hanging out with his sober friends, and thinking about the type of person he wanted to become. He also tried to ignore her.

Infusion of Creativity

My office is set up with two chairs sitting across from the couch. I sit in one and the other is often empty. I decided to utilize the empty chair technique. Killian finally saw himself as separate from his addiction and I felt that allowing him an opportunity to verbalize his feelings and thoughts would benefit his personal growth and development. I asked Killian if he could say anything to his "Lover," what would it be? I asked him to imagine her sitting in my other chair, and he could say anything he wanted. Killian looked at the chair and said, "You know me so well. You know what I like and what makes me feel good. I don't like that I need you, but I do." At the young age of 16, I felt Killian demonstrated incredible insight, and I shared my feelings with him. He then looked at me and said that he wished he could defeat his "Lover," but her strength continuously defeated him. "How does she defeat you?" I asked. He replied, "Because she knows me, she knows what I like. She tempts me with television, movies, magazines, images of smoking and sex, and makes me think of those things. Then, I want to do them." I responded by telling him that knowing so much about his "Lover" is a positive thing. "The more you know, the better you can prepare to defeat her." My next steps included Killian identifying how he could limit the activities that led him to temptation, and to figure out what he wanted to do with his life.

We spent the rest of the session making a list of situations when he resisted his "Lover," and looked for common factors that could help him continue to defeat her. This started a conversation about goals. I handed him a goal-setting worksheet and gave him 10 minutes to complete it. Once he finished, he shared his goals aloud. Killian wanted to (a) stay sober, (b) complete drug court, (c) have integrity and tell people who he really was, (d) move out, and (e) go to college. Killian also shared that he looked forward to turning 18 and moving out of state to live with relatives who influenced him positively.

We began making short-term objectives to reach each goal. During this session, I felt that Killian began to see himself and his situation differently. I believe he felt hopeful that his story could be different and he could be more than a heroin addict. As the session came to an end, I reminded Killian of our short time frame. Three weeks remained in his IOP, and he continued to make progress. I encouraged him to think about who he was, other than a heroin addict. Later that week in group, he completed a Step-2 and Step-3 worksheet, and expanded on the goals he set in his individual session.

OUTCOME

Throughout his time at our IOP, Killian grew by interacting with peers who struggled with addiction. For at least 2 hours, four nights a week, he received care for his emotional, cognitive, physical, and social needs. Killian gained the ability to be authentic with me, his peers, and the other counselors. I feel those connections allowed Killian to trust the process of individual counseling and the different techniques I utilized. Unfortunately, I also believe the lack of good connections with his family and his unmet needs, coupled with seeing a few of his peers relapse, made it difficult for his new connections to remain intact. Those instances set Killian back.

Killian eventually decided he wanted to continue doing drugs. He did not finish his last 2 weeks of the program. Killian used again and went back to an inpatient treatment facility. While attending our IOP, he learned valuable lessons and hopefully saw himself as more than a heroin addict. Unfortunately, he did not sustain his progress. I recently read the following: "When a flower doesn't bloom you fix the environment in which it grows, not the flower" (Garcia, 2016). Killian's environment did not change, and he easily went back to what he knew, to the comfort of his "Lover."

Reflecting on my time with Killian, I would work harder to get his parents active in sessions. I would paint a clearer picture of Killian's life or death situation. Lastly, I would be diligent about providing him with tangible resources that offered support for his family system. I rate this case a "success in progress." Killian did not return to IOP, but attended numerous inpatient facilities to gain and maintain sobriety. I asked myself the miracle question: If I woke up tomorrow and everything looked as I wanted it to, there would be sober living homes for adolescents so they can be planted in a growth-fostering environment. Therefore, as they change and improve, so do the environments they are in.

REFERENCES

Alcoholics Anonymous. (2001). *Alcoholics anonymous* (4th ed.). New York, NY: A. A. World Services.

Garcia, G. (2016, February 26). Re: Personal motivation correspondence [Online forum post]. Retrieved from https://www.linkedin.com

Jordan, J. V. (2008). Recent developments in relational-cultural theory. *Women & Therapy, 31*(2–4), 1–4. http://dx.doi.org/10.1080/02703140802145540

Vernon, A. (2009). *Counseling children & adolescents* (4th ed.). Denver, CO: Love.

Walsh, F. (2016). *Normal family processes: Growing diversity and complexity* (4th ed.). New York, NY: Guilford Press.

White, M., & Epston, D. (1990). *Narrative means to therapeutic ends.* New York, NY: W. W. Norton.

Young, M. E. (2013). *Learning the art of helping: Building blocks and techniques* (5th ed.). Upper Saddle River, NJ: Pearson.

CHAPTER 25

UNCOVERING MIKE

Tamarine Foreman

I would like to introduce you to Mike. Mike presented as a tall, slender, 15-year-old African American male. He attended a midsize suburban high school where, until recently, he successfully navigated his freshman year of high school. Mike's parents, Joe and Martha, were a Caucasian couple married for 25 years. The family resided in a middle-income suburban neighborhood outside a major city in a midwestern state. Mike was their only child. Both parents worked full time. Joe worked as a physical education teacher at a middle school and Martha worked as a nurse at the local hospital.

SYSTEMIC INFLUENCES

Mike talked about his many friends. He clarified that many of them came from various racial and ethnic backgrounds, both White and Black. Mike described his school as attended by both Black and White students, along with some Hispanic students. During our third session, I reflected to Mike his comments about having difficulty being around his friends.

> *Mike:* "They just don't get me."
> *Counselor:* "Hmmm. That sounds kind of rough to have friends who don't understand you."
> *Mike:* "Yea it is. I mean, they were cool with me asking Stephanie to the dance, but when she said no, they said I should just move on."
> *Counselor:* "Sounds like moving on is difficult."

Mike: "Yeah. I really like Stephanie. (Silence) It just burns me that her parents told her she was not allowed to go with me to the dance. I have been to her house many times to help her dad with some repairs and they treated me just fine. That is until I wanted to take their daughter to the dance. They told her I was not allowed to come over anymore. I just don't get it. Just because I want to date her, they think I am not good enough. But I know it is more about me being Black."

Internally, I experienced a strong reaction to what Mike shared with me. I became angry because the family treated him differently after he became romantically interested in their daughter. Mike trusted this family and enjoyed being around them. I wondered how this experience might be impacting our therapeutic relationship. Due to my strong internal emotional reactions, I sought supervision and consultation to explore how I might more effectively work with Mike around issues of experienced racism. In a later session, I shared with Mike that I wondered how his experience with Stephanie's parents might impact our sessions. I asked, "What is it like to share this information with me, especially since I am a White woman who is not adopted?" Mike responded he felt okay talking to me and stated he did not view me as judging him. This resulted in a pivotal moment in our therapeutic relationship.

Family History

When I asked about the family medical history, Joe and Martha shared they adopted Mike as an infant, and knew little of the birth family's medical or psychiatric history. The parents reported Mike's birth mother was incarcerated at the time of his birth, and chose to place him for adoption prior to his birth. Joe stated they lacked additional information about Mike's birth mother and had no knowledge of Mike's birth father. Martha shared they tried having children for 7 years, but could not have children of their own, and wanted to care for a healthy newborn. Martha stated it did not matter to them that their skin color differed from the infant they would eventually hold in their arms. They realized in that moment that they became responsible for a beautiful baby boy who needed their love and attention.

The parents reported their immediate families lacked excitement about their choice to complete a transracial adoption, but stated this changed once the family met baby Mike. Both Joe and Martha said their families accepted Mike as one of their own, and they never heard any negative comments or questions. Martha reported they received questioning looks and stares when they went out in public together, but that the stares and comments diminished over time. The parents reported they maintained relationships with a diverse group of people to provide Mike the opportunity to make friends and connect to people of his own race.

Strategies for Mike and His Parents

To assist the treatment in moving forward, I referred the family to the agency's postadoption psychoeducational group. The psychoeducational group is an 8-week series that provides a different group for adoptive parents, adolescents, and youth. Each session is designed to facilitate parallel information on specific adoptee issues such as trust and identity, separation and loss, dealing with anger, and exploring birth parent situations. The groups also foster a sense of support and belonging, as participants are encouraged to share their own experiences. Both Mike and his parents agreed to participate in the psychoeducational groups. I continued to see Mike individually every other week while Mike and his family attended the 8-week series.

DEVELOPMENTAL CONSIDERATIONS

In exploring Mike's early development, the parents described Mike as a fussy infant who did not sleep well. Despite the sleeping challenges, the parents reported Mike met all developmental milestones on time and without any concerns. Mike's parents described him as an active child and teen who enjoyed playing baseball and hanging out with friends. The parents described Mike as an average student who did well in both academic and extracurricular activities. Martha shared that they never received any negative reports from Mike's teachers or coaches. In addition, the parents stated that Mike grew into a typical teenager, with some disagreements and testing of limits, but nothing out of the ordinary.

RELATIONAL CONSIDERATIONS

Parental Perspective

When I asked about current concerns, Mike's parents became markedly distressed with worry and anxiety. The parents shared that recently Mike's grades declined and that he received failing grades on assignments. Additionally, they reported Mike received a 1-day suspension from school for fighting. Joe stated Mike did not usually get so angry, let alone fight. Both parents reported that when they would approach Mike to ask what happened, Mike would stomp away and go into his bedroom, slam his door, or storm out of the house. The parents stated Mike would often return to the house after storming out in an angry or depressed mood. They both saw a decrease in Mike's motivation to complete schoolwork and help around the house. They also reported Mike would rarely hang out with his friends and seemed disinterested in extracurricular activities. The parents described Mike as more argumentative lately, his sleeping and eating habits as sporadic and irregular, and noted frequent outbursts and moodiness. Joe shared that Mike said he did not want to play baseball that year. Martha commented that Mike played baseball since elementary school. His parents conveyed distress about Mike and his unwillingness to talk to them. During this meeting, the parents expressed concern about Mike's overall well-being, and they felt at a loss with what to do. They asked me to see Mike for counseling.

Client Perspective

In my first meeting with Mike, he presented as closed off, sullen, and quiet. I noticed Mike walked slowly into my office. He did not initiate conversation and instead spoke only when I asked a question or made a comment. He made little eye contact and he sat with his shoulders slouched. Mike spoke in a quiet tone with an uneven rhythm and blunted affect. When I asked if he knew the reason for his visit, Mike replied his parents worried about him, and because he got into a fight at school. He quickly stated he did not start the fight, and that the other guy deserved it. He refused to provide any additional information. I did not know Mike well enough yet, so I decided to save this conversation for another time. Mike reported having friends, but that right now they are just hard to be around. Mike shared he originally thought about going to college to major in communications or business, but could not be sure about his plans anymore. When asked to share about his family, Mike became more animated in his speech and appeared somewhat angry. Mike reported that "White people adopted him and he has no idea who his 'real' parents are." Mike then shared he wished people would stop reminding him of how different he is—especially when asking about his parents. Due to the signs of depression and irritability, I completed a suicide risk assessment with Mike. Mike denied having any suicidal thoughts or ideation during our initial meeting. When I asked Mike if he would be willing to see me for a few more sessions, he responded with a shrug.

MULTICULTURAL CONSIDERATIONS

From a multicultural perspective, I wondered about Mike's experience— sharing his thoughts and feelings with a White middle-aged woman

who did not go through adoption, and how that impacted our therapeutic relationship. I wondered if Mike knew other adopted youths
who lived in a multiracial family. I also wondered how Mike perceived
his own identity and how he described himself. Finally, I wondered
about the family's perception of their own multicultural family, and
how their experiences shaped the family's identity.

CONCEPTUALIZATION

As a counselor who works with adoptive families, I strive to be in tune
with how the parents and child view the adoption. I am aware that even
if an adoptive youth does not mention his or her birth parents, it is very
likely he or she has thought about them. In meeting with Joe and
Martha, I noticed they discussed the birth parents, but did not share
any information about what they discussed with Mike regarding his
birth parents. This would be an area to gather additional information. I
began to wonder what Mike knew about his birth parents and if he
struggled with how to view his adoption, while also navigating his own
identity. I also became aware that Mike may feel different due to being
adopted, and because his race differed from that of his parents. I would
explore these questions with him in subsequent sessions.

Assessing Mike's Strengths

In considering Mike's strengths, I observed his parents supported him,
and they expressed concern and a willingness to proceed with counseling. Mike had a history of being a good student, having friends, and
participating in extracurricular activities. Mike demonstrated some
awareness about his parents' concerns. In addition, Mike denied suicidal and homicidal ideation, plan, and intent. Despite Mike's nonverbal communication during the initial session, Mike cooperated and
responded to my probing questions.

Conceptualization of Presenting Concerns

My immediate concerns were related to Mike's level of depression,
school performance, and family communication. I felt concern about the
possibility of underlying grief and loss issues related to his adoption.
I would need to pay attention and continue to assess Mike for suicidal
risk. Also, within the context of a developmental life-span perspective,
I viewed Mike as being in the middle of developing his identity, which
was compounded by elements of his adoption. I perceived Mike as not

giving voice to his thoughts and feelings related to his adoption, with an inability to express these thoughts and feelings to his parents.

COUNSELING PROCESS FLOW

Theoretical Consideration

In considering person-centered theory (Rogers, 2003), I conceptualized Mike's condition of worth. It revolved around his inability to express his anger and confusion about his identity, for fear of rejection. In Mike's real self, he is sullen, angry, may feel abandoned and confused, is unable to express himself, and is struggling socially and academically in school. Mike's ideal self would be able to safely express a range of emotions, possess a clear identity, and would be doing well in school. Freud was one of the first psychoanalysts to describe depression as anger turned inward (Kahn, 2010). I wondered if Mike's outward expression of anger represented his depression. This seemed reasonable as Mike's situation showed his angst related to self-identity and unresolved questions about his birth family. Furthermore, I wondered if there might be some fear that discussing his birth parents might upset his adoptive parents.

Goals and Target for Client Change

Treatment goals involved both individual and family counseling sessions to address and improve communication while decreasing family conflict. In working with Mike individually, treatment would focus on establishing a therapeutic relationship, decreasing symptoms of depression through improving coping skills, improving sleep quality, improving eating habits, and helping Mike more effectively express his thoughts and feelings. These goals would also indirectly impact Mike's academic and interpersonal skills. I continued to inquire about school performance and peer relationships, and would implement academic and social skill building as needed. However, I first wanted to elicit more information pertaining to Mike's underlying thoughts and feelings, as I saw these as being related to his depression. I decided to implement a creative intervention to help Mike give voice to his thoughts and feelings in a nonthreatening and indirect manner.

I continued to meet with Mike individually on a weekly basis over the course of 3 to 4 months interspersed with family sessions. As I began to work with Mike individually, he began to share more information with me, but continued to present with a blunted or flat affect, quiet and irregular speech, and poor eye contact; in addition, he sat in a slouching posture. His mood ranged from irritable to sullen, with outward expressions of agitation. This prompted me to implement questions from the SIMPLE STEPS (McGlothlin, 2008) model of suicide assessment. This provided me with the opportunity to ask Mike to scale his level of pain based on his depressive symptoms. Mike continued to demonstrate a low risk for suicide and denied suicidal ideation, plan, and intent.

Infusion of Creativity

In later sessions, Mike became more open with me regarding the fight at school. I learned the fight began over a comment another classmate made about students dating people of their kind. I continued to struggle with Mike's experiences of racism and how coming from a multiracial family posed different situations for him to navigate. To engage with him further around his identity, I asked Mike to create a book cover. The book cover is a creative intervention where a person makes a book cover to explore external information that is known, while completing the inside with information that is not readily seen or observed. First, I asked Mike to fold the sheet of paper in half, thus making outside and inside sections. On the outside of the book cover, I asked Mike to draw or write things that people knew about him or could readily observe. Once he completed the outside, I asked Mike to open the book cover to the inside. I then asked Mike to color, draw, or write things about himself that others might not know or be able to observe. This intervention allowed me to glimpse some of the things that Mike found difficult to share, and gave voice to areas where he still struggled. Mike's book cover is shared in Figure 25.1.

It took Mike a little longer to complete the inside of the book cover. The activity provided me with a level of insight into Mike's concerns

Outside Cover

- Male
- I am adopted
- My parents are White, I am Black
- I love my parents
- I am a good student
- I can play baseball

Inside Cover

- I don't know where I fit in
- I feel angry a lot
- I wonder about my birth parents
- I worry that talking about my birth parents will upset my mom and dad
- I am constantly reminded that I am different, that I was adopted, and my birth parents ddn't want me

FIGURE 25.1 Mike's book cover.

and feelings about his development and identity as a transracially adopted youth. It also allowed me to shape the direction of treatment toward the goal of Mike being able to share the inside book cover with his parents.

OUTCOME

In my final session with Mike and his family, each member articulated what he or she learned during our counseling sessions, as well as what he or she gained from his or her experiences in the postadoption psychoeducational groups. The parents shared they would begin attending the adoptive parent support group. Mike revealed he did not want to attend a support group, but stated he would like to stay connected with some of the other youth he met during the group sessions. The family presented as congruent with a positive outlook for the future. Mike's grades improved, he spent time with his friends more regularly, and he received no other suspensions or incidents of fighting. The parents also reported Mike seemed to be sleeping more regularly and eating better. Mike agreed with their report. The family shared there are still some heated discussions, but that they do not escalate to the point that doors are slammed or people storm out of the house. Mike demonstrated that right now he wanted to focus on finishing high school and getting into college. I shared with Mike and his parents that my door would be open for future counseling sessions, even if just for a brief check-in or update.

In hindsight, I wonder how I could utilize the book cover intervention with the entire family. What would the outcome be if each family member created a book cover? I wondered if it might have facilitated a richer discussion related to unexpressed thoughts and feelings, and opened the discussion about Mike's thoughts about searching for his birth parents. However, the postadoption psychoeducational groups provided an opportunity to explore these issues with other adoptive parents and transracially adopted youth.

Although I worked with other transracial adoptive families, Mike's case represented the first time an adolescent openly shared his personal experiences of racism with me. I recognized racism occurred, but seeing and hearing Mike's personal experiences further awakened my observation and realization of the suffering racism causes. Mike's experiences disturbed me, but I am thankful for the opportunity to work with Mike and his family. This case served as an early experience that stayed with me throughout my personal and professional journey as a counselor. Personally, I am a White woman raised in a working-class family with limited multicultural and multiracial experiences. As an adult, I frequently seek out experiences that are different than what I experienced in my youth—exposure to people of rich heritage, culture, and diversity. Professionally, I realize I walk a fine line between my White privilege and how it potentially impacts my relationship with others. My experiences in supervision helped me process my thoughts and feelings surrounding my internal reactions to Mike's experience of racism, and enhanced my competence in working with multicultural families. Since then, I continue to move forward to enhance my own personal and professional experiences through trainings and supervision related to clinical experiences that arise in the counseling office or classroom.

REFERENCES

Kahn, D. (2010). Ask the experts. Retrieved from http://asp.cumc.columbia .edu/psych/asktheexperts/ask_the_experts_inquiry.asp?SI=76

McGlothlin, J. (2008). Models of a suicide assessment interview. In J. McGlothlin (Ed.), *Developing clinical skills in suicide assessment, prevention, and treatment* (pp. 35–46). Alexandria, VA: American Counseling Association.

Rogers, C. (2003). *Client-centered therapy: Its current practice, implications, and theory.* London, UK: Constable.

CHAPTER 26

THE GIFTED GIRL

Michelle Robinson

For 3 years, I worked as a professional school counselor at the largest high school in the South Texas area. With a school population of nearly 3,800 students, I worked with nearly 570 freshmen students the first 2 years of my counseling experience. During my third year, I worked with all grade levels with a caseload of nearly 400 students. Angel, a 14-year-old White female, self-referred to my office concerning her anger management and anxiety issues. As a gifted ninth grade high school student, she experienced difficulty belonging and fitting in with her peers. While she involved herself in church activities, made good grades, and participated in athletics and the high school fine arts program, she felt disconnected from school. After consulting with her father, he claimed that Angel often sought attention from authority figures, but gave consent for Angel and me to meet regularly to discuss Angel's concerns.

SYSTEMIC INFLUENCES

Both of Angel's parents held bachelor's degrees and both retired from the military. Her mother continued to work with the military while her father stayed at home. Her parents wanted children and chose to adopt after failed attempts to give birth to children of their own. Angel's parents adopted Angel and her three siblings—two sisters, who lived out of state with families of their own, and one brother, age 17, who resided with Angel and her parents.

Angel's parents always expected their children to do well academically and to be involved in school. Her brother participated in the choir and received a lot of recognition for his musical accomplishments. Angel joined orchestra and track and received recognition for her musical accomplishments.

Angel and her brother shared the same biological mother. Angel disclosed that her brother, an upper classman at her high school, turned 18, which made it possible for him to seek out their birth mother. This concerned Angel. From Angel's 14-year-old point of view, she perceived her adoptive parents as "older parents" (mid-50s) and worried about changing the relationship with them if her brother searched for their birth mother.

DEVELOPMENTAL CONSIDERATIONS

Cognitive Development

Based on assessment data, the school identified Angel as a gifted student in elementary school. She scored in the exemplary range on her elementary school state assessments. At the middle school and high school levels, she continued to score above grade level. She never failed a state assessment and currently maintained a 94 grade point average (GPA). She ranked in the top 10 percent of her class. School records showed no discipline, truancy, or attendance issues. This school year, Angel's teachers reported that she worked hard and sought their approval. She often spent time during lunch and advisory with her teachers instead of with other students. This assessment of Angel appeared contrary to the reports received during the last school year, and could possibly be explained by the classes that she took. In the previous year, Angel enrolled in pre-advanced placement (Pre-AP) classes; this year, the school implemented the Gifted and Talented (GT) program in a manner that students would be enrolled and serviced through GT classes.

Angel and her parents shared a concern about the amount of work that Angel's teachers assigned and the level of expectation that her teachers held. They also became troubled by Angel's lack of focus in school. Her parents expected Angel to earn grades of 90 or above. Although Angel possessed the capability to meet this expectation, she did not consistently perform to her parents' expectations. This led to stress on her behalf. The school recognized Angel as gifted even though Angel did not enroll in classes designated for GT students. Instead, the school serviced her through Pre-AP classes. The demands of the Pre-AP coursework potentially contributed to her stress level. In addition to these classes, Angel participated in extracurricular activities inside and outside of school. Angel and her parents requested assistance in helping Angel develop time management skills.

Personal, Social, and Emotional Development

Angel appeared to be functioning within the social and emotional development appropriate for her age group. She tended to argue with her mother while, at the same time, seemed very caring and empathetic. She reflected on situations and determined how she could better handle them in the future. She appeared to respect authority figures but challenged them at times. She observed others, paid attention to detail, and liked order. She experienced difficulty asking for assistance when needed. Some of these characteristics also depicted her giftedness.

In general, Angel presented no health or medical concerns. During our counseling sessions, she revealed that she injured her heel while running track and suffered from severe shin splints. These setbacks, she felt, contributed to her missing track meets. Angel's parents expressed no concerns about Angel's general personal, social, or emotional needs. Instead, they focused on her attention-seeking behavior. They also did not validate any of Angel's expressed concerns (e.g., feelings of not fitting in, anxiety toward school, or perceived anger management problems). However, I worked with Angel in counseling regarding these concerns.

RELATIONAL CONSIDERATIONS

Angel described herself as a member of the "popular" group in middle school. Since coming to high school, she felt this to no longer be true. Angel felt that she seemed more mature than other freshmen in high school. She often commented that people agitated her for asking stupid questions or not walking fast enough in the hallways. With her older brother attending the same high school, she believed her friends used her to get to her brother. She believed this contributed to her anger issues. When I observed Angel in social settings with friends and teachers, she appeared comfortable as she developed positive relationships with those around her. She also developed a positive relationship with me since knowing that I attended school with her older sister, which occurred before Angel's birth. Her parents recognized me and shared this information with Angel. Due to this past relationship with her sister, Angel seemed comfortable opening up to me.

MULTICULTURAL CONSIDERATIONS

Angel came from a middle-class family. The fact that the school labeled her a gifted student and her parents adopted her added to her uniqueness. As mentioned earlier, she involved herself in her church activities and proclaimed herself a Christian. These factors impacted my counseling because while I identify as a proclaimed Christian, we belonged to different churches. Also, not being adopted myself, I knew I needed to learn more about adoption or try to gain some perspective on being adopted. This led me to reach out to a close friend of mine who became adopted as an infant. According to Howe (2006), "Within the affective exchanges between parents and infants, children begin to build up an understanding of how their own and other people's minds work at the emotional, intentional and behavioral level, and how these mental states affect social interaction and relationships" (Introduction, para. 2). As an educator, understanding the brain and personality of a gifted student also impacted my counseling. Giftedness can be showcased in many different ways. I attended an in-service training session provided by the school district. My friend's personal accounts and the in-service training assisted me in expanding my awareness about adoption and giftedness. Additionally, Angel completed several different personality tests and the results of these tests, along with information from other sources, gave me a better understanding of her as a gifted student.

CONCEPTUALIZATION

In speaking with Angel, I believed a lack of self-esteem and self-confidence presented as her main concerns. Due to this developmental need, I believed she shared other situations or problems that appeared to be presented on the surface due to her unwillingness to look deeper.

Goals and Strategies for Myself

The counseling theories that I used included reality therapy with the inclusion of WDEP (wants, doing, evaluate, and plan; Glasser, 2010) and solution-focused brief therapy (SFBT; de Shazer & Berg, 1997). These theories, combined with an approach to counseling called impact therapy (Jacobs & Schimmel, 2013), truly impact students through the use of props or writing. They provide students with tangible evidence that is easily remembered and is presented in the form of writing, pictures, or visual stimulations. When working with Angel, my goal involved keeping Angel focused and engaged in the session by using multiple methods. Using these theories helped provide different strategies to use in the counseling sessions.

The school setting lends itself to frequently using brief counseling as a preferred modality. With a caseload of over 400 students, individual counseling for all students became a challenging goal. As a professional school counselor, I held no expectations from teachers to allow students to miss entire class periods; however, I worked collaboratively with them to gain access to students. The typical length of sessions with students usually lasts about 30 minutes. Due to time constraints, professional school counselors generally choose brief counseling techniques in an attempt to meet the needs of all students. Brief counseling sessions also allow students to set goals, make plans, and evaluate them within a specified time period.

Goals and Target for Client Change

As my first counseling goal, I wanted Angel to determine the difference between her perception or irrational thoughts and her reality. This goal addressed most of her present concerns. Through this, I hoped to assist her in building self-esteem and self-confidence; help her find the origin of her anger issues; and determine her support system. As my second goal, I taught and helped Angel develop strategies for time management skills to decrease her stress levels. I also assisted Angel in determining her feelings about her brother's choice in finding their birth mother. I wanted her to process how to handle this. Finally, because of Angel's identified giftedness, I wanted her to become aware of the ideals she and her parents held for her. The gifted label gave her an identity to hold on to; however, through our counseling sessions, I wanted her to see that being gifted did not mean that she fit into only one category of people. People demonstrate giftedness in different ways and she did not need to assume that she should be the same as other gifted persons.

COUNSELING PROCESS FLOW

Angel and I decided to meet Friday mornings, which allowed her to process events that occurred during the week and share what she felt she needed to focus on mostly. We decided to meet eight times, but ended up meeting four scheduled times due to Angel not showing up for some of our scheduled time. I presented her with the opportunity to meet with me as needed outside the four scheduled sessions.

Session 1

In our counseling sessions, I preferred using creative techniques often derived from impact therapy (Jacobs & Schimmel, 2013). I used the creative techniques to keep Angel involved without overreliance on talk therapy. Through the creative techniques, Angel took on a more active role in our counseling sessions because impact therapy allowed her to produce something tangible. During the first counseling session, we discussed her week. She consistently brought up her inability to control her anger. When pressed for clarification, she reported that she wanted to scream and yell at people all of the time. Together we created a chart of possible situations that served as reasons individuals lose control of their anger. The chart included a red face, hitting people, and yelling at people. On the other side of the chart, we indicated with a check mark if she reacted in similar manners. She charted no check marks for herself, so I asked her to tell me more about these results. She responded by saying, "I guess I don't have anger control issues, but people make me so mad when they don't move in the hallways." Her self-reflections revealed that her problem appeared to be anger and frustration with people who did not do things her way as opposed to anger control. This realization, to me, appeared to be going in a positive direction. Angel tried to analyze her inability of not being able to control her anger. After her self-reflections, we discussed that it seemed normal for people to become angry. This helped normalize her anger feelings. Instead of feeling as though she could not express her anger, she seemed to understand that it happened to be okay for her to feel anger, which helped her focus more on how to handle her anger. Being a gifted student, she liked having things done on her terms and in a certain way; and when done differently, she responded with frustration. I emphasized that her feelings of being frustrated happened to also be okay. People do things differently every day. Her lack of patience did not translate to an anger control issue. To help develop her patience, we discussed strategies that she could incorporate when she started to feel her frustration rise.

Session 2

The next session focused on her lack of belonging. Angel indicated that she felt different from every student on the campus and that she did not fit in. Using Rational Emotive Behavior Therapy (REBT; Ellis & Dryden, 1997), we again created a chart for her to write down her thoughts. The first column indicated her thoughts; the second column indicated the reality; and the third column indicated the truth and positive self-talk she could use instead of her negative thoughts. Her thoughts included: (1) "I do not have any friends"; (2) "Everybody thinks that I am annoying"; and (3) "I do not trust anybody."

We started to dispute those thoughts. She mentioned at least two friends previously, so we wrote down their names next to number 1. We also rephrased her thoughts in the third column as, "I have at least two friends." To address her second thought, we wrote down my name because I did not think she came across as annoying. In the third column, we re-wrote, "Not everybody thinks I am annoying." Lastly, we used friends from her church group she trusted and rephrased the sentence in the third column to, "I trust my friends from church." Borrowing from impact therapy, we called the first column ANTs in her head. ANTs stands for Assumptions Not Truths. We discussed keeping the ANTs out of her head and reflected back to the third/truth column when her ANTs tried to sneak back into her head (Jacobs & Schimmel, 2013).

Session 3

The third session focused on her brother's upcoming 18th birthday that made it possible for him to seek out their birth mother. Angel appeared very conflicted about this. She indicated that she did want to meet her birth mother. Her two major concerns appeared to be about how to share this with her adoptive parents and her anger toward her brother for possibly doing this without her. She appeared jealous that her brother would be able to know her biological mother 3 years before she became able to do this. To focus on her conflicted thoughts, we used WDEP from reality therapy (Glasser, 2010). She determined what she truly wanted. Her "W" in WDEP represented wanting to meet her birth mother without upsetting her mom. She also wanted her brother to wait for her to make contact. The "D" represented her inability to act on what she wanted. This helped with the "E," or evaluating what worked and what did not work. She determined that not doing anything did not get her where she wanted to be in her relationship with her birth parents and her adoptive mother, or with her communication with her brother. This realization leads to her "P." She planned to speak with both her brother and her adoptive mother. She preferred not to speak to them together, so she planned to speak with her mother first and her brother second. She wanted to make sure her mother became aware of her desires from her without the worry that her brother would "tell on her." Angel appeared nervous about speaking with her mother, so she wrote a letter instead. She felt she could speak to her brother openly about why she wanted him to wait until she turned 18 as well.

Session 4

At the beginning of Session 4, I came up with a goal to review the letter and conversation with her mother and brother. She did not engage in either conversation. She wrote the letter to her mom, but became afraid to give it to her. She also did not want to discuss another plan of how to arrange for the conversations because she thought school seemed too overwhelming at the moment. On her plate, her load included her first track meet, choir concert, and two projects due within 3 days. She said she felt overstressed with little confidence in getting it all done. She felt pressure from her parents because she did not seek perfection. She felt like crying. I did not know if she used these reasons to hide her feelings about her impending conversations with her adoptive mother and brother, but I reminded myself that Angel remained my client, so I focused on her needs. I assessed her stress level using a scale of 1 to 10, with 10 being the highest. She indicated a 12. I became doubtful that she ranked 12, but we continued to develop a plan for her. Using the miracle question (de Shazer & Berg, 1997), I asked her how she would know everything would be completed within 3 days. She responded with winning a ribbon at the track meet, having a perfect performance at the concert, and making 100s on her projects. There seemed to be so many ways to address this response, but I chose to help her create a time and task schedule, instead of focusing on her high expectations. Using an excel spreadsheet and one of our time management resources, we filled out an hour-by-hour schedule for Friday through Sunday. After she filled in her requirements of sleep, eating, concerts, track meets, and church, we started to fill in time for her to work on her projects. By the end, she completed a full schedule. Her scale of stress still ranked an 8, but she said at least she developed a plan and could see it getting done. I wanted to discuss more fully her expectations, but we ran out of time.

OUTCOME

Angel and I did not meet regularly after the fourth session. She stopped in randomly to my office and very briefly shared her status. When she came to our assigned meeting time, she told me that she could not think of anything new to share and disclosed that she overcame her stressors. We continued to plan individually for her academic success; and in those planning meetings, we addressed her desire for perfection. Most of those discussions occurred within 10 minutes and we discussed her reality instead of her expectations. This became a common theme in our short meetings. I believed that Angel became comfortable with me so she did not feel the need to stick with a scheduled meeting time. She knew that I had an open door policy, but she also did not stay longer than a few minutes.

At the conclusion of last year, I became uncertain about the effectiveness of the counseling sessions with Angel. In observing her on campus, I saw her spending time with her friends. Through tracking her grades, I also noticed that she maintained an A/B average. I felt lucky being on the same campus with Angel this year. While the school did not schedule her into my caseload, I became designated as the GT Counselor, so I saw her in the classroom setting once a month.

The school's implementation of a GT program at the high school level to address academic and emotional needs of GT students seemed invaluable for Angel. Being in a smaller classroom setting with other gifted students presented her with a smaller circle of people to interact with. I noticed that her friend circle expanded and her grades increased. She also continued to stop by my office to update me on her choices and discuss her boyfriend and her friends. We maintained a good counselor–client relationship. Angel developed better relationships with her teachers and felt she minimized her disagreements with her parents. She did not mention her birth mother this year, but overall seemed more confident and happier in the choices she made for herself. I would like to say that our counseling sessions contributed mostly to this, but I also know, developmentally, she grew and matured. I occasionally asked about her ANTs and she would laugh.

Addressing her needs as a gifted student in individual counseling sessions and placing her in gifted classes aided in her growth. This is a special population and the smaller settings presented teachers the opportunity to more effectively meet individual student needs; and, for myself, to address classroom concerns within the GT identified population. Angel learned to manage her time better, which helped decrease her stress. She also developed strategies to look at her reality and not her beliefs. I look forward to watching her grow over the next 2 years; and, of course, I remain available to provide social and emotional support to her.

REFERENCES

de Shazer, S., & Berg, I. K. (1997). "What works?" Remarks on research aspects of solution-focused brief therapy. *Journal of Family Therapy, 19*, 121–124. http://dx.doi.org/10.1111/1467-6427.00043

Ellis, A. E., & Dryden, W. (1997). *The practice of rational emotive behavior therapy.* New York, NY: Springer Publishing.

Glasser, W. (2010). *Choice theory: A new psychology of personal freedom.* New York, NY: HarperCollins.

Howe, D. (2006). Developmental attachment psychotherapy with fostered and adopted children. *Child and Adolescent Mental Health, 11*(3), 128–134. http://dx.doi.org/10.1111/j.1475-3588.2006.00393.x

Jacobs, E., & Schimmel, C. (2013). *Impact therapy: The courage to counsel.* Star City, WV: Impact Therapy Associates.

CHAPTER 27

GINGERBREAD SENTIMENTS

M. Michelle Thornbury Kelley

Dean Barber is a well-mannered, friendly, adolescent male. Concerns about him came to my attention when Ms. Vicks, his English teacher, recounted a phone conversation with Dean's mother. Ms. Vicks called home regarding missing assignments and Dean's uncharacteristically disrespectful behavior. Mrs. Barber told her that Dean's father received a prison sentence a month prior. Mrs. Barber also reported to Ms. Vicks that she contacted the middle school counselor for advice regarding changes in her younger son's behavior, but her elementary-aged daughter and Dean seemed to manage well during the lengthy trial and legal proceedings. However, in the past couple of weeks, Dean often became irritable and quick to anger. Mrs. Barber asked Ms. Vicks to share the information with me, Dean's professional school counselor.

SYSTEMIC INFLUENCES

Dean is the oldest child in a family of five; he has a sister and a brother. His mother is the sole provider while his father is in prison. At school, coaches report that Dean is one of the better players on the junior varsity football team and he is a natural leader. He also plays baseball. Although he does not excel in that sport, his positive nature and dedication make him an asset to the team. He retained many of the same friends since elementary school and the same girlfriend for almost a year.

DEVELOPMENTAL CONSIDERATIONS

Historically, Dean excelled academically. Dean attended school regularly, and always made good grades in pre-advanced placement (Pre-AP) courses. He earned high school credits in math and foreign language while he attended middle school. Prior to the referral associated with this case study, Dean visited with me regarding course selection and schedule concerns, and we discussed his future college and career plans.

RELATIONAL CONSIDERATIONS

Dean is in the 10th grade at a comprehensive high school in South Texas where his outgoing personality and bright smile make him stand out, even among 2,500 other students. For 15 years, Dean lived in the same neighborhood near friends and extended family members. Prior to his father going to prison, Dean had not experienced significant loss. The grief associated with his father's sudden absence from everyday life left Dean feeling frustrated and disconnected.

MULTICULTURAL CONSIDERATIONS

Dean describes his mother as Hispanic and his father as Caucasian. Dean identifies as Hispanic, as he is very close to his mother and extended family members. He never met some members of his father's family. Prior to Mr. Barber's incarceration, the family held an upper middle-class status. Currently, the family is struggling to remain in their house and they are receiving financial assistance from relatives.

CONCEPTUALIZATION

Because the changes in Dean's behavior began when his father went away, I suspected I would learn about the hardships related to his father's incarceration and how they impacted him and his family. Although I did not know Dean well, I also wondered if he might be grieving the loss of daily interaction with his father. I further surmised he acted out in response to these things.

My professional goals while working with Dean consisted of becoming acquainted with him and gaining his trust. I also wanted to understand the situation from his perspective and help him relate his feelings to his actions without inflicting any of my own biases. I hoped Dean would gain introspection and the ability to identify and navigate the emotions surrounding his father's incarceration.

The first time I met with Dean I used a time-efficient scaling method from solution-focused brief therapy (Murphy, 2008), and I introduced the WDEP (wants and perceptions, direction and total behavior, evaluation, and plan) system of reality therapy (Corey, 2009). It did not align with my original goal of helping Dean explore the feelings related to his father's imprisonment, but it helped him address a problem he viewed as a priority. It also served to build rapport between the two of us and it helped Dean begin to trust the counseling process.

Because grief is not only associated with a death loss, and because Dean felt apprehensive about addressing emotions regarding his father's incarceration, the second time I met with Dean I employed a creative technique I learned at a training session at the Children's Bereavement Center of South Texas in San Antonio, Texas. Using an expressive arts activity, children are asked to identify feelings of grief using markers and the outline of a gingerbread person. After Dean identified his emotions via this activity, I used parts of Meichenbaum's cognitive behavior modification approach (Corey, 2009) to help him learn how internal states can impact behavior. I also consulted with Mrs. Barber and then facilitated a conversation between the two of them. I provided a list of community resources and a consent form for release of information because I believed Dean would benefit from counseling services beyond those provided by a professional school counselor. Additionally, I coordinated a meeting with Dean, his mom, all of his teachers, and myself to discuss how to support Dean. If Dean and his family decided not to seek counseling from a community provider, I would follow up with Dean individually and seek permission from Dean's mother to include him in small group counseling on campus.

COUNSELING PROCESS FLOW

I saw Dean three times over a 2-week period. The first time, I sent for him during Ms. Vicks's class. His mother told him about her conversation with his English teacher the evening before, so he anticipated a pass to my office. I could not tell how he felt about being there, so I asked him how he felt about the concern of his mother and teacher. He said, "I guess its nice, but I'm fine." I told him it made me glad to hear that, but I wondered why his mom and Ms. Vicks would think otherwise. I invited him to sit and tossed him a stress ball.

I told him about the limits of confidentiality in the counseling department and, as he played with the ball, he told me his grades in many of his classes dropped from As to Cs and Ds. He only partially completed assignments, but his grades would improve when he turned them in if his teachers would take late assignments. He said he needed to "take care of it" so he could be eligible for football, although he added he struggled with focusing and did not play as well as he usually did. Also, his mom grounded him for missing curfew too many times and he did not see his friends or girlfriend outside of school. His punishment ended the coming weekend, but his family planned to travel to the prison to visit his dad. He said his mom stressed out all the time, and it made things tough at home. Dean did not get specific, but added that he felt bad for the way he treated her. I told him, "It seems like there is a lot going on in your life and I can see why people might be worried about you." He conceded, so I asked if we might spend a bit more time together. He hesitantly agreed.

Dean identified more than one problem, so the two of us decided to find a way to help him identify a single area of concern on which to focus. To help Dean narrow it down and to ensure I did not make assumptions or assert my own priorities, we used a solution-focused scaling activity (Murphy, 2008). I asked Dean to use sticky notes and a marker to write one problem per note. He stuck the notes to the back of the door, ranking the problems in order of significance from 1 to 5, with 5 being the most troublesome. I anticipated he would rank his father's incarceration as the primary concern, but he did not. He ranked it at 1. He ranked low grades and football at 5. He put his mom at 4. He ranked his girlfriend at 3.

Dean explained he did not worry about his dad because he could not do anything to change the situation. On the other hand, if he improved his grades it would give his mom one less thing to worry about and he would be eligible for football. His rankings surprised me, but I stayed with Dean's thinking in order to continue to build rapport and because I felt Dean did not want to discuss his feelings about his father or did not trust me enough to do so.

I chose to introduce the time-efficient WDEP system (Corey, 2009) as a way to help Dean find a solution to the problem regarding his grades, and to gently broach the topic of his strained relationship with his mother. I asked him if his existing approach to homework and studying brought him closer to being eligible for football or further from it. Obviously, his current actions impeded his goal, so he used a piece of paper and wrote out his plan. He indicated he *wanted* to improve his grades. We already *evaluated* his current actions and acknowledged what he was *doing* did not work, so he devised a clear *plan* to complete assignments and talk to teachers about turning in his work late. I told Dean that WDEP would also work for relationships, and mentioned what he had said before, regarding feeling bad for the way he treated his mom. He said he would think about that later. We agreed to talk again the following week.

A couple of days passed, and I saw Dean in the hallway. He flashed a bright smile in my direction as he walked by. I checked his grades online and felt good when I saw a dramatic increase. His improved academic performance pleased me, but I remained concerned about his unwillingness to acknowledge his feelings about his father's incarceration.

Early the following week, Dean's science teacher, Mr. Pauls, referred him to me. He earned a low score on an exam and, when he saw his grade, he cursed, crumpled the paper, and threw it in the trash. Because Dean did not usually act this way, Mr. Pauls wrote a pass for him to come see me instead of writing a discipline referral to the assistant principal. Dean arrived with a furrowed brow, his fists clenched, and he paced in my small office. After a few minutes, he told me he felt fine and wanted to go back to class. I told him I disagreed and asked him to stay a bit longer. He grabbed a stress ball from the basket on my desk and sat down. He squeezed, pulled, and twisted the animal-shaped ball. After a long silence he said, "I don't know what to do." His mother grounded him, so he could not attend a party over the weekend. In his absence, his girlfriend Beth spent time talking to a junior on the football team. He said he felt like all of the hard work and time he spent last week talking to teachers and turning in late work would be undone if he kept failing tests, and he could not seem to control his temper at home. He said everything felt like chaos again. He relaxed as he continued to talk, and we laughed when we realized he pulled the stress ball animal apart. We talked about our previous meeting, and I asked him if we could revisit something he said. He agreed.

> *Counselor:* "You told me there is no need to worry about your dad because there is nothing you can do about it."
>
> *Dean:* "Right. I can't do anything about him being there. I don't think he did everything they say he did, but if a jury says he did then I can't change that. I think he was the easiest one to catch. If he did all of it, he deserves to be in prison, but I don't think he did. And besides, I just think I should concentrate on things I can change."
>
> *Counselor:* "And you can change your grades, and you can control your behavior."
>
> *Dean:* "Right."
>
> *Counselor:* "It would not be helpful to spend time or energy trying to change something we have absolutely no control over; I agree with you. You seem committed to making changes where you can, but you're getting tripped up. What's tripping you up?"

Dean: "I don't know. I do great for a few days, and then something sets me off. It's not like anything happens, you know? Not anything big, anyway."

Counselor: "I have an idea that might help sort some of it out. Are you willing to try something?"

Dean: "Yeah."

Infusion of Creativity

I wanted to use cognitive behavior modification to work with Dean to identify the true nature of the problem (Corey, 2009), and I wanted to incorporate the creative arts technique I learned at a training hosted at the Children's Bereavement Center of South Texas. I drew the outline of a gingerbread person on a sheet of paper and gave Dean a box of markers. I asked him to assign feelings to colors, and then color the gingerbread person where he felt those feelings. I turned on some music and, hesitantly, he began. He worked independently for about 10 minutes. When he finished, he sat in silence for a moment and fought back tears as he stared at the picture.

Dean used yellow on the head to represent confusion because he did not know the truth surrounding the events that led to his father's imprisonment. Red on the head and hands represented anger. Dean shared his anger toward his father and the judicial system. Sometimes he experienced anger toward his mom for being so unconditionally supportive of his dad. A blue heart sat in the middle of the gingerbread person's chest to represent sadness. Dean said evenings and weekends at home did not seem the same without his dad there, and he missed having his father in the stands during football games. A large purple circle represented fear in the pit of Dean's stomach. Although Mr. Barber let his family know he felt safe, Dean experienced nightmares concerning his father's well-being. Brown and orange outlined the gingerbread person. They represented embarrassment and anxiety, respectively. Dean felt embarrassed about his dad's conviction and told very few people. When he spoke to his teachers the previous week, he told them his parents separated and his dad moved out of the house. He experienced anxiety about the future and the well-being of his mom and siblings. His brother continuously got in trouble at school, sometimes he could hear his mom crying at night, and the family struggled with money. Dean wished he could get a part-time job to help.

As we continued to talk, Dean told me he tried to focus on staying strong for his mom and younger siblings, and he reiterated that he believed people should focus on what they can control and not worry about the rest. We discussed the difference in ignoring things we cannot change versus choosing how to respond to them. Dean recognized that his response to the confusion, fear, anxiety, anger, embarrassment, and sadness he felt manifested in negative behaviors. I applauded his willingness to be introspective and acknowledge how emotions can affect us. Dean told me he felt better, but he still did not know what to do. He jokingly added that it would take all of the sticky notes in my office to sort everything out.

Now that Dean recognized his problems as negative by-products of the real issue, he wanted to address the actual concern. We discussed effective ways he could manage the stress that accompanied his emotions. He indicated that recognizing where his stress came from brought great relief, and that he felt he would benefit from taking time to draw his feelings in a sketchpad. Also, in Dean's younger years, he took martial arts and he said he would use breathing and relaxation techniques he learned to help remain calm. Finally, we talked about ways to improve communication, and therefore the relationship, with his mom. We agreed that, although he revealed no information that dictated I break confidentiality, we would invite his mom to come to school to talk immediately. We also agreed that I would facilitate the meeting and he would do the talking. Dean went back to class until she arrived.

When I sent for Dean later that afternoon, he greeted his mom with a smile and hug. He pulled the gingerbread drawing out of his backpack and explained it to her. He recapped our conversation and explained what he realized regarding the implications of ignoring his feelings versus having the power to control his reaction to them. Mrs. Barber listened patiently to Dean, even when he said things that she might find difficult to hear. She indicated she felt guilty for having lost the list of community counselors given to her by the professional school counselor at her son's middle school. I gave Mrs. Barber a new list of community resources and a consent form for release of information to give to a counselor in the community. We also contacted the principal's secretary to schedule a conference with all of Dean's teachers. I told Dean I would check in with him in a few days.

OUTCOME

Toward the end of the week, I sent a pass for Dean to come to my office. He told me he and his girlfriend remained together, and his mom scheduled appointments with a licensed professional counselor for him, his siblings, and herself. Things seemed a little better at home since he and his mom talked, and they agreed that he might not go to the prison with the family for an upcoming visit. The following week, the meeting with Dean's teachers went well; they provided support and understanding. I received the consent form for release of information signed by Mrs. Barber and Dean's licensed professional counselor. I continued to check Dean's academic progress and to speak to him when I saw him on campus.

I recognize that Dean's case is not typical of all students with an incarcerated parent. In many cases, families do not obtain community counseling services. Some students are not as introspective as Dean, and others may be grateful their parents are incarcerated due to the nature of their crimes. When I began working with Dean, I tried not to make assumptions about his feelings and attitudes toward his father's imprisonment because experience taught me students' responses cannot be predicted.

In hindsight, I wonder if I should have addressed Dean's conflict with his mother more assertively. I backed away from the topic after his abrupt response when I attempted to discuss it in Session 1. I also wonder if I should have spent more time talking about the relationships with his friends and girlfriend. I suspect Dean felt isolated during his punishment because he could not spend as much time with his friends as he usually did. The feelings of disconnection from his mother, friends, and girlfriend may have contributed to Dean's overall affect, and may have warranted more attention than I gave them.

Overall, I consider my time with Dean a success. Unattended emotions surrounding Dean's father's incarceration impeded his academic success and damaged his relationships. As his professional school counselor, I wanted to help him see the connection, and ultimately he did. Being able to identify emotions and understand that internal conflict carries external implications is a valuable life-lesson, and learning to apply the WDEP concept to problem solving is a useful skill. I believe my success extended beyond the walls of my office, as I contributed to building positive relationships between members of the Barber family and other members of the school community. I helped an entire family by coordinating the services of a therapist in the community. The last time I spoke to Dean, he reported doing well academically and he thanked me for the help I provided.

REFERENCES

Corey, G. (2009). *Theory and practice of counseling and psychotherapy* (8th ed.). Belmont, CA: Thomson Brooks/Cole.

Murphy, J. J. (2008). *Solution-focused counseling in schools* (2nd ed.). Alexandria, VA: American Counseling Association.

CHAPTER 28

BRITTANY—THE SOCIAL MEDIA QUEEN

Mona Robinson

Brittany presented for counseling accompanied by her mother, Karla Lane. During the first part of the intake session, Ms. Lane provided background information about Brittany. Brittany was a 14-year-old African American female. She was short in stature with a slender build. She had light brown skin with freckles on her nose and cheeks. She had long, reddish brown hair with purple streaks throughout. She appeared dressed appropriately in casual attire. She carried her pink cell phone in her manicured hands. Brittany was a freshman and attended an urban high school where she was an honor student and a member of the volleyball team.

SYSTEMIC INFLUENCES

The Family System

Ms. Lane shared that Brittany's family consisted of herself and her younger brother, Marcel, who was 8 years old. Brittany does not know her father and does not get along with Marcel's dad, Jerry, who is in the home off and on. Ms. Lane never married and lived in a low-income housing community in a Midwestern city where she worked full-time as a cashier in a major retail store. She had strong beliefs in the family system and felt protective of her children. Ms. Lane stated that she wanted Brittany to go to college and have a better life than she had. "I want Brittany to make something of herself."

The Peer System

I spoke with Brittany's mother at length in my effort to gain more information about Brittany and to understand the concerns that led them to
counseling. Ms. Lane stated that Brittany spent too much time on the
telephone and computer. She was in trouble at school due to bullying
other students through social media comments. Ms. Lane also noted
that Brittany has been on the receiving side of bullying from other students and states she believes that Brittany was "doing what has been
done to her."

The School System

Ms. Lane reported that the administrators at Brittany's school also dis-
ciplined her several times recently due to exhibiting oversexualized
behaviors at school. Ms. Lane brought Brittany to counseling because
"she needs help. I am concerned about the amount of time she spends on
her phone and on the computer." She said Brittany has been "acting out
lately and I don't know how to handle her." Ms. Lane shared that Brittany
"got into the altercation" with me because I tried to take her telephone.
Ms. Lane also noted that Brittany's grades recently dropped and she is
worried Brittany may have to repeat a grade. Ms. Lane described Brittany
as being irritable and isolating herself from her family, spending hours in
her room on the computer and telephone. Ms. Lane also discussed concerns that Brittany dressed in provocative clothing. This change in dress
was new. Brittany usually dressed very conservatively. Ms. Lane often
found Brittany in her room crying and regularly came home from school
in tears, feeling like she had no friends. These feelings and behaviors
were new. Brittany had always been active socially and had a couple of
"good friends that she hung out with." Brittany generally attended multiple birthday parties throughout the school year and often spent time
with friends shopping, going to the movies, and talking/texting on her
telephone or computer. Ms. Lane reported that Brittany experienced a
growth spurt within the last year and feared she received too much
attention from boys, wondering if this contributed to her oversexualized
behaviors. Brittany's suspension from school again last week for texting
inappropriate pictures prompted Ms. Lane to bring her to counseling.

During the last part of the intake session, Brittany and I discussed
her reasons for coming to counseling. Brittany appeared hesitant at first
and declared she was not going to talk to me. When I asked her why
she did not want to talk, she said, "I don't like to talk to people. I am only
here because my mother made me come and there's nothing wrong with
me." I explained to Brittany that I wanted to help her and wanted her to

have someone to talk to about anything that was going on. I informed Brittany that anything she said to me was confidential as long as it was not harmful to herself or others. After a short time, Brittany seemed to relax and became more comfortable with sharing her concerns.

DEVELOPMENTAL CONSIDERATIONS

Cognitive Development

Ms. Lane described Brittany as an intelligent, energetic, and independent thinker. She recalled that Brittany quickly achieved all milestones and understood the difference between right and wrong at an early age. She indicated that Brittany developed language skills early and communicated well with others. She stated, "Brittany is my 'old soul' child. I feel like she is way ahead of her time, a mini adult."

Personal, Social, and Emotional Development

Ms. Lane stated that Brittany's developmental history was unremarkable and she reported that Brittany was in good health. Ms. Lane recalled that Brittany walked, talked, learned toileting, and met all developmental milestones at the appropriate time. She said Brittany has always had good sleep patterns even as an infant. Ms. Lane did not encounter any feeding difficulties with Brittany as a child and Brittany has no known allergies. She reported that Brittany was a lovable child who was well behaved. She said Brittany related well with others while growing up and made friends easily. Brittany developed appropriate thinking skills by age 11 and moved from concrete thinking to abstract ways of thinking. She said she would consider Brittany to be a model child up until about a year ago when she reached puberty.

RELATIONAL CONSIDERATIONS

Brittany and I discussed the incidents at school that resulted in her suspensions. We explored her use of social media and how it affected her relationships with others. We talked about how her style of dress changed within the last year. We discussed self-esteem in relation to what it feels like to go from an underdeveloped pre-teen to a well-developed teenager in such a short time period. Brittany said her "so-called" friends felt jealous because she started receiving attention from boys. Brittany said that while she sometimes felt scared adjusting to all of the changes, she enjoyed the attention. She coped by posting pictures of herself dressed "sexy" so boys would want to spend time with her. She became tearful during the session and relayed her occasional feelings of sadness and hopelessness. Brittany said she escaped by sending pictures. Because suicide is a common concern with girls of this age, I conducted a suicide assessment as a safety measure. Brittany denied suicidal ideation. Brittany agreed to work with me to help resolve her current conflicts and help her feel better about herself.

MULTICULTURAL CONSIDERATIONS

As an African American counselor, I often approach my work with clients from a multicultural lens. I recognize the importance of stepping out of one's own comfort zone and respecting the culture of others. Through my work with others who look very different from me, and from my work with those clients who look similar to me, I gained experiences that help me to work successfully with diverse cultures. I believe it is important to meet the clients where they are and validate any concerns they may have about me. Brittany shared that she expected a Caucasian counselor who would not understand what she was going through. She felt pleased to meet an African American counselor who looked like her but, more importantly, listened to her. I believe Brittany would have problems forming an alliance with me regardless of my culture if I approached her situation from a deficit perspective.

According to research, solution-focused therapy is a good choice to use with African Americans, especially those who come from disadvantaged backgrounds. Counselors and clients have witnessed success with this model and some clinicians indicated that it is very inspirational to see a client reach his or her goals.

CONCEPTUALIZATION

My initial concerns focused on addressing Brittany's feelings of sadness and hopelessness related to her low self-esteem. I conceptualized that Brittany suddenly turned from a child to an adolescent and felt unsure how to adjust to all the changes that came along with this growth. I wanted to provide a sense of safety while addressing Brittany's adolescent identity role confusion. So, rather than targeting her inappropriate social media behaviors, I focused on improving her self-esteem.

To gain a better understanding about Brittany and her usage patterns related to social media, we discussed the influence of social media on adolescents and adolescent identity development as topics to assist us in making gains in counseling. Our discussion about the influence of social media on friendships and the prevalence of adolescents posting inappropriate pictures of themselves on social media would be a part of the counseling process.

We spent time on Brittany's attention-seeking behavior of sending inappropriate pictures. We explored how getting in trouble did not seem to deter her from continuing this practice. Brittany shared pictures of herself in provocative clothing because she enjoyed the attention. Therefore, I believed a major counseling goal would be to help Brittany realize why this was so important to her and learn how it influenced her feelings of sadness and hopelessness. I also wanted to address Brittany's practice of posting unflattering pictures of friends on social media because they "did the same thing" to her.

The therapeutic alliance is the foundation for counseling effectiveness. I hoped that as I listened to Brittany's concerns and affirmed that her input was important, our rapport would develop. I hoped my efforts to display genuineness and convey unconditional positive regard allowed Brittany to feel safe in counseling and invite her to share her feelings with me.

My Goals and Strategies

My goal in counseling centered on increasing Brittany's self-esteem and decreasing her reliance on approval by friends via social media. I believed that making improvements in these areas would decrease Brittany's feelings of sadness and hopelessness. I used psychoeducation to help Brittany gain a greater understanding of the stages of identity development and the influence of social media on adolescents. I helped Brittany explore alternatives to social media use. I chose solution-focused brief therapy to guide our work around resolving her issues relating to her friends. I employed solution-focused brief therapy because it is useful when trying to find solutions quickly to a problem rather than trying to focus on solving the problem quickly. This method works well with adolescents who sometimes lack mature cognitive skills. Second, due to the constraints of managed care, solution-focused brief therapy offered an alternative that worked. In the end, it is always my hope that a solution will be found quickly and the issue will be resolved quickly (Sklare, 2014).

COUNSELING PROCESS FLOW

Over the course of 3 months, Brittany and I met on a weekly basis. Brittany seemed somewhat reserved and a little closed off at the initial interview, but we quickly formed a therapeutic alliance. While Brittany seemed reluctant to talk in our first meeting, she seemed eager to meet with me in subsequent meetings. Brittany typically arrived on time and appeared to be in a good mood.

Infusion of Creativity

During the first 4 weeks of counseling, Brittany participated in self-esteem building activities. I provided her with homework assignments that required her to keep a journal and record her feelings. I encouraged Brittany to journal using electronic means such as her phone or computer. I encouraged her to explore her feelings about herself and her friends.

During the second and third months, we integrated psychoeducational activities into our sessions and in the homework assignments. We explored various theories of life-span development, specifically those that focused on adolescent development. Brittany became more confident and better understood the changes in her body. I watched as Brittany's self-esteem continued increasing. By the end of 2 months, Brittany no longer responded that she felt sad and hopeless. Instead, she described how her relationships with her friends had improved. She told me that she related better with her mother and she received no school suspensions for oversexualized behaviors or bullying.

Time-Efficient Methods

In an effort to better understand Brittany and assist her through the process of solution-focused brief therapy, I prepared myself by engaging in practice activities using problem-focused and solution-focused questions as suggested by Sklare (2014). I used the practice exercises to experience the same results Brittany might experience when the focus shifted from problems to solutions.

I met with Brittany for individual counseling once a week for an hour each visit over a period of 3 months. During our second session, we worked on finding solutions as opposed to focusing on her problems. My focus on Brittany's strengths and utilizing them in session enlivened her cooperation and contributed to her growth. Brittany began to build confidence as she engaged in activities that helped build her self-esteem. I often reframed her negative statements into positive ones in my quest to focus on solutions.

OUTCOME

Goals and Targets for Client Change

We tried to set limits on social media usage. Initially, we set such strict limits that Brittany could not follow through. We scaled back the time limits and Brittany successfully reached her goals. I made it a point to de-emphasize Brittany's social media usage. Instead, I focused on activities that fostered raising her self-esteem. I felt that if we could make improvements there, the rest would fall into place.

Brittany benefitted from counseling and her feelings of sadness and hopelessness diminished each week. Two months into counseling, she no longer reported the feelings of sadness and hopelessness at all. Subsequent check-ins with Ms. Lane revealed that Brittany was "her old self again." She was no longer concerned about Brittany's safety and Brittany appeared happy and well adjusted. She said Brittany now used social media appropriately. She no longer worried about Brittany's provocative dress, inappropriate texting, and suspensions from school. Brittany developed meaningful relationships with her girlfriends and enjoyed spending time with them. She no longer dressed provocatively or spent inappropriate amounts of time on the phone or computer. Brittany ceased isolating herself in her room crying. Her grades improved and she started playing volleyball again.

Strategies for the Client

Brittany connected with me as her counselor on an individual level. She opened up and shared her personal experiences with me. I believe Brittany used the techniques she learned in counseling to assist her with improving how she felt about herself. Increased self-esteem motivated Brittany to make changes in her relationships with other people. She expressed that she no longer "craves attention from boys." She said, "If a guy does not like me in my regular clothes, then he does not get to talk to me when I am dressed up." She said she felt good about herself and her main concern centered on getting good grades in school so she could go to college. She did not care what girls who are not her "true friends" said about her anymore.

Using brief solution-focused counseling with Brittany was a good choice. Brittany made progress in counseling almost immediately. By approaching her and her situation from a multicultural perspective, we developed initial rapport quickly. I believe Brittany will continue to thrive and make responsible choices regarding social media. I think she made the connection between her developmental identity issues and her inappropriate social media usage. By coming to terms with her feelings of sadness and hopelessness and recognizing the effect of her sexualized behaviors, Brittany made positive changes in her lifestyle. Brittany was an active participant in counseling and worked diligently to meet expectations discussed early in her treatment.

I continue to work on my professional growth as a counselor and continually stay abreast of new techniques that may be beneficial to my client's varying needs. I make it a point to ensure I am practicing from the most appropriate theoretical perspective as well as utilizing appropriate interventions that suit my client's problems. I will continue to look for solutions to problems as opposed to focusing on the problem.

REFERENCE

Sklare, G. B. (2014). *Brief counseling that works: A solution-focused therapy approach for school counselors and other mental health professionals* (3rd ed.). Thousand Oaks, CA: Corwin.

CACREP Signature Assignments

CACREP Standards serve as markers to ensure that counselors-in-training acquire the necessary knowledge and skills for effective professional practice. Signature assignments may be used by professors and students as evidence of coursework accomplishment. They are created or modified to allow students to apply learning addressed in a wide variety of circumstances and settings. Additionally, they provide professors continuous and systematic assessments that depict how student learning outcomes are measured and met—in this case, the assessment of multiple CACREP Standards that are aligned to the assignments (i.e., utilizing essential interviewing and counseling skills and behaviors; practicing counseling theories that provide models for case conceptualization, appropriate counseling interventions, techniques, and strategies; counseling in developmental, systemic, relational, and multicultural contexts; and facilitating academic, career, personal, and social development of children and adolescents).

Four of the contributing authors for this textbook submitted five CACREP signature assignments for classroom use. Each designated the targeted CACREP Standards for the assignments submitted. Dr. Thomas Anthony Chávez submitted an assignment for his case study, *Imprisoned Identities*. Dr. Taryne M. Mingo submitted an assignment for her case study, *A Gift for Jeffrey*. Dr. Brenda L. Jones submitted two signature assignments: a role-play assignment for a child and adolescent counseling class and an assignment that serves as case study critiques. Dr. JoLynne Reynolds presented a role-play assignment with a focus on anxiety issues experienced by children and adolescents. Both assignments submitted by Dr. Jones and Dr. Reynolds may be used with any of the case studies listed in the textbook. Professors may use these assignments as presented or modify them to fit specific coursework.

CACREP Signature Assignment
An assignment written specifically for the case study,
Imprisoned Identities

Submitted by
Thomas Anthony Chávez, PhD, LMHC (NM)
University of New Mexico
Albuquerque, New Mexico

2016 CACREP Standards, Section 2: le; 2a, b, c, d, e, f, g, h; 3a, c, f, h, i; and 5a, b, f, g, h, k.

Activity Title: Exploring Biases and Stereotypes Toward Justice-Involved Adolescents

Purpose: The purpose of this activity is to enhance self-awareness and understand deeply embedded biases and stereotypes of adolescence, criminality, mental illness, and values regarding successful parenting. This activity is modeled after an activity designed by Singaravelu (2011) that helps students explore diverse race and cultural stereotypes and generalizations.

Learning Objective: As a result of this activity, students will have a greater understanding of their own biases related to adolescence, criminality, mental illness, and values regarding successful parenting. They will be able to identify the source of such biases and beliefs and better focus on systemic issues that come into play with high-risk, high-need adolescents.

Target Population: Master's-level counseling students learning about contextual factors and theory.

Time Required: 30 minutes

Setting: Classroom with chairs arranged in a circle so that students face each other. The students will explore individually their biases and then turn to a group discussion.

Materials: Index cards or blank sheet of paper.

Instructions: The instructor will instruct the students to write, without their names, on one side of their index card or paper the words "adolescence," "criminal," "mental illness," and "parenting." Once they do so, they should be asked to write words or phrases that immediately come to mind with each word. Once they have completed this task, the instructor should ask the

270

students to reflect on and write on the other side of their paper on the question: "Where did I learn these ideas and beliefs?" Upon completion of the task, the instructor collects all papers and shuffles them. The instructor then redistributes the papers among the students. If a student gets his or her own, it is okay. The instructor should ask the student to read aloud to the group his or her list starting with "adolescence" in the first round, followed by "criminal" and such until each list for each term has been read aloud. The instructor will then ask where their ideas, images, and beliefs stemmed from. To further prompt discussion, the students should be asked to discuss what it felt like to listen to the representations, stereotypes, and beliefs about this population as well as how it has affected how they interact with youth with behavioral concerns. Finally, students should be asked how this may serve as a barrier toward developing a therapeutic relationship with adolescents dealing with criminal behavior, mental illness, and disruptive family issues.

REFERENCE

Singaravelu, H. (2011). Stereotypes and generalizations. In M. Pope, J. S. Pangelinan, & A. D. Coker (Eds.), *Experiential activities for teaching multicultural competence in counseling*. Alexandria, VA: American Counseling Association.

CACREP Signature Assignment
Assignment 1 written specifically for a child and
adolescent counseling class

Submitted by
Brenda L. Jones, PhD, CSC, LPC, NCC
The University of Texas at San Antonio
San Antonio, Texas

2009 CACREP Clinical Mental Health Counseling Standards: A2; B1; C8; E1; F3;
2009 CACREP School Counseling Standards: A2, A6; B1; C1, C3; D1, D5; E4; F1,
F4; H1; M1, M5; 2016, Section 2, 2c, 3f, h, and i; 5a, b, f, g, h, i, j, and n.

Instructions for the Instructor: Select enough cases from the case study text-book that will allow each student to have a role. Usually for a class of approximately 35 students, about six or seven cases will need to be selected. Choose five to seven roles (depending on class enrollment) from each case study. Following are the two cases (not found in this case study book) that can be used as examples for writing modified situations for cases found in this book.

Before the full role-play assignment is given, prepare a role-play sign-up sheet for students and have them choose a role from one of the selected cases. Type the selected case study roles next to the students' names as listed in the first column of the given table. The case number listed is the chapter number in the case study textbook.

First, have students read the originally assigned case study from the case study textbook. Afterward, they are to read the instructor's modification of the case (as listed in the second column). This modification reflects a change in the client's situation. Each group will incorporate the modifications in the newly created role-play skit.

Group Members—A	Case 1 Modification
Roles	*Case Study Title and Author*
Counselor: (Name of student)	Three years after termination with the
Student, Paul: (Name of student)	case study counselor, Paul, now 7, is
Grandmother: (Name of student)	living with his paternal grandparents
Supervisor: (Name of student)	who now have custody of him. Paul's
Tekki: (Name of student)	mother is incarcerated for a drug
Narrator: (Name of student)	possession charge. Paul's recurrent
	nightmares have returned. His
	grandmother reported to see you at
	the Community Family Life Center.

Group Members—B	Case 5 Modification
Roles	*Case Study Title and Author*
Elementary School Counselor: (Name of student) Co-counselor: (Name of student) Mother, Maria: (Name of student) Father, Julio: (Name of student) Supervisor: (Name of student) Tekki: (Name of student) Narrator: (Name of student) Maria and Julio are Angelica's parents.	Maria and Julio see you and another professional school counselor at your school 2 months after their last conference with the case study counselor. Their child, Angelica, is backsliding academically. Maria is scheduled for chemotherapy. She is fearful that Julio will not be able to manage the kids and take care of her at the same time. She wonders how to tell them she is dying and how Angelica will get back on track academically.

Role-Playing Assignment Instructions for Students

- The roles that you have selected by groups have been posted on the blackboard.
  - Students who are selected to be *tekkis* are to work with the group in the development and recording of the role-play skit. Tekkis are to use a personal laptop or cell phone to record the session and make sure that the recording is done correctly before the group is dismissed. The recorded session should be *no more than* 25 minutes. Tekkis are also responsible for transferring the recorded audio/visual session onto a DVD that will be submitted to the instructor after the case has been presented to the class.
  - Students who are selected to be *supervisors* are to assist in "pulling the group together"; assist in the development of the skit; assist the tekki in taping; and serve as a replacement in the case of an emergency during taping.
  - *Narrators* are to summarize for the class, before the start of the presentation, the original chapter that the case is based on. The narrators also prepare the audience for the newly modified recorded role-play situation and assist in the development of the skit.

- Although the narrators will summarize the chapters/cases, the entire class is expected to read all assigned chapters/cases in order to more effectively provide critical feedback to groups after the group presentations.

- Evidence of the following should be incorporated into the recorded role-play or narration.
  - Evidence of understanding and practice of ethical and legal considerations specifically related to the practice of school and clinical mental health

counseling (i.e., attention to intake procedures [if applicable]; an explanation of the counselors' roles, confidentiality, and the counseling process; and an assessment of the client's needs [personal, social, and emotional])
- A review of previous session(s), if appropriate
- The opening, working, and closing stages of the counseling session
- An assessment of the client's developmental level (i.e., atypical growth and development, health and wellness, language, ability level, multicultural and relational issues, and factors of resiliency on student learning and development such as strategies for helping clients identify strengths and cope with environmental and developmental problems and their effect on student ability level and achievement)
- Evidence of a theoretical orientation (single theory or integrated) with an infusion of creativity
- Counseling strategies and techniques that are aligned with the theoretical orientation
- Evidence of including a systemic approach to counseling to enhance the academic, career, and/or personal/social development of students
- Time-efficient methods, if appropriate

Role-Play Feedback Sheet/Rubrics

2009 CACREP Clinical Mental Health Counseling Standards: A2; B1; C8; E1; F3; 2009 CACREP School Counseling Standards: A2, A6; B1; C1, C3; D1, D5; E4; F1, F4; H1; M1, M5; 2016, Section 2, 2c, 3f, h, and i; 5a, b, f, g, h, i, j, and n.

Group Number: _____ Case Title_____ Date_____

Instructions to Students: Take notes as each group presents the counseling role-play video. Follow the given outline. Be prepared to provide constructive feedback and point totals to group members after they present. Each bullet is worth two points, totaling 10 points for this assignment.

- The opening section
  - Establishment of rapport with client
  - Review of previous counseling session (if appropriate)
  - Explanation of the counselor's role (if this is the first session)
  - Discussion about the parameters of confidentiality
  - Evidence of mutually set goals for this session (client and counselor)

- The working section
  - An assessment of the client's needs (personal, social, academic, etc.)
  - Good conceptualization of the client's presenting problem
  - Evaluation of the counseling process

- Evidence of a theoretical orientation (single theory or integrated)
- Counseling strategies and techniques that are aligned with the theoretical orientation
- Evidence of including a systemic and relational approach to counseling to enhance the academic, career, and/or personal/social development of client
- Infusion of creative or expressive arts techniques

- The closing section
  - Summarization of session
  - Check for client understanding
  - Plans for follow-up session (date and preliminary goals)

- Evidence of the following should also be incorporated into the recorded role-play or narration.
  - Evidence of understanding and practice of ethical and legal considerations specifically related to the practice of school and clinical mental health counseling including attention to intake procedures (if applicable)
  - An assessment of the client's developmental level including atypical growth and development, health and wellness, language, ability level, multicultural issues, and factors of resiliency on student learning and development (i.e., strategies for problems and their effect on student ability level and achievement)
  - Multicultural or diversity considerations

- Other comments (e.g., time-efficient methods, if appropriate)

CACREP Signature Assignment
Assignment 2 written specifically for a child and
adolescent counseling class

Submitted by
Brenda L. Jones, PhD, CSC, LPC, NCC
The University of Texas at San Antonio
San Antonio, Texas

2009 CACREP II G.3.c., e., f., G.5.b., c., d., e., f., g.; G.6.a., b., c., d.

Students are to choose two cases/chapters from the listed book and do a critical analysis on each by answering the following questions:

1. What are your thoughts about the case conceptualization for each case/chapter that you chose?
2. What techniques and strategies used by the counselor(s) in each case seemed to be most effective? Explain why you considered them to be effective.
3. Choose a different counseling approach, technique, and strategy from those presented in each of the selected case studies and describe what that would look like.

CACREP Signature Assessment
An assignment written specifically for group work
for gifted children and used in child and
adolescent counseling classes

Submitted by
Taryne M. Mingo, PhD, NCC
Missouri State University
Springfield, Missouri

2009 CACREP Clinical Mental Health Counseling Standards: C8, F3; 2009 CACREP School Counseling Standards: A6; C1, C3; D1, D5; E4; F1; H1; M5.

This assignment is linked to the description of the "peer system" approach mentioned within Chapter 3. This can be used with graduate students enrolled in group counseling courses for children and adolescents. See the attachments associated for students to incorporate.

Scenario for Group Intervention

You are working in a rural elementary school that has limited access to a variety of educational and community resources and a high number of children requiring specialized, direct counseling interventions for anxiety. Unfortunately, most of these children live in families of economic disadvantage, and as a result their families are unable to afford or transport their children to a community mental health counselor. The teaching faculty at your school have recently expressed concern about many of these students' ability to adjust to the new state-mandated expectations for increased student performance, and the administration is worried about their social adjustment to peers as well as bullying issues. Your principal asks you to develop a group intervention for those students struggling with anxiety and requiring specialized, direct counseling services to address these concerns.

Forming Stages of Group

1. What type of group would you form to support this population of students?
2. What further data might you want to collect to help you better clarify what might be useful?
3. Who else would be included in the group with the student?
4. What would be the general goals and purpose of this group?

5. How would you want to set up your group in order to best meet your goals and objectives? Think about leadership variables, participant variables, group format and structure, group process, etc.).

Norming Stages of Group

1. What goals will you set for this group?
2. In order to help your group members reach the group goals, what objectives might you set?
3. How will you account for setbacks in the group process?
4. Would you use techniques? Why? Why not?

Storming Stages of Group

1. How would you control for some of the risks involved for each student's participation in your group (particularly as it relates to anxiety)?
2. How would you address difficult clients from your theoretical approach?

Performing Stages of Group

1. How will you use group members' strengths and weaknesses to move the group process forward?
2. Is your group counseling approach culturally sensitive?

Termination Stages of Group

1. How will you ensure skills developed during group will continue into the classroom?
2. How will you determine your group's effectiveness in assisting members to handle anxiety beyond the group?

Lastly, provide an imaginary sample interaction between the case study client and you as group facilitator *from your assigned theory.*

CACREP Signature Assignment
An assignment written specifically for
co-creating therapeutic stories with clients

Submitted by
JoLynne Reynolds, PhD, LPC, NCC, RPT-S
Regis University, Bloomfield, Colorado

2009 CACREP Objectives: Standard F.5.g. essential interviewing, counseling, and case conceptualization skills; Standard F.5.h. developmentally relevant counseling treatment or intervention plans; Standard F.3.i. ethical and culturally relevant strategies for promoting resilience and optimum development and wellness across the life span; Clinical Mental Health Standard 5C.3.b. techniques and interventions for prevention and treatment of a broad range of mental health issues; School Counseling Standard: Section 5.G.3.f. techniques of personal/social counseling in school settings.

Each person, in a small group of three people, will select one of the following roles: a child or adolescent, a counselor, and an observer.

Role-play a situation where a child has anxiety related to a life problem. The child/adolescent first tells the problem facilitated by the counselor. The person acting in the role of the counselor implements a mutual storytelling intervention with the child/adolescent using the three steps outlined in this case study:

• Step 1: Mutual Story Introduction
  The counselor retells the problem in a story format, co-authoring with the child to select characters, describing feelings and reactions to the problem, and including a strategy where the main character seeks help from an imaginary character he or she trusts.
• Step 2: Imagining Problem Strategies
  Continue the second part of the story, where the imaginary character offers a solution or strategy to solve the problem suggested by the counselor and then a second solution or action suggested by the child.
• Step 3: Retelling With New Solutions and Improved Outcomes
  Retell the problem situation a second time in the story format, this time using the solution-focused questions and then with new more favorable outcomes for the main character.

Questions for the Discussion:

1. How did the counselor validate the child's view of the problem, including summarizing the child's feelings and reactions to the problem situation?

2. How did the counselor implement creativity and imagination into the storytelling format?
3. What strategies were suggested by the counselor? Did they seem to offer new ways of acting or viewing the problem appropriate to the child's developmental level and cultural background? Did the counselor enlist the child's help in developing strategies?
4. In the retelling of the problem with new solutions, did the counselor engage the child in coming up with new feelings and new positive outcomes?
5. How did the counselor incorporate sensitivity to the child's culture, including developmental age, ethnicity, gender, and so forth?
6. How might this intervention increase the child's coping skills and resiliency?
7. What improvements or adjustments to this technique might you suggest in making this work with the population each member of your team either currently counsels or plans to counsel?

INDEX

Lightning Source UK Ltd.
Milton Keynes UK
UKOW07f0623170817
307440UK00001B/27/P